PROTESTANT PLURALISM
AND THE
NEW YORK EXPERIENCE

Religion in North America

Catherine L. Albanese and Stephen J. Stein, editors

PROTESTANT PLURALISM
AND THE
NEW YORK EXPERIENCE

A Study of Eighteenth-Century Religious Diversity

RICHARD W. POINTER

INDIANA UNIVERSITY PRESS
Bloomington and Indianapolis

For My Parents,
Roy and Else Pointer

Portions of my article, "Religious Life in New York"
(*New York History,* October 1985), are reprinted herein by permission
of the New York State Historical Association.

Manufactured in the United States of America

Library of Congress Cataloging-in-Publication Data

Pointer, Richard W., 1955–
  Protestant pluralism and the New York experience.

  (Religion in North America)
  Bibliography: p.
  Includes index.
    1. Religious pluralism—New York (State)—
History—18th century. 2. Protestant churches—
New York (State)—History—18th century. 3. New York
(State)—Church history. I. Title. II. Series.
BR555.N7P65 1988   277.47'07   87-45371
ISBN 0-253-34643-6

1 2 3 4 5 92 91 90 89 88

CONTENTS

FOREWORD

Richard W. Pointer joins cause with an expanding number of contemporary scholars who are countering the conventional obsession of colonial historians with the religious life and traditions of New England and Virginia. The search for historical precedents for the development of religious pluralism in the United States has turned new attention to the situation of the Middle Colonies, where religious diversity of a kind unknown elsewhere in colonial America existed from the beginning. Until now, Pennsylvania has attracted most attention, for William Penn's "Grand Experiment" welcomed religious groups as diverse as Quakers and Anabaptists, Lutherans and German Reformed, Presbyterians and Anglicans. In this new work, however, attention shifts away from Pennsylvania to its neighbor to the north.

The northern neighbor, New York, proves an excellent choice for examining the evolution of Protestant pluralism in the eighteenth century. Recent historians who have explored the social, economic, and political consequences of diversity in that colony have offered only preliminary insights into the religious effects of heterogeneity. Pointer now carries forward the quest for understanding, examining the separate religious traditions and the relationships among the denominations. The situation in New York was complex and varied, an anticipation of the later pluralistic pattern in nineteenth- and twentieth-century America.

Working through the complexities, Pointer concludes that the process leading to the development of Protestant pluralism in New York was not simply a pragmatic evolution with little reflection on the part of denominational New Yorkers. On the contrary, churched New Yorkers embraced religious pluralism in a thoughtful and positive manner, all the while recognizing its implications for liberty and toleration.

Likewise, Pointer challenges the now standard depiction of the Revolutionary era in America as a time of spiritual drought or religious declension. The documentary evidence in New York, he argues, gives the lie to the picture of churchly decline in that colony and thus undercuts older generalizations about religious apathy in the late eighteenth century. Pointer raises questions about the relationship between denominational vitality and the number of available ministers. He also examines anew the process of religious reconstruction after the Revolutionary War.

This research suggests an underlying gradualism about religious developments instead of the "instantism" associated with the evangelical revivals that is traditionally used to explain the surge of religiosity at the beginning of the nineteenth century. In the picture that emerges, there are continuities of both time and space in the story of New York's religious history. Events in the post-Revolutionary period are linked with earlier developments in seventeenth-century New York as well as with circumstances in the larger fellowships spanning the Atlantic Ocean.

Finally, Pointer's work demonstrates how popular attitudes toward religious pluralism changed among Protestants in New York during the eighteenth century. It shows us how these changing attitudes contributed to the formation of a Protestant culture that became increasingly characteristic of much of America during the nineteenth century. In fact, this study of the religious impact of diversity in New York has a new timeliness in the late twentieth century as Americans debate the implications of the accelerating heterogeneity in the nation.

The research presented here rests upon an impressive documentary base. Pointer has searched archives carefully and has discovered important unused sources. His work suggests that new insights are still obtainable from traditional historical approaches. It also stands as an invitation to continue the investigation of this formative period by intensive local studies of particular communities in New York and by comparative analyses with other colonies.

CATHERINE L. ALBANESE and
STEPHEN J. STEIN, *series editors*

PREFACE

Traveling through the Middle Colonies in 1759, Englishman Andrew Burnaby could not precisely characterize eighteenth-century New Yorkers because they were "of different nations, different languages, and different religions."[1] He thus highlighted New York's most distinguishing social feature—its religious and ethnic heterogeneity. Diversity was the rule rather than the exception in the rural villages of Long Island and the Hudson Valley, as well as in New York City and Albany. Provincial newspapers, sermons, diaries, letters, and conversations all testified to the plurality of sects whose churches dotted the countryside and dominated Manhattan's urban landscape.

That colonists found themselves living, working, and worshiping alongside persons of different backgrounds and beliefs has always been known. But what difference this simple but profound social reality made in the world of eighteenth-century Americans, and particularly New Yorkers, remains something of a mystery. Robert Kelley and Henry May have illustrated pluralism's key role in the political and intellectual development of early America.[2] Stephanie Grauman Wolf, in a pioneering study of Germantown, Pennsylvania, has shown that, on a local level, a town's heterogeneity was likely to affect all aspects of community life.[3] Students of colonial New York have discovered that the multiplicity of religious and ethnic groups contributed to its political and economic factiousness, as well as to its cultural richness.[4] Milton M. Klein has argued that pluralism was not only the central fact of New York's colonial history, but that largely on this account the province is the place to look for the origin of the American tradition, rather than either New England or Virginia.[5] Similarly, Michael Zuckerman has suggested that "in religion, the Middle Atlantic exhibited more fully than any other colonial region the shape of things to come."[6] All these studies have shed important light, then, on the wide impact of religious diversity on life in colonial America and have illustrated that contemporary Americans can find the roots of their own plural religion primarily in the colonial societies of New York, New Jersey, and Pennsylvania.

Nevertheless, much darkness remains. Ironically, among the poorest lit subjects is how pluralism affected colonial religion itself. Scholars have long been convinced that diversity encouraged toleration and eventually set the stage for full religious liberty. Yet beyond this conviction little progress has been made. For example, John Webb Pratt's excellent study of the church-state theme in New York details how the colony's multiplicity of religious groups "always worked for religious freedom," but it says almost nothing about pluralism's other consequences for New York's churches.[7] How did diversity affect the institutional development of colonial religious communities still wedded to European state churches? What did pluralism mean for men and women interested in finding religious truth? What difference did diversity make in the struggle by some New Yorkers for religious equality and religious disestablishment? In what ways did the colony's heterogeneous religious opinions influence Revolutionary behavior? Was pluralism an asset or a liability in the task of religious recovery after the war?

None of these questions has relevance only for New York. On the contrary, during the eighteenth century all colonial regions were following to one degree or another the model set by the Middle Colonies in becoming religiously diverse. Still, the longer and more complete encounter of New Yorkers with religious pluralism suggests this colony as the most ripe for study.[8] What this book seeks to provide, therefore, is a close examination of the effects of diversity on individuals, congregations, and denominational communions in New York. I shall summarize in the following chapters what I have concluded are the major ways it shaped the organizational structure, spiritual practice, theological beliefs, and political ideology of the colony's religious bodies in the eighteenth century. In addition, because pluralism's impact was always tied closely to colonial perceptions of its value or harm, I shall also trace the evolution of provincial attitudes toward diversity and explain how it came to be accepted as the cornerstone of the new state's religious order.

For most of New York's residents in the colonial era, religious pluralism meant Protestant pluralism. While individual Jews and Catholics could be found throughout most parts of the province and clusters of both groups had settled in New York City, the vast bulk of the population was Protestant to one degree or another. "Typical" New Yorkers were acquainted with persons of these other religious faiths, but their primary experience with diversity came in the form of repeated contact with members of other Protestant denominational traditions. This Protestant interaction dominated the colony's religious environment and constituted the raw material out of which most New Yorkers built their opinions about religious heterogeneity. For this reason, I shall concentrate in this study on Protestants and their pluralism as it evolved during the 1700s. The stories of Jewish and Catholic experiences amid New York's diversity are equally rich, but the limits of space and evidence preclude any thorough consideration of them here. Instead, I shall occasionally introduce Catholic and Jewish examples for comparative purposes to illustrate both what they shared and how they differed with their Protestant neighbors.

If New York's Protestants are an obvious choice for analysis, not so immediately evident are the reasons for concentrating on the eighteenth century. While a good case can be made for studying an earlier era, the eighteenth century, and especially the sixty years from 1740 to 1800, seem preferable for several reasons. By then, New York's churchgoers had had more time to think through and articulate their opinions about diversity, as well as to respond in practical ways to its demands. These years also witnessed the interplay of New York's pluralistic culture with the most significant religious events of early American history, the First and Second Great Awakenings, and with the American Revolution. Finally, taking the story up to the turn of the century makes it possible to see what role religious diversity was likely to play in American religion during the 1800s.

To highlight the dynamic character of pluralism's impact, the study is divided into two parts. Part I focuses on the period from 1700 to 1775 and shows in separate chapters how diversity both reinvigorated and reduced popular spirituality, encouraged a drive for ecclesiastical self-sufficiency, and spurred periodic attempts at eliminating religious inequalities. It also demonstrates that with the spread of New Light evangelicalism and rationalistic liberalism after 1750, colonists began to view their own diversity in a more favorable light. Part II investigates in chronological sequence pluralism's effects on religious life during the Revolution and the two postwar decades. It finds that New Yorkers readily affirmed religious diversity in the remaking of their church-state relations, granting liberal portions of religious liberty to Protestant, Catholic, and Jew alike. It illustrates further that, while the presence of competing groups made the task of rebuilding congregations after the war much tougher, leaders of the dominant Protestant denominations saw the discovery of unity amidst diversity rather than sectarian exclusivism as the wave of the future. By the late 1790s, they and their lay supporters were ready to engage in a host of cooperative ventures aimed at nothing less than bringing the kingdom of heaven to earth. Such ventures were the best, if only one, indication at the century's end of what New York's religionists had deemed necessary for survival in a pluralistic milieu.

These conclusions stand in sharp contrast at a number of points to the arguments advanced in the many fine essays of Sidney Mead. Mead's work has probably exerted more influence over what American religious historians believe about religious pluralism than anything else written on the subject. Because his conclusions stand as a tour de force for any student of American pluralism, it is worth summarizing his key propositions here at the outset: first, that American Protestants and Catholics in the middle to late eighteenth century came to accept and adopt religious freedom and religious diversity as practical necessities without intellectually or theologically coming to terms with them and all their implications; second, that the late eighteenth-century American rationalists were the only ones who intellectually wrestled with the theoretical meaning of religious freedom and pluralism; third, that American pietists and rationalists joined in a temporary coalition of convenience on behalf of religious liberty in the Revolutionary era; and fourth, that American churches largely gave up the goal of religious uniformity in the eighteenth century but retained their exclusivistic claims to being "the Church" well into the next century.[9]

Sweeping in scope and powerful in argument, Mead's assertions have too often been taken as the final word on colonial pluralism rather than as a stimulus to further inquiry. My research into one colony's experience with religious diversity suggests that it is time for a reevaluation of what Mead and his followers have asserted about America's experience as a whole. For in New York at least, provincials responded to the reality of their own pluralism in ways unaccounted for by the standard interpretation. Mead is right in his claim that practical necessity pushed most colonial Protestants toward acceptance of freedom and diversity. But this kind of pragmatic acquiescence did not preclude serious and thoughtful reflection about pluralism's religious meaning. On the contrary, strong evidence exists that throughout most of the eighteenth century in New York religionists of various theological stripes, and not just those who had embraced Enlightenment rationalism, pondered whether the multiplicity of Protestant communions could be squared with a biblical understanding of Christ's church, whether religious truth would suffer where all opinions were free to compete, and whether religion itself could survive if detached from state financial support. Not surprisingly, they reached widely divergent conclusions on these and other issues, a divergence that became most pronounced in the years surrounding the American Revolution. Among those who by that point had fully embraced religious liberty and the religious diversity that accompanied it were evangelical proponents of the new birth and liberal advocates of latitudinarian Christianity, or deism. Their joint efforts to secure religious disestablishment and religious equality for all sprang less from convenience than from their mutual regard for the religious and political benefits of pluralism. Both groups had decided that plural religion, or more specifically Protestant pluralism, was consonant with the rest of their creed and dictated that they give up not only the goal of religious uniformity but the tendency to equate the Christian church solely with their own communion. Not all New Yorkers shared these views, of course, and therefore repudiations of diversity and sectarian claims could still be heard at century's end. Yet their voice was not the dominant one in New York as the 1800s began. Instead, those citizens who had theologically and politically reconciled themselves to pluralism and who had now made it the central feature of the state's religious order held the day and entered the nineteenth century confident that New York's pluralistic future was bright.

ACKNOWLEDGMENTS

It has now been almost a decade since I began to explore New York's religious pluralism, and over those years I have accumulated many scholarly and personal debts. First and foremost I must thank Timothy L. Smith, under whom this project originated at The Johns Hopkins University. Professor Smith is that rare mentor who is able to play the roles of critic, counselor, and confidant equally well. A host of other scholars have read drafts of parts or all of the book and provided suggestions along the way, including Jack Greene, J. G. A. Pocock, Jon Butler, Patricia Bonomi, Milton Klein, Michael Zuckerman, Mark Noll, William Brackney, and Steven Pointer. Librarians and archivists at the research institutions listed in the bibliography gave invaluable assistance in tracking down sources and providing congenial work environments. Series editors Catherine L. Albanese and Stephen J. Stein have taken their job seriously and, as a result, many of the glaring inadequacies of my work have been eliminated. Still, whatever errors of fact or judgment remain are wholly my responsibility.

This book is dedicated to my parents, Roy and Else Pointer. For as long as I can remember their sense of the importance of what has come before has been passed on in fun and loving ways. For better or worse, it has netted them two historians for sons. They have also passed on a vibrant hope for the future, for which I am equally grateful.

My three daughters, Katie, Kristy, and Julie, have been models of patience and encouragement while Daddy has toiled at his desk. Their sweetness has often helped moments of despair to pass quickly. Finally, my wife, Barb, has put almost as many hours into this book as I have, typing, editing, proofreading, critiquing. Without her, none of this would have been possible.

PROTESTANT PLURALISM
AND THE
NEW YORK EXPERIENCE

INTRODUCTION

New York's pluralistic character originated in its New Netherland days. During the four decades of Dutch rule, from the 1620s to the 1660s, Calvinists from the mother country predominated, but their hopes for a religiously uniform colony were never realized. Efforts by Governor Peter Stuyvesant (1647–64) and the Dutch Reformed dominies to enforce religious conformity to their church failed in the face of religious and ethnic diversity. Immigrants from a wide variety of nations and faiths trickled into the colony, encouraged by the tolerant policies of the Dutch West India Company and the prospects for economic gain.[1]

As the focal point of commercial activity, New Amsterdam (later New York City) attracted many of the newcomers. When Jesuit missionary Isaac Jogues visited the port town in 1643, he found smatterings of English Puritans, Dutch Lutherans, and French Catholics, along with a handful of Anabaptists (probably Mennonites) and the preponderant Dutch Reformed.[2] If he had stayed longer or looked harder, he would have run into seamen, merchants, and artisans from Spain, Portugal, Scandinavia, and various parts of central Europe. If he had returned a decade later, he could have welcomed New Netherland's first Jews, Sephardic refugees from Brazil.

Other religio-ethnic groups established footholds elsewhere in the colony. New England Congregationalists and Presbyterians formed communities on Long Island and in Westchester County; English Quakers put down roots on western Long Island; French-speaking Walloons settled on Staten Island; and French Huguenots clustered around New Paltz in Ulster County. In some cases, these settlers formed culturally homogeneous villages. But their presence in the province added to New Netherland's overall heterogeneity.

So, too, did the presence of black Africans and American Indians. Set off from whites not only by race but also by religion, blacks and Indians were almost completely unchristianized under Dutch rule. Their traditional rituals and beliefs were carried on apart from Europeans and served as counterpoint to the Western religiosity of whites in New Netherland's religious landscape.

By the time the English conquered the colony, in 1664, no greater mixture of religions, nationalities, races, and tongues could be found anywhere in colonial America. And in the years that followed, New York's religious diversity only broadened. The influx of new royal officials from England created a fledgling Anglican community in New York City. At the same time, the "papist" sympathies of the Duke of York (later James II) attracted English Catholic settlers, at least until the backlash of Jacob Leisler's rebellion in 1689. Covenanters from the Lowlands of Scotland arrived during the 1670s and '80s in the first of several waves of Scottish and Scots-Irish immigration to the colony. The Revocation of the Edict of Nantes (1685) brought hundreds of French Huguenots to New York City, Staten Island, and New Rochelle. All these groups added to the plurality of religious expression in New York in the late seventeenth century. No wonder that Governor Thomas Dongan's long list of provincial sects in 1687—Anglicans, Catholics, Singing Quakers, Ranting Quakers, Sabbatarians, Antisabbatarians, Anabaptists, Independents, Jews, and Dutch Calvinists—was still incomplete.[3]

A heterogeneous immigration continued throughout the eighteenth century, thanks to European political conflict, England's Act of Toleration, and New York's economic opportunities. From the mother country came many more Anglicans along with several types of dissenters, including Baptists, Quakers, and Congregationalists. The first English Methodists reached New York via Ireland in the 1750s. Germans and Swiss of Moravian, Reformed, Lutheran, and Catholic persuasions appeared, settling on farms and in hamlets along the Hudson and Mohawk rivers. Among these newcomers were the more than two thousand Palatines who emigrated between 1708 and 1710 as part of a royal scheme to populate upper New York. A steady flow of Presbyterians from Scotland and Ulster began arriving around 1720. Most of these Calvinists crossed the Hudson and formed villages and congregations in Orange and Ulster counties. Ashkenazic Jews immigrated from the Continent in sufficient numbers to make them the majority in New York City's Jewish community by the 1730s. French and Spanish Catholics also landed there more frequently after 1700. Unfortunately, they came as English prisoners of war, captured in the European wars of succession. Just before another war, the American Revolution, Catholics from the Scottish Highlands settled temporarily in the Mohawk Valley. Finally, thousands of "heathen" Africans arrived in slave ships, making blacks one-sixth of the province's population in 1775.

Eighteenth-century New York therefore continued the pluralistic pattern in religion established early on by New Netherland. Colonists could scarcely complain of having little choice of religious affiliation. By the 1770s, the more than twenty thousand inhabitants of New York County could select among congregations belonging to no less than eleven Protestant denominations and Judaism. The extent of this religious pluralism rivaled that of Philadelphia.[4] Throughout the rest of the colony, the distribution of churches in villages and towns largely reflected the settlement patterns of the previous 150 years. The upper Hudson and Mohawk Valleys were still dominated by the Dutch and German Reformed, followed by a strong Lutheran minority and a small but growing Anglican constituency centered in Albany. Dutch Reformed congregations were also numerous in Dutchess and Ulster counties (central Hudson Valley), due largely to the internal migration of colonists of Dutch descent from lower New York after 1730. Migration westward from Scotland and New England brought even larger numbers of Presbyterian and Congregational churches to this region by mid-century. These same two groups predominated further south in Westchester and Orange counties, as well as on eastern Long Island, though Anglicans and Quakers provided stiff competition in the former counties. On Staten Island and western Long Island, a host of communions had organized congregations, with the Dutch Reformed, Presbyterian, Anglican, and Quaker bodies leading the way.

In the colony as a whole in the eighteenth century, the Dutch Reformed and Presbyterians were far more numerous than the Quakers, Anglicans, Lutherans, German Reformed, Congregationalists, and Baptists. The French Protestant, Moravian, Methodist, and Jewish bodies each had fewer than five congregations in the province before the American Revolution, but they were spread out in such a way as to intensify the heterogeneous character of particular communities (table 1). Likewise, many New Yorkers lived in areas where their own denomination was not institutionally represented so that the religious mix of a town was always greater than the variety of congregations present there. Frenchman J. Hector St. John de Crèvecoeur gave a classic description of this situation in rural Orange County, where, separated from others of like faith, Roman Catholic, German Lutheran, Scottish Presbyterian, and Dutch Reformed farmers lived as neighbors in apparent harmony.[5]

Then, too, there were those colonists who had no ties to any Christian (or Jewish) tradition or body. These people were not simply the unchurched but rather those who identified neither in public nor in private with the Judeo-Christian religious heritage. Instead, they either ignored religion completely (if that is possible) or became involved in various kinds of folk religion in which magic and occult arts were practiced. How many New

TABLE 1.   **Protestant Congregations in New York in the Colonial Period**[6]

Denomination	1650	1700	1750	1775
Anglican	0	2	20	26
Baptist	0	0	4	10
Congregational	4	9	5	12
Dutch Reformed	2	19	48	76
French Protestant	0	4	4	4
German Reformed	0	0	7	10
Lutheran	2	2	26	26
Methodist	0	0	0	1
Moravian	0	0	1	2
Presbyterian	1	4	35	50
Quaker	0	8	14	22
Total	9	48	164	239

Yorkers fell into this category in the colonial era is impossible to say, but some colonial historians have suggested that it may not have been uncommon for provincials to embrace a syncretic religion that included elements of Christianity and necromancy.[7]

In being religiously and ethnically diverse, New York was a typical Middle Colony. Yet, its Protestant pluralism was clearly different from that in adjoining provinces in at least two ways. First, New York, unlike Pennsylvania and New Jersey, was dominated by church as distinguished from sectarian groups. With comparatively few Quakers and even fewer Moravians, the colony lacked a strong sectarian wing. Instead, its major denominations—Anglican, Reformed, Presbyterian, and Lutheran—were all accustomed to tax support and had strong traditions of alliance with the state.[8] Not surprisingly, then, New York also stood apart from its Middle Atlantic neighbors in having a religious establishment. After the Glorious Revolution in 1689, the Church of England was established in the four counties centering on New York City (New York, Queens, Westchester, and Richmond). The establishment continued until the Revolutionary War, giving Anglicans a religious and political clout greatly disproportionate to their numbers.[9]

While New York's religious milieu was unique, it nevertheless was a part of the larger Western religious world. To understand what was happening there, the colonists' transatlantic religious ties to Europe cannot be ignored. Throughout this period, the Atlantic Ocean was as much a highway as a barrier to cultural exchange. A constant stream of religious ideas, practical

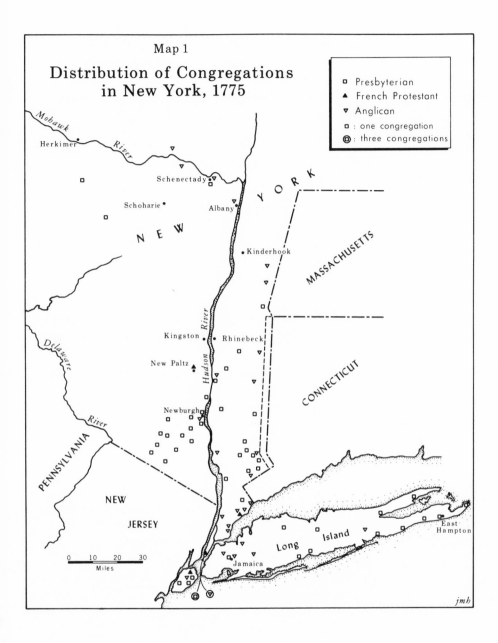

Map 1

Distribution of Congregations
in New York, 1775

□ Presbyterian
▲ French Protestant
▽ Anglican
□ : one congregation
◉ : three congregations

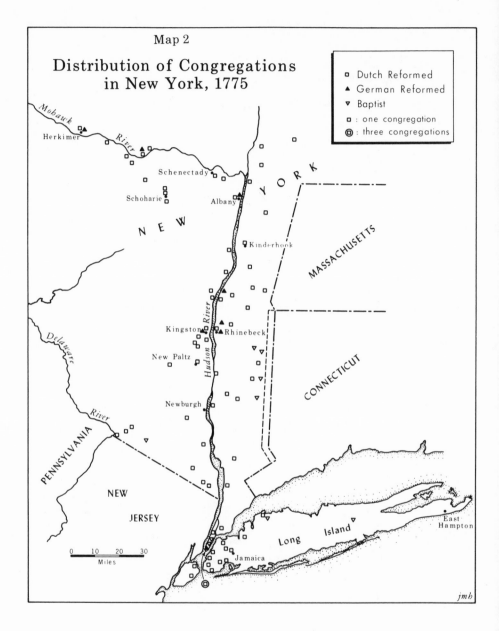

Map 2

Distribution of Congregations in New York, 1775

□ Dutch Reformed
▲ German Reformed
▽ Baptist
□ : one congregation
◎ : three congregations

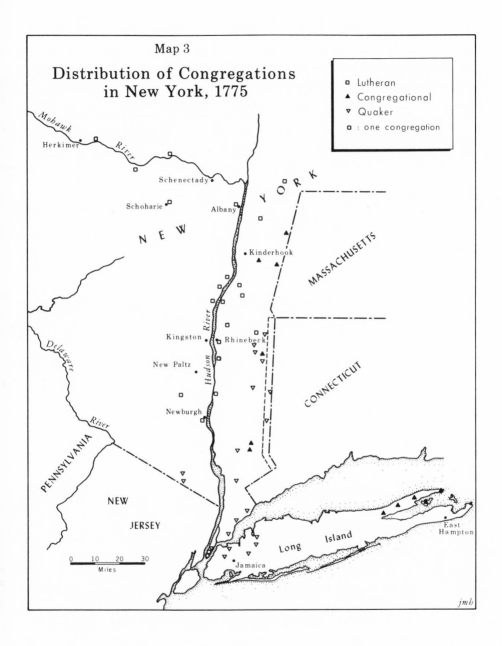

Map 3

Distribution of Congregations
in New York, 1775

□ Lutheran
▲ Congregational
▽ Quaker
□ : one congregation

innovations, and political points of view flowed in both directions. It is entirely appropriate, therefore, that this study begin by looking at the intense interest certain New Yorkers displayed during the middle decades of the eighteenth century in the ecclesiastical relationshps between their churches and those in the homelands.

I

Plural Religion in a New World Environment, 1700–1775

I

"A SPIRIT OF INDEPENDENCE"
THE QUEST FOR ECCLESIASTICAL
SELF-SUFFICIENCY

Drawing on eighteen years of firsthand observation, Michael Christian Knoll, Lutheran pastor in New York City, described religious conditions in the colony in 1749 for the Lutheran Consistory at Rothenberg, Germany. Congregations were scattered miles apart in the largely rural province, he wrote, and their average size was far below their European counterparts. With no local ecclesiastical overseers, "everyone does what he considers right" in religious affairs. Members were tempted to stray away from their faith through "marriage, pride and bread, so that one who is today a Lutheran, he or his child may tomorrow be a Reformed, a Moravian, or a Quaker, etc." Faithful ministers were opposed by the "evil-minded" and had to ward off the teachings of many "false preachers" who were not ordained and paid little attention to the Augsburg Confession. On top of all that, the large German immigration to the colony during the past decade had completely changed the makeup of his Lutheran congregations, prompting a long controversy over what language should be used in their worship services.[1]

While Knoll's description is far from complete, it does highlight a number of the problems New York's churches shared in trying to survive and grow in this New World environment. These problems, although present elsewhere in the Middle Colonies, were exacerbated in New York by its greater geographical expanse and partial church establishment. In assessing how best to succeed, Knoll and other colonial observers generally agreed that institutional survival required above all adequate human and material resources. Without money to build houses of worship or sufficient ministers to supply them, religious groups were hard pressed to retain the loyalty of their lay participants, especially when attendance at a competing congregation was possible.

Knoll's letter also illustrates, however, that Lutherans, as well as other colonial churchmen, were not entirely on their own in trying to meet these needs. Most congregations were still either formally under the supervision of European ecclesiastical bodies or informally dependent on them. That was particularly true of congregations in the state church tradition—Anglicans, Lutherans, and Dutch and German Reformed—and, to a lesser degree, Presbyterians and French Huguenots. But it was partially true also of Jewish, Methodist, Quaker, and Moravian fellowships. Twice in the 1750s, for instance, Congregation Shearith Israel wrote to the Sephardic congregation in London requesting that a young man be sent to be their hazzan (cantor, or leader). Similarly, New York's Methodists in 1768 wrote to John Wesley requesting "an able and experienced preacher" for their church.[2] On the whole, nearly all the congregations in the colony looked to Europe for spiritual guidance as well as for ministers and mission funds.

This dependence stemmed from the infant state of their organizations and their understanding of the ministerial office. Deprived of the powerful ecclesiastical leadership and state support many of them had enjoyed in Europe, they found it difficult during the seventeenth and early eighteenth centuries to mobilize the larger units that were beginning to be called denominations.[3] Hence, most provincial congregations found identity beyond the local level in only one place—with their fellow religionists in Europe. In addition, their prevailing high view of the ministerial calling emphasized the absolute necessity of proper educational preparation and ordination and inhibited the growth of an indigenously trained and locally ordained ministry.[4]

The relationships they enjoyed with their homeland churches afforded them a variety of benefits. Communication with ministers and laypersons across the Atlantic kept colonists abreast of religious and political developments in their mother countries. Such contact generally reinforced their determination to retain the sense of national pride and ethnic identity that tied them to the Old World. Theologically, the European bodies sustained their rich traditions of belief and practice by supplying Bibles, prayer books, Psalters, hymnals, and other liturgical and devotional works. The Dutch Reformed and Lutherans in New York used their Amsterdam and Hamburg advisers to review and settle disputes between and within congregations. The Bishop of London served the same purpose for colonial Anglicans.[5] Anglicans also depended on British contributions to the Society for the Propagation of the Gospel (SPG) to pay the salaries of their missionary ministers. Even those bodies without any formal ties to Europe, such as the Baptists and Quakers, relied upon transatlantic correspondence and occasional visits for spiritual as well as political counsel.[6] Participants from virtually all colonial denominations thus derived some form of aid from their European fellows.

Unfortunately, these benefits were often overshadowed by the failure of the European bodies to send an adequate supply of clergymen. Religious hierarchies in Europe had difficulty attracting suitable young men to fill their own pulpits, let alone convincing enough clergymen to leave family and friends for the low salaries and physical hardships of colonial life. The reasons Dutch Lutheran Woltherus Conradi gave in 1668 for declining a call to the colonies were still being invoked a century later:

> First, the not only long, but also perilous and uncertain voyage, not knowing whether one can indeed sail across without danger. Second, one does not know the conditions of the country, whether it is expensive to live there or not. Third, one does not know for certain either whether one is to have free dwelling there or not. Fourth, whether, after I had been there two or three years and should be inclined to return hither, I should be promoted to the first vacant place.[7]

At the same time, the danger and cost to colonials of sailing to Europe for education and ordination set such a high price on a ministerial career that relatively few provincial souls had sufficient courage and money to pursue it. Within the Church of England alone, as many as ten prospective ministers were lost while making the trip during the eighteenth century.[8]

As a result, a large disparity arose between the number of congregations and the number of ministers in New York during the first half of the eighteenth century, as immigration and natural growth swelled the population to over eighty thousand.[9] As the numbers increased, so too did the geographical spread of settlement. Lay groups founded new congregations, but were usually frustrated in their first attempts to secure ministers. Of the more than 160 congregations in the province in 1750, about a fourth had full-time pastors who conducted worship services and oversaw other congregational activities on a weekly basis. In contrast, some went months at a time without any pulpit supply.[10] Most congregations were forced to share the services of their ministers with several sister churches. Typical were the colony's Lutheran parishes in which one pastor was responsible for three to six congregations.[11]

Based largely on this shortage of ministers, Martin Lodge has argued that here and elsewhere in the Middle Colonies the churches institutionally failed in the era preceding the First Great Awakening.[12] "Organized religion seemed on the verge of collapse," in his view, especially in rural settlements flooded with new immigrants.[13] Similarly, Michael Kammen has insisted that eighteenth-century New York was becoming increasingly secular, largely because of the undistinguished and inadequate quality and quantity of clergy.[14] These historians are accurate, I believe, in asserting that burgeoning lay needs simply could not all be met under the prevailing circumstances. Moreover, the colony's pluralistic environment often heightened the importance of a minister for the welfare of a congregation. Large-scale transfers of members sometimes took place solely on the grounds of who had a pastor and what language he spoke. In addition, even when the number of clergymen was sufficient, as one observer put it, "the progress of the gospel here depends much on the qualifications of the preachers."[15]

Yet, the suggestion that the churches were institutionally failing or suffering a "crisis of faith" is overdrawn when applied to New York, both because it exaggerates the seriousness of the problem and underestimates the resourcefulness of the laity. Between 1700 and 1750, the number of congregations in New York steadily grew from 48 to 164, thereby almost keeping pace with the colony's fourfold population increase.[16] Moreover, much of this church growth took place in the newly settled areas of the Hudson and Mohawk Valleys, where pastors remained scarce until later in the century.[17] In such spots, groups of committed laypersons sometimes kept religious interest and practice alive for years while receiving only occasional visits from a pastor or missionary. That was clearly the case in a half dozen or more of the Lutheran fellowships formed in this era, for besides a periodic service performed by Albany minister William Berkenmeyer, or an occasional sermon from a traveling preacher like Johan Van Dieren, laymen were completely on their own.[18] A parallel situation held sway in various Dutch Reformed, German Reformed, and Presbyterian congregations along the Hudson River, not to mention the numerous pockets of active Quaker worship that by design were maintained without benefit of a formal ministry.

While this evidence indicates that no pervasive institutional crisis was occurring, it is nevertheless noteworthy that after 1740 colonial churchmen devoted much attention to resolving the ministerial shortage. In fact, probably no other ecclesiastical issue was more talked or written about by New York's religious leaders in the pre-Revolutionary era. Earlier in the century, the several communions had made little corporate effort to deal with this problem because the challenge of keeping individual congregations going absorbed the time and energy of ministers and laypeople alike. By the 1740s, however, members of every religious body realized that the issue could no longer be ignored, for the future of each group in America depended ultimately (if not immediately) upon its resolution. Lay efforts to provide for their own religious life were commendable, but long-term success depended on an adequate clergy since there were certain things (e.g., administering the sacraments) they alone could do. During the following three decades, therefore, colonists debated among themselves and with their coreligionists in Europe how best to respond to the need for more pastors.

These debates took place against a backdrop of continued institutional growth at the congregational level, as another seventy-five new congregations were formed prior to 1775.[19] Nevertheless, because the lack of pastors stemmed largely from the colonial churches' dependency on European bodies unable to supply them, the stakes in these debates were very high. Churchmen did not merely discuss where to find more ministerial recruits but instead confronted such vital issues as the proper relationship between the colonial and European churches, the best form of ecclesiastical organization in the New World, the essential requirements for a successful ministry, and the prospects for autonomous American denominations. Nothing less than their whole future institutional development hung in the balance, and colonial religious leaders were anxious to implement whatever decisions were reached. These discussions therefore merit close attention. They were a key shaping influence upon the organizational development of New York's churches and thus help to reveal the ways diversity was molding the colony's religious scene.

Overall, two basic conflicting positions emerged among those seriously concerned about the continued well-being of provincial churches. Large groups within the Dutch Reformed and Anglican communions and smaller groups within the Lutheran and Presbyterian bodies saw ecclesiastical reliance on Europe as the lifeline to which their church's existence clung. They argued that any alteration of it would mean certain decay and probable death. In their view, the only hope for religious progress lay in continued deference to European authorities—and greater benevolence from them. As one Lutheran minister put it, "If the mother church in Europe does not have mercy on us, then the Christian religion in America in general, and the Evangelical Lutheran in particular, is done for."[20] After years of frustrated hopes and unanswered petitions, however, many pastors and laypersons in these same communions and others concluded that such expectations were chimerical. They adopted the alternative view that congregations in each faith tradition must form a self-sufficient denomination, with an organization empowered to recruit, educate, and ordain a new generation of native-born pastors.[21]

While advocates of these alternative solutions were committed to the common goal of ensuring the spiritual welfare of their religious communities, they found little else to agree on in the twenty-five years preceding the American Revolution. Within denominations, and even within congregations, they disputed over ordination powers, ministerial education, and the language of worship services. The underlying source of disagreement, however, was usually the contrasting perceptions of what the relationship of colonial to European churches should be. "Traditionalists" understood the new call for self-sufficiency to imply an actual ecclesiastical independence that would cut the ancient bonds in which they found their doctrinal and cultural identity. "Accommodationists" insisted that self-sufficiency was their communion's only chance of liberation from a transatlantic dependence that was slowly paralyzing the American congregations.[22]

What accounts for this fundamental division between two emerging parties within the several communions? Perhaps one way to answer this question is to study the general composition of the opposing sides. The Dutch Reformed clergy, where battle lines were sharply drawn, is the best example with which to begin. While forty-five of the seventy-five pastors who served in New York and New Jersey from 1714 to 1776 came from Europe, twenty-five of the forty-one still active in 1776 were native-born.[23] This dramatic shift was closely paralleled by a gradual increase in the proportions trained and ordained in America.[24] Furthermore, the vast majority of those who received their theological education in the colonies trained under clergymen who were deeply committed to the Pietist doctrines and style popularized in the earlier part of the century in the Raritan Valley by Theodore J. Frelinghuysen.[25] These Pietist beliefs and practices differed significantly from those of Continental Dutch Reformed Orthodoxy. In light of these facts, it is significant that most of the New York and New Jersey pastors who favored self-sufficiency, known as the Coetus party, were born in America and virtually all, whether native-born or not, had studied under colonial pastors in the Pietist tradition. They also were located primarily in settlements west of the Hudson River. Conversely, their opponents, known as the Conferentie party, were generally natives of Europe educated in Germany, Holland, or Switzerland. The few of the latter group who were educated in America had tutored with clergymen committed to more traditional European styles of worship and belief. In addition, Conferentie ministers more often than the accommodationists served in older areas of Dutch settlement and in towns where the high concentration of Germans or Dutch seemed to mandate the continued use of European language and customs.[26]

The evidence suggests, then, that such factors as place of birth, educational experience, theological orientation, and geographic location contributed to the conflicting views among the Dutch Reformed in America. These differences, taken together, seem also to help explain why one group of members within other colonial communions wished to follow closely the model of their church "at home" while another group moved to develop in the American branch a genius and character of its own. Among Lutherans, the key governing factor in the split, according to Johannis Mol, was acceptance or rejection of pietistic theology.[27] Among the Presbyterian ministers involved in the Old Side-New Side split in 1741, place of birth and education were important distinguishing features. Like the Dutch Reformed Conferentie, virtually all of the Old Side pastors had been born and educated abroad, while most of the revivalists had been tutored by evangelical ministers in America.[28] Within Anglicanism, traditionalists were strongest in those areas (New York, New Jersey, Connecticut) where the Church of England was a minority faith with little or no state support and High Church sentiments prevailed among the clergy.[29]

Among the Dutch Reformed advocates of the accommodationist view was John Frelinghuysen, son and successor to Pietist leader Theodore J. Frelinghuysen. John participated actively in the debates in his own communion prior to his premature death in 1754. The previous year he had written to the Classis of Amsterdam urging it to approve the calling of Thomas Romeyn to the two congregations in Queens County, Oyster Bay and Jamaica. Frelinghuysen argued that Romeyn was particularly suited to this field because he was born in America and "accustomed to the ways of the people." He urged the classis to overlook the "makeshift procedures surrounding this pastoral call." They were not unusual in the special circumstances that prevailed in America, he reasoned; and the two congregations had been so long without a minister that some members were drifting to the Baptists or joining the Church of England, whose "pelagian principles and political bulwarks" were "so agreeable to the corrupt nature."[30]

Frelinghuysen's letter represents a remarkably complete presentation of the accommodationist view that colonial congregations required a self-sufficiency based on innovative adaptations of European traditions. Stated briefly, accommodationists argued for the inherent advantages of native ministers, practical church government and discipline, and a substantial transfer of authority to the colonial churches.

The case for American-bred clergymen emphasized the time and expense required to import pastors from Europe, as well as the frustration often incurred in the process. There were many examples to draw upon. Between 1766 and 1771, for instance, Lutherans in Loonenburg, New

York, wrote four times to the Amsterdam Consistory requesting a minister, without success. After the final refusal, the congregation wrote the consistory and sarcastically expressed its disappointment:

> . . . Your Right reverences will please not trouble yourselves further on our account, but let it go at that, in order that we may make use of other assistance. You will excuse us, however, if we hereby express our gratitude for the altogether too great and abundant love and solicitude, yes, quite fatherly care and efforts in our behalf, which your Right Reverences have indeed bestowed upon us.[31]

Similarly, in 1772 French Protestants in New York City petitioned their congregation in London for a pastor, only to be told that no candidates could be found because of the physical and financial sacrifices of ministering in the colonies.[32] Even when congregations were able to locate a willing European candidate, the expense of transporting him to America was prohibitive.[33]

Furthermore, many immigrant clergymen lacked proper education and ordination, or worse, any degree of moral and theological integrity. (On this point, accommodationists and traditionalists agreed.) American churchgoers of all persuasions could have echoed Baptist minister John Gano's statement that his New York City congregation had lived in harmony in the 1760s except for the difficulties aroused by two or three schismatic preachers from England.[34] Members of the Dutch Reformed church on Staten Island were deeply discouraged when they discovered that their minister, Peter de Windt, had lied about his education and ordination.[35] Lutheran pastors William Berkenmeyer and John Weygand resolutely opposed the "vagabond" clergy who, whether formally trained for the ministry or not, had no call from a congregation and were usually not ordained.[36] Many of these preachers, like their fellow immigrants, tied themselves to no specific place or religion for any long period of time. Presbyterians became so concerned about the heterodoxy of English and Irish ministers that they temporarily violated their rules and empowered their synod to review all pastoral appointments of candidates from overseas.[37]

Despite such examples, accommodationists admitted that many "faithful shepherds" had been called and sent from Europe. There was no guarantee, however, that such men would adapt to the New World. Lutheran leader Henry Muhlenberg confided that during their first years in America immigrant ministers were "not in a position to put up with our work and manner of life."[38] One such Lutheran pastor was Muhlenberg's Pietist ally,

John Hartwick. After close to a decade of colonial service in the Hudson Valley, Hartwick confessed disgust with having to endure "the poorly constructed houses they call churches," the lack of a tolerable parsonage, the widely scattered nature of his parish, and the religious ignorance and doctrinal indifference of the people.[39] Such declarations convinced a growing number of colonial leaders that clergymen reared in America were preferable, if only because they knew what to expect when they chose their calling. As Anglican Samuel Johnson put it, such men knew the "genius of the people."[40]

Central to understanding this "genius" was their ability to speak the language of their flocks, both literally and figuratively. Perhaps no other factor accounted for so much movement from one group to the next as the presence of a minister who could speak a desired language. The Dutch Reformed, Dutch Lutheran, and French Protestant congregations in New York City witnessed a growing exodus of members because of language difficulties.[41] In the Dutch Collegiate Church (Reformed—New York City), a debate over whether to hold services in English extended for forty years before an English-speaking minister was called in 1763.[42] Thereafter, English preaching gradually spread to other Dutch Reformed congregations around the province, although the majority retained the old language at least until after the American Revolution.[43] Their reluctance to make this change had been costly, however. John H. Livingston, one of the ministers of the Collegiate Church after 1770, observed:

> . . . had the English language been timely introduced in the public service, how many of our chief & largest families wo'd have been preserved among us? had . . . vigorous effectual methods been pursued to educate divines from amongst ourselves who co'd also have served in the english language & been an ornament in the learned world as well as the Church, how large, how numerous, how flourishing sho'd we at this day [1772] have been?[44]

This pastor and many others agreed with Presbyterian layman William Livingston's conclusion that the increasing pervasiveness of the English tongue dictated the eventual disuse of all foreign languages, including Dutch.[45] Only the calling of English-speaking clergymen could stop the decline of their congregations; and what better place to find such men than among those born and reared in America?

Proficiency in the English language was, according to the accommodationists, only one among many natural abilities native American ministers possessed.[46] Others were habituation to the climate, firsthand knowledge of the needs of young people, the sense of a common brotherhood and heritage with other colonists, and, in some cases, personal acquaintance with their future parishioners. When set against the liabilities of immigrant pastors, these advantages seemed to many to be overwhelming.

Colonial birth, of course, was not a benefit unless ministers allowed their familiarity with the environment to shape their pastoral methods and message. The realities of American church life made it next to impossible for clergymen to maintain European standards of worship. Although efforts to do so may have been honorable, they were nevertheless futile.[47] Accommodationists did not propose watering down central doctrines, but they encouraged pastors and laypersons to accept, for the sake of their congregations, simplification and, in some cases, relaxation of traditional church practices, rituals, and rules.

Since readiness to adjust European usages to American conditions was more a mental disposition than a hard-and-fast principle, its practical manifestations were as varied as the persons involved. To help meet the language needs of a group of Welsh-speaking Presbyterians, the New York and Philadelphia Synod in 1758 ordained John Griffith, who had had little formal theological training. In this case, the spiritual commitments of Griffith and his fellow Welshmen caused the synod to overlook its educational requirements.[48] Henry Muhlenberg demonstrated remarkable flexibility in altering the content of his catechetical exams, in broadening the invitation to his communion table, and in preaching in whatever language his audience best understood.[49] His policy was to use whatever resources were available to meet the spiritual needs of his parishioners.[50] In contrast, traditionalist William Berkenmeyer sought to repeat Old World ritual completely, even to the point of insisting that the shape of the communion wafer be identical to that used in homeland churches.[51] German Reformed leader Michael Schlatter departed from European customs by democratizing the congregational election of pastors.[52] More out of necessity than choice, the French Protestant Church of Saint-Esprit in New York City depended for ten years on the presence each third Sunday of a minister who, though neither French nor fully aware of the particular doctrinal emphases of this congregation, could at least speak their language and administer the sacraments.[53] Finally, New York's earliest Methodist congregation decided, though it was later overruled, that a permanent pastor was preferable to John Wesley's plan of a rotating ministry.[54]

Accommodationists became convinced that failure to make such adaptations would spell certain decline for their churches. Dutch Reformed advocates of a stronger denominational organization pointed to the case of their congregation in Stone Arabia, New York. Because the pastor, J. M. Goetschius, had never been ordained and therefore could not administer the sacraments, the church had finally dropped both him and the Dutch Church Order and become "prey to confusion and to German tramps."[55] Others observed that Moravian growth in New York was sharply curtailed by adherence to the European definition of the society as "a Church within the Church," called only to lead souls to Christ. Converts were encouraged to remain in their respective churches in order to persuade others of their need for redemption. This policy made the idea of membership in a Moravian congregation problematic and prevented the organization and expansion of new Moravian groups.[56] On the other hand, Presbyterians and Baptists prospered because they established synods and associations that could respond to the demands of their environment and the needs of their people. These general bodies consistently devoted a portion of their annual meetings to assigning pastors to supply temporarily "vacant" or "destitute" congregations. In this way, the congregations were not left to die out, although it was rare that such places experienced significant growth.[57]

An American-bred clergy reconciled to the realities of colonial religious life could only be ultimately successful, however, if invested with sufficient power to perpetuate itself. Hence, the third and most important part of the accommodationist objective was to secure means to train and authority to ordain ministers in the colonies. This required that provincial groups establish their own seminaries and receive European permission for an expansion of their ecclesiastical powers. Among bodies with a state church tradition, Presbyterians alone had taken these steps prior to 1750. The founding of the first American presbytery took place as early as 1706; ten years later there were enough congregations to justify the formation of the Synod of Philadelphia, comprising four subsidiary presbyteries.[58] The synod, established with the approval of the Church of Scotland, brought together annually ministerial and lay delegates from each Presbyterian congregation to deal with matters of polity, discipline, and doctrine. Scottish recognition of the synod's authority not only gave its decisions a degree of validity but, more important, affirmed the authenticity of the ordinations its constituent presbyteries conferred.

Possession of the power to ordain did not, however, guarantee consensus among Presbyterians on the qualifications necessary for ordination. As evangelical revivals swept through the Middle Colonies in the 1730s and '40s, this issue became divisive. The revivalists, known as the New Side, left the Synod of Philadelphia in 1741, and four years later formed their own body, the Synod of New York. Initially, many of the revivalists opposed the notion of a learned ministry, fearing that study might dampen their enthusiasm. By the time the New York Synod was established, however, the New Side had firmly committed itself to educating pastors. The spread of the

Great Awakening convinced the new synod that its supply of ministers from European universities, New England colleges (Yale and Harvard), and William and Gilbert Tennent's Log College was inadequate. Only a strong college located in the Middle Colonies could make readily accessible the quality education necessary to attract able young men into the ministry.[59] When the College of New Jersey began classes in 1747, therefore, American Presbyterianism took a giant step toward ecclesiastical self-sufficiency.[60]

Members of other denominations in New York quickly recognized the advantages the Presbyterians had gained. A group of Dutch Reformed ministers declared that Presbyterians were growing because they had received "the advice and help of the Church of Scotland," including especially "the privileges of admitting their young men locally to the ministerial office."[61] Likewise, Henry Muhlenberg attributed Presbyterian progress primarily to the fact that "they have established seminaries in various places, [and] educate their own ministers. . . ."[62]

Strong Presbyterian development produced first envy, then imitation among competing denominations. The Dutch Reformed ministers of New York and New Jersey made their first strides toward organizing corporately in the late 1740s. Concerned with maintaining their church's influence in a region where they were rapidly losing their numerical and cultural dominance, they followed the advice of their Amsterdam overseers and organized themselvs into a representative body, known as the Coetus. Principally designed to serve as consultant and arbiter for its member congregations, this assembly lacked the authority it needed to resolve the problems brought before it. When the Coetus in September 1754 moved to be changed into a classis, with full examination and ordination powers, it sparked a division in the denomination that lasted until 1772.[63]

Similar developments occurred in other colonial communions. In 1747, German Reformed churches in Pennsylvania created a coetus that gradually asserted rights and privileges virtually identical to those being claimed by the Dutch Reformed Coetus. Henry Muhlenberg oversaw the formation of a Lutheran ministerium in Pennsylvania in 1748. Composed of ministerial and lay delegates, it was to meet regularly, assume the full powers of ordination, and exercise oversight through an elected president. By the 1760s, four of New York's five Lutheran parishes were controlled by it. Members within each of these groups, contending for a more powerful coetus or a local ministerium, tried to persuade their European brothers that sharp changes in the supervision and oversight of colonial congregations were necessary.[64]

Despite the variety of their requests, the provincials used similar arguments in their appeals to overseas authorities. Virtually all insisted on the inability of the colonial bodies as presently constituted to compete effectively against other religious groups and irreligion. Typical was Albany pastor Theodore Frelinghuysen's lament to his Amsterdam supervisors that Presbyterians and Anglicans had a clear advantage over the Dutch Reformed because they had their own colonial colleges.[65] Accommodationists were also fond of emphasizing their congregations' need for the continuous and consistent oversight that European bodies could not provide. For example, members of the Dutch Reformed Coetus pointed out the frustrations imposed upon their efforts to settle disputes quickly by the necessity of referring all decisions to the Amsterdam Classis for final approval.[66] Finally, advocates of change openly expressed their conviction that spiritual leaders in the homelands failed to appreciate the special problems facing American believers. Lutherans, in particular, suggested the impossibility of Europeans having a clear conception of the spiritual and moral struggle confronting the colonial congregations.[67]

These arguments demonstrated the basic agreement among accommodationists on their primary objective, local examination and ordination powers. This authority would provide their communions with the guidance, leadership, and discipline necessary to recruit and maintain growing congregations by persuasion and consent. Furthermore, religious bodies could then oversee the establishment of the colleges needed to train a native ministry. Such powers, once obtained, would release the colonists from dependence on European bodies and enable them to assume control over their own religious destiny.

To the great frustration of the accommodationists, large numbers in their several communions were unconvinced by these arguments. In fact, the "traditionalist" or "formalist" pastors and laymen considered the accommodationist plan an anathema upon them and their congregations. From this conservative perspective, the prospect of ecclesiastical self-sufficiency was both unrealistic and undesirable. Although these conservatives were not blind to the institutional needs of New York's churches, they had made no attempt to formulate a plan to meet them until confronted with the accommodationist proposals. Consequently, they stated their position primarily in the form of a response to or reaction against those proposals. Their arguments lacked the consistency and cohesiveness their opponents had displayed, but several common themes were pervasive.

Conservatives argued first of all that the proposed changes would only make bad situations worse. They conceded that local ordination of native ministers might be helpful, but only if proper educational institutions came into being first. Otherwise, the quality of the ministry would inevitably decline. Without careful restriction of candidates, a less learned, less respected, and perhaps less orthodox clergy would result.[68] Members of the conservative Dutch Reformed Conferentie feared that any steps toward self-sufficiency might undermine the legal and other privileges their denomination enjoyed by virtue of being regarded as a national church by the Anglicans.[69] Another objection formalists raised sprang from their inability to conceive of an alternative to religious establishment. They argued that even if colonial bodies gained greater ecclesiastical powers, their decisions would be meaningless without the sustaining authority of the civil government.[70] Lutheran minister John Hartwick explained: "In Europe our churches are intertwined with the state and are supported by the state. Here in America . . . the church is like a vineyard without door and lock."[71] The circumstances were so difficult in pluralistic New York, Hartwick believed, that the churches could not survive without a civil establishment. Accordingly he recommended that all the Lutheran congregations conform to the Church of England.[72]

Second, traditionalists maintained that the calling and training of pastors in America would inevitably cause the separation of colonial congregations from the churches of the homeland. The Consistory of the Dutch Collegiate Church in New York City, in a letter to its Amsterdam superiors, noted that some already called the relation with the classis "a father's yoke, which must be shaken off."[73] Rather than loosening transatlantic bonds, they suggested the opposite course. The Conferentie declared, "Our object is that the tie between us and the churches of the Fatherland, instead of being broken, may become stronger and stronger."[74] Long accustomed to looking toward their mother countries for spiritual leadership and cultural ideals, these pastors sought to promote steps they thought would bind parent and child more closely. Nowhere was that more evident than in the efforts of some Anglican clergy to gain bishops for America. Throughout the generation preceding the Revolution, Samuel Johnson, Thomas B. Chandler, and other ministers maintained that Anglican congregations could not resolve the shortage of pastors nor keep up with other bodies until they received their proper disciplinary and spiritual head, a bishop in America.[75] In their minds, an American episcopate would not only allow Anglicanism to compete more effectively but would bring the colonial church more fully under the supervision of her English mother and more closely in line with English ecclesiastical practice.[76] Their accommodationist opponents, on the other hand, were Anglican ministers and laypeople in New York and elsewhere who opposed a bishopric and preferred instead to preserve colonial innovations (e.g., lay control over the selection of the minister) that promised self-determination.[77]

The desire to preserve the colonial-European bond prompted formalists to charge that the real goal of their opponents' cry for self-sufficiency was individual gain. Far from being motivated by a genuine concern for the welfare of their congregations or the Christian faith, the accommodationists' suggestions seemed to them to mask a desire for power.[78] Old Side Presbyterians made numerous protests against what they considered abuses of majority rule by their New Side colleagues.[79] Similarly, Conferentie members, seeing their influence receding and fearing the domination of an opposing majority, suggested that decisions on major issues should require unanimous rather than majority approval. And they urged the Synod of North Holland to commission the Dutch ambassador at the British Court to protest that their churches in America were being "oppressed in their privileges and liberties by a band of ministers, who, through a spirit of independency, have turn[ed] . . . from the Netherlandish Church, and cast off their relations to that Church."[80] Hence, in traditionalist eyes, a "spirit of independence" enveloped all accommodationists and represented a selfish zeal for partisan rule.

During the long controversy, both sides sought the approval of their European advisers. Their repeated appeals forced religious leaders in Britain, Holland, and Germany to face these divisive issues. Churchmen overseas thus became major participants in the discussions of how to ensure a prosperous future for the colony's churches.

Although I shall not be able in this study to examine in full detail European perceptions of colonial religious developments, I will venture at the outset a few suggestions. For the most part, European church leaders showed more compassion than indifference. When convinced that the colonial situation required changes, they frequently accepted them, as when the Amsterdam Classis reprimanded opponents of English-speaking ministers for being more concerned with the "external utterances of the Gospel in a particular language" than with the "ruin and loss of a whole congregation."[81] On the other hand, this same body, when threatened by a challenge to its exclusive right to examine and ordain ministers, resisted doggedly, claiming that to do otherwise might result in an inferior colonial ministry.[82] Both responses show the difficulty Europeans experienced in determining what was best for a dynamic colonial church set in a world far different from their own. Simply understanding the new realities of provincial religious life was so complex a task as often to prompt frustrated denunciations of the "wretched condition and disorder in America."[83] Anglican authorities, moreover, had to consider the impact in England of their colonial policies. While some sympathized with colonial calls for an American episcopate, they repeatedly insisted that such a move was impossible until it became politically expedient at home.[84]

Despite the difficulties Europeans found in discharging their responsibilities toward colonial churches, one goal nevertheless seems to have
been the governing factor in most of their decisions: the desire to retain the
closest possible relationship with the pastors and people of their persuasion
in America. Inspired by this aim, the Moravian General Synod in Saxony
judged that its colonial congregations required closer supervision and more
immediate control.[85] Given New York's pluralism, however, others adopted
the opposite course, with the same objective. After two decades of trying to
mediate the Coetus-Conferentie dispute, the Amsterdam Classis concluded
in June of 1768 that unless a resolution was accomplished soon, the consequences would be "the complete severance of the greater portion of the
ministers and churches there from the Church of the Netherlands." Fearful
that the mother church would lose "all relationship with a daughter" and be
forced "to see that daughter departing from the ancient purity of doctrine,"
the classis proposed a plan that gave the colonists de facto independence
but allowed for a continuing "close Alliance" between the Dutch and
American churches.[86] The threat of losing all its prerogatives had in fact
prodded the classis to surrender some of them.

The Moravian and Dutch Reformed cases illustrate that the Europeans,
no less than the colonial accommodationists and traditionalists, held differing opinions on what was best for New York's churches. In retrospect, it
seems clear that all three groups understood that the province's pluralist
environment, as well as the practical reality of being separated by three
thousand miles, made continued dependence on the Old World more and
more difficult. Once they recognized this problem, they realized they had to
consider all possible ways to resolve it. That a portion of the colonial
religionists decided that the only sensible course was ecclesiastical self-
sufficiency was not due, as their opponents claimed, to a desire to sever all
connections with Europe. If that had been the case, they could have simply
suspended all correspondence with the mother churches.[87] Far from desiring what all parties described as spiritual isolation, proponents of self-
sufficiency wished to continue receiving the advice of their cousins in
Europe even after independence was gained.

What ecclesiastical independence did imply, however, was the transformation of the transatlantic relationship from colonial subservience to a
degree of parity that assured practical autonomy. Influenced by the ideas of
political independence and self-rule germinating in the colonies in the
1760s and '70s, accommodationists gradually became more aggressive in
denouncing a subordination they now perceived as unjust and obsolete. In
a dramatic declaration in June 1765, the Dutch Reformed Coetus stated
that it would no longer argue on the basis of past history whether the

colonial churches should remain in a subordinate position but would argue instead from "inherent rights." As a "free people" the coetus members insisted that the decision whether or not to correspond with the European body was theirs alone to make.[88] By 1771, they had succeeded in gaining independence for their congregations from the Netherlands, and thereafter began molding them into a full-fledged American denomination.

Thus did the Dutch Reformed join the progress of New York's Presbyterians, German Reformed, and Lutherans, as well as Baptists and Quakers, toward the independence all were to realize fully after 1775. Within each of these bodies important steps were taken in the preceding three decades to construct the denominational institutions required for maintenance of their congregations in a free and pluralistic society. As they formed representative governing bodies, founded colleges, and ordained ministers, these groups not only became self-sufficient but also established themselves as autonomous partners with their European coreligionists. At the same time, they retained some degree of deference toward their European brothers and continued to look across the Atlantic for guidance and Christian fellowship. Collectively they stood as a clear witness to other colonial, as well as European, bodies of the dominant direction of American church life.

By the time the Revolution began, therefore, the accommodationist-traditionalist debate was essentially over in most of New York's religious groups. The colony's Moravian and infant Methodist congregations, however, had little choice but to remain reliant on Europe. And traditionalist Anglicans kept up their fight for an American episcopate. They remained in the ironic situation of being denied a local bishop, whose presence would surely have brought them into closer corroboration with their mother church. During the late 1760s a group of disgruntled Anglican clergymen informed the English hierarchy that they would only remain subordinate if their request for an American bishop was granted.[89] The rhetoric of the plea made them sound like accommodationists. At heart, however, they were firmly traditionalist, for they thought an American bishop would tighten, rather than loosen, their bonds to the Church of England. They could scarcely help becoming impatient when repeated attempts to be an obedient child went unrewarded by a parent they deemed increasingly negligent.

The realities of the social and religious situation, especially the colony's religious pluralism, seem almost to have demanded that its churches become self-sufficient. While no pervasive institutional crisis was occurring, the growing shortage of pastors made competing in a diverse environment more difficult and left some lay needs unmet. Concerned with finding a solution, a majority in most provincial religious groups—and perhaps in all of them—came to believe after 1745 that indigenous ecclesiastical structures were needed to supplant an outmoded dependence on Europe. Self-sufficiency promised to colonial churches the dual benefits of better care for their own members and recognition as an equal participant in the Christian world community. Traditionalists, shaped in the cultural and ideological womb of Europe, balked at these prospects. Their opponents, fearful that the conservative policies would permanently retard American Christianity, chose the path of autonomy in order to give colonial communions the chance to grow into mature religious communities.

II

"THE VITAL PART OF RELIGION"

THE SEARCH FOR A SATISFYING FAITH

Because colonial religious institutions were created by groups who perceived themselves to be the people of God, the organization and development of New York's Protestant churches were always closely associated with the theological ideas and spiritual values of their members. The colonial religious bodies were never simply, or even primarily, institutional structures; rather, they were communities of believers, spiritual organisms concerned both with the salvation of individuals and the redemption of society. Consequently, the province's religious life involved the quest for a vital personal faith anchored in coherent structures of belief, as well as for forms of church organization that would sustain both the faith and the beliefs.

How and to what extent New York's pluralism affected this quest is the main concern of this chapter. In other words, in what ways did pluralism influence the religious practices and beliefs of New Yorkers during the colonial era, especially in the middle decades of the eighteenth century?

Students of this question traditionally have been persuaded that diversity had only debilitating effects and that, largely on this account, the religious factor in New York was "singularly weak."[1] They have been quick to quote the testimony of ministers like Gualterus Du Bois, Dutch Reformed dominie in New York City, who in 1741 denounced diversity as producing a "spirit of confusion" among laypersons.[2] Convinced that the heterogeneous and acquisitive character of provincials in this colony checked religious fervor, they have accepted as accurate the observations of Anglican minister John Miller, who, after visiting the province in 1695, characterized the spiritual interests of New Yorkers as their "least concern, and as if salvation were not a matter of moment, when they have opportunities of serving God they care not for making use thereof"; if they went to church, he added, "'tis but too often out of curiosity and to find faults in him that preacheth rather than to hear their own. . . ."[3]

This depiction of New Yorkers as religiously lethargic has recently been challenged, however. In a provocative article, Patricia Bonomi and Peter Eisenstadt have argued that the American colonists, New Yorkers included, were a predominantly churched population from at least 1700 on. Relying on wide literary evidence rather than only ministerial jeremiads, and on the ratio of colonial churches to population rather than unreliable church membership figures, they have concluded that colonists were not slack in their religious observance. On the contrary, it was "the exceptional person in any colony who deliberately stood apart from the fellowship of a religious community." Specifically, they contend that throughout the first half of the eighteenth century, at least three of every four colonial Americans identified or associated with institutional religion. In the Middle Colonies, they say, religious interest was strong, demonstrated by, among other things, the significant institutional growth experienced by Presbyterians, Lutherans, German Reformed, Anglicans, and Quakers in the decades both before and after the First Great Awakening. In fact, as a result of this growth, this region had a closer ratio of churches to population in 1750 than either New England or the South. Furthermore, Bonomi and Eisenstadt deny that religious diversity either hampered the growth of organized religion or produced a religiously apathetic laity. They admit that in pluralistic settings "some persons of weak conviction were undoubtedly alienated by the competition between denominations." But they see this group as a distinct minority, balanced at the time, if not in later historical writing, by other colonists whose religious commitments were "invigorated by the challenge" of a diverse environment.[4]

Bonomi and Eisenstadt's research raises serious questions about the prevailing interpretation of religion's place in the lives of colonial New Yorkers. Were provincials more religiously active than traditionally supposed? Did diversity sometimes spur religious commitment instead of doubt? How did pluralism affect individual spirituality?

One way to begin to answer these questions is to apply Bonomi and Eisenstadt's quantitative methods to New York. Some slight modifications are in order, however. In determining the size of the "churched" population in colonial America at different points in the 1700s, Bonomi and Eisenstadt used a constant figure of eighty families per church and included only the white population. Because New York's population density changed over time, so too did the average number of families per church. Hence, I have used different figures for each date (tables 2 and 3). Also, because blacks made up a significant proportion of the colony's population

TABLE 2.   **Ratio of Churches to Population in New York, 1700–1775**

Year	Population	Congregations	Ratio
1700	19,000	48	1:396
1750	80,000	164	1:488
1775	193,000	239	1:808

TABLE 3.   **Church Adherents and Population in New York, 1700–1775**

Year	Population	Congregations	Families per Church	% Church Adherents to Population
1700	19,000	48	50	77.5
1750	80,000	164	60	73.6
1775	193,000	239	80	59.2

and participated in the same congregations as whites, total population figures are used. Both of these adjustments, along with my conservative estimates of the number of congregations, serve to minimize the levels of church adherence. Nevertheless, my results suggest that New York's pattern of church adherence closely resembled the pattern Bonomi and Eisenstadt found for the colonies as a whole.[5]

This data is helpful in pointing out that, institutionally, New York's religionists were keeping pace with the levels of religious activity and observance common among colonists elsewhere. As such, it casts doubt on the traditional notion of New York as a colony sorely lacking in religious interest.[6] But these numbers cannot tell us much about the impact of diversity beyond suggesting that it had certainly not completely crippled religious involvement in the province. What is needed therefore is a more complete analysis than previous studies have made of the available literary evidence concerning how religious pluralism shaped colonial spiritual life. This analysis must pay close attention to the changes that occurred over time in both the character of New York's pluralism and the theological meaning ascribed to it by provincials. In addition, it must be set in the larger context of New York's cultural and theological development. Only then will we have a clearer understanding of diversity's influence on the religious practice, spiritual commitment, and theological belief of eighteenth-century New Yorkers.

The most obvious by-product of pluralism for contemporary Americans is the wide variety of religious options from which they may choose. Among the diverse colonists who settled New Netherland and New York in the seventeenth century, however, pluralism often had no such effect because of the social and cultural distance separating the ethno-religious groups. While their various religious and ethnic backgrounds encouraged a policy of toleration, many immigrants arriving during the first decades of settlement had, practically speaking, little choice of religious affiliation for themselves or their families.7 In the Long Island community of Newtown, for instance, the highly mobile English-speaking colonists from old and New England remained overwhelmingly Congregationalist throughout the century (there were a few Quaker families), while the town's Dutch-speaking freeholders exclusively practiced the Dutch Reformed religion.8 Even though religious gatherings of a number of persuasions were present, differences in both language and doctrine among the denominations were so great as to force most newcomers to join the one with which they had some familial or national ties. The result here and elsewhere was not that religious competition and conflict were entirely absent but that individual choice was sharply circumscribed by social reality.9

This situation was further enhanced in the seventeenth century by the pockets of religious and ethnic homogeneity in the colony. Individual villages along the Hudson River and on eastern Long Island were culturally homogeneous, composed of either Dutch or English Calvinists. Within these local settings, both religious pluralism and religious choice were essentially missing.10

That, however, did not keep diversity from leaving marks on the colony's spiritual life in the 1600s. If colonials had yet to reap from pluralism the luxury (or burden) of having many religious alternatives, they had felt its impress on the worship styles and church polity of their religious communities. For within the province's plural religious world, religious borrowing or imitation between groups occurred. One of the most noteworthy instances of religious borrowing took place among New York City's Lutherans. During their first generation in the colony (1640s–1660s), the fledgling status and questionable legality of their religious worship left Lutherans dependent on the dominant Dutch Reformed Church for their religious rites (baptism, marriage, burial). As a result, by the time their own congregational life began to function regularly in the 1670s, they had been "so completely under the influence of the Reformed environment, that . . . they took over bodily many of the customs of the [previously] established church."11 The Reformed influence was particularly prominent in the Lutheran congregation's worship order, for in place of the typical European Lutheran liturgy was a Calvinistic emphasis on the use of the Psalms. Likewise, the Lutherans adopted the same church officers the colonial

Dutch Reformed congregations had—elders, deacons, overseers, church masters, and lay readers.[12]

Religious imitation within New York's diversity continued throughout the eighteenth century, assuming a host of forms and affecting various aspects of the religious practice of provincial churches. Sometimes this mimicking involved a single congregation, as when Episcopalians in Rye followed the democratic lead of their Congregationalist neighbors in seeking complete control over the selection and maintenance of their minister.[13] Other times it cut across the colony's entire religious landscape. Intensified Anglican efforts to Christianize blacks and Indians, for example, quickly heightened spiritual and moral concern among other groups (especially Presbyterians) for the colony's nonwhites and led to parallel attempts at evangelization and catechization. Similarly, the establishment of Anglican schools prompted New York's other leading denominations to reemphasize the importance of providing religious education for their own young people. In these ways and others, the 1700s witnessed pluralism molding the religious governance, moral emphases, and spiritual priorities of New York's churches.

At the same time, diversity came to exert much greater influence over individual spirituality in the eighteenth century. Significant changes occurred in the colony between about 1690 and 1730 to bring it about. For one thing, the population's religious and ethnic heterogeneity increased as new waves of immigrants arrived, chiefly from the Rhineland and Great Britain. They brought entirely new communions to New York and intensified the religious diversity of local communities throughout the province. As a result, the religious options within the several language groups were broadened. Here again the case of Newtown is illustrative, for with the establishment of an Anglican church and the increasing respectability of Quakerism, English-speaking residents now had viable alternatives to Congregationalism.[14] Similarly, farther north in the upper Hudson Valley village of Germantown, the influx of Calvinist settlers from the Palatinate led to the formation of a German Reformed congregation in 1728, giving community residents a choice between attending this congregation and the previously organized Lutheran church.[15]

During these same years, the arrival of Scottish and Scotch-Irish Presbyterians, along with many more English immigrants, enhanced the growing political and economic ascendancy of the English and encouraged the gradual Anglicization of New York's culture.[16] As Dutch, French, and German colonists became Anglicized and the trend toward social and cultural homogeneity appeared certain to dominate the future, language and other ethnic differences gradually became less formidable obstacles to freedom in the selection of a church. Young people from these ethnic groups were the first to take advantage of the enlargement of their religious options. By the mid-eighteenth century, their familiarity with the English language made them free to join any one of a wide spectrum of religious groups.[17] For them and the church bodies trying to retain their allegiance, pluralism clearly took on a new significance. Simply put, it now provided persons with much greater opportunity to decide on their own which brand of Christianity, if any at all, they wished to believe and practice. Thus, the addition of new religious communions and the Anglicization of the colony's culture had by 1730 dramatically magnified the meaning of diversity for individual religiosity.

This development took place alongside a greater incidence of friction between provincial relgious bodies. First, England's Glorious Revolution set off a wave of anti-Catholic hostility that found expression in New York in the rebellion led by Jacob Leisler.[18] Then, after fears of a Catholic takeover had subsided, both old and new sources of strife arose to divide provincial Protestants in the early 1700s. While New York's major denominations acknowledged one another's right to freedom of worship and shared a common Reformation heritage that left them mutually opposed to Roman Catholicism, each perceived itself as the best expression of Christian faith and showed little reluctance in casting doubt on the validity of others' theology and polity.[19] In many cases, the conflicts that developed were limited to a local time and place and soon became overshadowed either by positive signs of common brotherhood or disputes within rather than between denominations. Nevertheless, amid New York's religious competition, many preachers made it clear that "true religion" was rarely found outside the confines of their own communions.[20] And even when they cultivated friendships with neighbors of other persuasions, as Anglican Thomas Colgan did with Quaker and Presbyterian folk in his Jamaica, Long Island, parish, the intention was to convert "many Souls . . . to the true Church of Christ" (in Colgan's case, the Church of England) rather than merely to associate with other believers.[21]

Much of the religious tension evident in the early eighteenth century stemmed from the establishment of the Church of England in a predominantly dissenter colony. Old World antagonisms quickly took root in New World religious soil. The most familiar case of Protestant bickering therefore was the series of Anglican-Presbyterian conflicts over the issues of congregational incorporation, ministerial appointments to tax-supported parishes, proselytizing by the Anglican Society for the Propagation of the Gospel (SPG), and the validity of Presbyterian ordinations.[22] Throughout the first half of the century, the SPG secretary received constant reports about the contentious competition between its missionaries and dissenters of all types, including Friends, Baptists, Lutherans, and Congregationalists.[23]

At one point or another, New York's denominational rivalries touched all religious groups. Quakers criticized the Calvinist doctrines of the Reformed bodies, and the latter, in turn, denounced the preaching and work of Moravians.[24] Lutherans maintained good relations with the German Reformed, but repeatedly complained of ill treatment from others, as when minister William C. Berkenmeyer observed in 1734 that the Dutch Reformed insisted their numbers entitled them to have everything their own way.[25] Not to be outdone, New York City's Jewish community divided in factious rivalry between its Sephardic and Ashkenazic segments.[26]

Given this religious environment in which diversity's importance was growing as both religious options and sectarian disputes increased after 1690, how were the religious beliefs and actions of New Yorkers affected in the first three or four decades of the eighteenth century? Investigation of a wide array of evidence suggests that pluralism's impact in this era on individual piety and conviction varied greatly.

As noted earlier, historians have generally cited as typical the comments of certain ministers reared in the more stable and less threatening state church environments of Europe. For these ministers, pluralism seemed an inescapable curse. Eight years of service amid the multiplicity of groups in the upper Hudson Valley led Lutheran John Hartwick to lament to his superior that "Whereas i had the Happiness to be born and educated in an Established Church, i have been very much griev'd and rent with the bad Affects wich the many Divisions in Religious Sentiments and Worship have [here] with Respect to the General Cause of Christianity."[27]

While Hartwick's statement and others like it are representative of certain contemporary attitudes toward diversity, they hardly tell the whole story. That he and other clergymen complained about pluralism is not surprising, given that it generally made their jobs tougher. But their views should not be taken as a just portrayal of how the vast majority of New York's residents (laypersons) thought about or were influenced by diversity.

Like the Pennsylvania Lutheran and Reformed Germans Patricia Bonomi has studied, some New Yorkers responded to their pluralistic environment with a firmer commitment to, and a heightened sense of, the distinct religious identity of their own group.[28] Among them, the presence of religious choices and religious competition sparked a resolute attachment to both the formal doctrines and rituals and the informal customs of their particular communion. In the process, diversity also led them to become more tightly bound spiritually and emotionally to other members of their congregation. Certainly that was the case in New Rochelle among a group of dissident Huguenots who carried on a long-standing opposition to their church's decision in 1709 to conform to the Church of England. Fearful (rightly, as it turned out) that Anglican conformity would destroy their community's distinctive religious and ethnic character, these dissidents sought to rekindle Huguenot loyalty by forming a separate congregation in which all services were in French and minister Jean Joseph Brumeau de Moulinars could preach a strong Calvinistic (and anti-Anglican) faith.[29]

The same kind of determined resistance to Anglican evangelism arose among some Dutch Reformed, German Reformed, and German Lutheran settlers. According to Ronald Howard, the early eighteenth-century quest to bring New Yorkers into conformity with the Church of England largely had the opposite effect. While Anglicanism gained some converts, majorities within most ethnic and religious groups responded to its aggression by seeking ways to reinforce and pass on traditional loyalties. In most cases, that meant establishing schools (to rival Anglican ones) where young people could be indoctrinated with the religious and cultural distinctions their parents and forefathers had brought from Europe. These folk stoutly rebuffed overt attempts at religious homogenization, even while succumbing to the subtler process of Anglicization.[30]

Meanwhile, Anglicans themselves often displayed a zealous fidelity to their church amid New York's diversity that belies the typical caricature of them as latitudinarian and lethargic. And this was true among laypeople as well as ministers. Unswayed by the dominant dissenter majority in Hempstead, Robert Tenney's Anglican parishioners begged him for prayer books in 1735 so they could participate more fully in the divine services of the Church of England.[31] Elsewhere in Queens County, the long and bitter struggle between Anglicans and Presbyterians to control Jamaica parish surely lacked Christian charity, but nevertheless reflected the determination of laymen on both sides to advance the interests of their churches.[32]

That Protestant bodies were not alone in having their members invigorated by religious competition is demonstrated by the generations of Jewish lay leaders who oversaw an active religious life in their community throughout the eighteenth century. It would have been understandable if this tiny fraction of the population, surrounded by the huge Christian majority in New York City, had relinquished its Judaism altogether. But instead, like their religious kin in so many other places, New York's Jews were intent on retaining their distinctive religious identity. To that end they established congregation Shearith Israel in 1706, constructed a building for it in 1730, opened a school for Jewish children in 1735, and consistently opposed the surest and quickest means of Jewish assimilation into the Protestant world—intermarriage.[33]

Diversity affected the religious convictions of other provincials quite differently. Confronted by both increasing options and what was sometimes a bewildering mix of sectarian claims, some laypersons found themselves becoming religiously "indifferent." Based on the testimony of those members of all denominations who encountered such persons, it appears that in most instances their indifference was less a matter of religious disinterest or outright irreligion than of doctrinal impartiality or confusion.[34] Few churchgoers questioned the basic importance of religion or even their own need for salvation. But a significant minority of them were finding it increasingly difficult either to know which one of the competing sets of beliefs and practices was worthy of acceptance or how to go about deciding.

For most, the loss of doctrinal rigor did not undermine their overall religiosity. While less sure about, and insistent on, the validity of particular doctrinal claims of their church or any church, they nevertheless maintained their basic religious interest and involvement. So, for example, Anglican minister James Wetmore reported in 1736 that the diversity of his Westchester County parish had left many persons doctrinally in "such an Indifferent Temper that Scarce themselves know what profession they are of."[35] Yet, it was these same people who principally made up the large rural congregations he attracted, and who, according to Wetmore, flocked to hear "all sorts of teachers."[36] The accounts of other SPG missionaries and schoolmasters during these decades similarly testify to the routine manner in which Anglican and dissenter inhabitants of their parishes attended each other's worship services on Sundays when there were no meetings in their own churches.[37] Arthur Worrall has found that among New York Friends, social contact with neighbors of various persuasions led to a growing incidence of marriage outside the meeting (performed by clergy of other denominations or a justice of the peace). But it hampered neither Quaker growth nor Quaker enthusiasm.[38] If such religious mixing left some churchgoers "unsettled in their principles," it also helped to reveal the shallowness of convictions that rested simply on group prejudices. A Dutch Reformed woman told Lutheran Minister Henry Muhlenberg on the eve of her marriage to a Lutheran that she had been taught to believe that his faith was "despicable and absurd" but had realized her error after hearing Muhlenberg preach.[39] Thus, as Crévecoeur observed in Orange County, the crucible of day-to-day living and worshiping in a diverse milieu gradually produced some persons who found their enthusiasm for particular sectarian claims curbed.⁴⁰ Rather than being the cause of religious apathy, however, this kind of religious indifference seems to have been a common corollary to maintaining an active religious life.

These observations are sustained by the diary of Mary Cooper, a remarkable document that contains perhaps the clearest and most complete lay description of popular religion in mid-eighteenth century New York. Although Cooper's journal was written close to the Revolution (1768–73), it nevertheless illuminates some of the ways in which religious diversity had been affecting individual spirtuality throughout the century. In particular, it highlights how some New Yorkers drew spiritual and moral nourishment from several (rather than only one) religious communities within their local setting.

Mary Cooper lived on a farm with her husband on the outskirts of Oyster Bay, an agricultural village on Long Island's north shore. She was a mature woman in her fifties when she decided to keep a diary. Its pages reveal a woman of deep religious sentiment who was accustomed to a routine of frequent religious observance. Mary and a number of her friends took advantage of the worship services held at the town's four churches— Quaker, Anglican, Regular Baptist, and New Light Baptist—as well as special meetings convened by itinerant or visiting pastors. After her nephew, Peter Underhill, joined her sister, Sarah Townsend, as a leader of the New Light congregation, Mary decided to become a formal church member within that body. As part of this congregation, she shared intensely in the elation of its revival in 1772 and in the sorrow of its division in 1773. But even while giving most of her attention to this fellowship, Mary attended other churches and listened to a wide variety of Protestant exhorters, including female, black, and Indian preachers. She did not always approve of what she heard or saw, as she suggested in a prayer she wrote down after going to one Quaker meeting: "O Lord, is not this peopel ignorant of the greate and needful doctrins of the gospel? O thou that has the residue of the spirite, I pray the, enlitein these that set in darkness." Nevertheless, Cooper's diverse religious contacts on the whole seem to have intensified her religious sensibility and left her far more concerned about the spiritual state of her own and others' souls than about any particular doctrine.⁴¹

Not all New Yorkers were like Mary Cooper, of course. It should come as no surprise, therefore, that among some colonists the loss of doctrinal certainty (which often accompanied living in a diverse environment) exacted a heavy toll upon their spirituality: a declining religious observance and a mounting spiritual perplexity that added up to a faltering religious interest. While retaining a sense of the importance of the "great truths of revelation," such persons showed less and less zeal for them.[42] The doubts pluralism raised about old verities were not easily allayed, and often the only spiritual "counsel" offered by ministers was another sectarian denunciation of the competition. Muhlenberg encountered a man who confessed that he had not baptized his son because he had not known which was best among the different communions in the area. Dialogue with the leaders of each helped little, Muhlenberg was told, since they all claimed "to possess the best medicine for the soul and the nearest road to Heaven."[43] Dutch Reformed minister Theodore J. Frelinghuysen preached about the expressions of uncertainty he and other pastors had heard from laypersons: "I would be religious, did I only know which religion is the true one; but how shall I who am young, arrive at a correct conclusion? One . . . professes this belief, and another that, and a third rejects both."[44] Writing on the basis of his own experience, Presbyterian layman William Livingston aptly summarized the religious frustration and confusion these persons felt while living amid New York's diversity: "Among which of these Systems shall a candid Inquirer after Truth, look for Christianity? Where shall he find the Religion of Christ amidst all this priestly Fustian, and ecclesiastical Trumpery?" They all, he continued, "claim to be orthodox, and yet all differ from one another, and each is ready to damn all the Rest."[45]

Although the literary evidence is difficult to quantify, it suggests that the number of people being adversely affected in this way by pluralism was growing by the 1740s. Anglican Samuel Seabury, for instance, told the SPG secretary in 1745 that within his Hempstead, Long Island, parish there were now "many who profess no Religion nor attend any place of worship but yet pretend they believe the Gospel."[46] Similarly, pastor Du Bois in New York City insisted that because "so many conventicles exist . . . so many are perplexed and misled; while others neglect or scoff at the divine service. . . ."[47]

The trend in this direction was being enhanced by a growing religious mobility and the influx of New Light or revivalistic religion. Contemporary records testify to a rising tide of shifting religious affiliations. The large number of Dutch, French, and German young people nurtured in the Reformed and Lutheran traditions who were now attending Anglican churches to hear services in English is the most prominent of many examples that could be cited.[48] Although this movement demonstrated the colonists' growing freedom of choice and often allowed persons to become more active in the life of a congregation, in some cases it contributed to, as well as reflected, religious uncertainty. Participation in a different communion often demanded a reevaluation of one's inherited conception of Christianity, for even the denominations that were most alike—for example, the

Dutch and German Reformed—emphasized different points of Calvinist doctrine and maintained varied communal customs and liturgies of worship. Confronted by these differences, individuals were vulnerable to the temptation to question the validity of both old and new ideas. Of course, the increasing incidence of movement from one communion to another was sometimes an effect rather than the cause of growing doubt. Some persons switched churches in search of a satisfying substitute for the creed in which they had lost confidence.

At the same time, the spread of New Light religion into the colony in the 1740s added, at least initially, another confusing element to New York's religious milieu and rekindled both intra- and interdenominational squabbles.[49] Evangelical preachers proclaimed a new style of piety and faith that raised questions about "true religion" even in the minds of those most settled in their beliefs. Such was the testimony of Dutch and German Reformed ministers concerning the impact of Moravian pietism upon their flocks in the Hudson Valley.[50] Similarly, SPG missionaries Thomas Colgan and James Wetmore wrote home about the disruptive influence of "methodist teachers" in their Jamaica and Rye parishes.[51]

In summary, then, during the first forty to fifty years of the eighteenth century, the presence of new religious communions, the Anglicization of New York's culture, and the growth of sectarian competition served to heighten dramatically the importance of diversity for individual spirituality. Overall, most New Yorkers had their religious beliefs and practices affected in one of three ways. Diversity encouraged many to reinvigorate their denominational commitment, while among others it spurred an increasing religious indifference that usually meant simply a loss of doctrinal rigor but occasionally contributed to spiritual confusion. What that meant for the overall state of religious interest and vitality in New York was that pluralism was neither wholly debilitating nor completely without ill effect. By curtailing the religious certainty of a small number of New Yorkers, diversity contributed to a growing laxness. Yet this laxness was more than counterbalanced by those who responded to their pluralistic milieu either with a new enthusiasm for their own sect or a willingness to feed on whatever spiritual food was available regardless of which denominational kitchen had prepared it.

Over the next twenty-five years (roughly 1750 to 1775), both the character and extent of diversity's impact on popular religiosity changed once again. At the root of this change was a more fundamental transformation in New York's religious culture: the gradual decline of European Orthodoxy as the colony's dominant theological and liturgical expression of

Christianity and its replacement by revivalistic Pietism and rationalistic liberalism. An "evangelical" understanding and practice of the Christian faith came to characterize a large minority, if not the majority, of provincial congregations by the 1770s, while a small but influential group of "enlightened" laypersons came to embrace a latitudinarian Christianity they considered more reasonable. Both served to reduce diversity's overall importance and to encourage churchgoers to adopt more positive attitudes toward pluralism.

During the first half of the eighteenth century, the colony's "church" clergy—Reformed, Anglican, Lutheran, Presbyterian—set the tone of provincial religious life and thought. The style and content of their pastoral leadership reflected their continued commitment to the theological standards and traditions developed by their seventeenth-century denominational forebears in Europe. For the Dutch Reformed and Lutherans, this commitment meant close adherence to the Continental confessions and catechisms that gave doctrinal definition to their churches and fidelity to the rigorous theological interpretations known collectively as Reformed and Lutheran Orthodoxy.[52] Similarly, Presbyterians and their Congregationalist cousins found their theological and ecclesiastical identity by subscribing to one or more of the doctrinal platforms set out by Puritans in the 1600s in either old or New England.[53] New York's Anglican leadership, meanwhile, generally followed the High Church party of the Church of England in emphasizing veneration for the church fathers, worship centered on the use of the Book of Common Prayer, and loyalty to England.[54]

Called variously confessionalists, traditionalists, and conservatives in this New World setting, these ministers and their followers as a whole might best be labeled simply Orthodox Protestants or promoters of European Orthodoxy.[55] For our purposes, these terms will refer to all those who inherited and affirmed the seventeenth-century conviction that religious faith springs from a rational understanding of the gospel. Drawing on that century's confidence in human reason, these Protestants believed that humans were—or should be—rational beings who derived their standards of moral behavior from studying the Scriptures and observing God's works in the external world.[56] For persons to experience God, they first had to apprehend him rationally. Once they recognized the infinite greatness and excellency of God, they could understand their own weakness and sinfulness. As one Dutch Reformed minister put it, "We must first discover the Divine Perfection and Beauty, before we can perceive our own utter Imperfection and most monstrous [moral] Deformity."[57] Within this scheme, then, the chief pastoral duty was to make parishioners aware of God's moral law, show them their transgression of it, and convince them of their need to seek righteousness.[58] That was to be accomplished primarily by preaching literate sermons, following prescribed liturgies, catechizing young people, and administering the sacraments. Persuaded of God's greatness and their own wretchedness and guilt, rational men and women would choose to worship God and to abide by his ethical will.

In light of these convictions, it is plain to see why most of New York's Dutch Reformed ministers, as well as their Anglican and Lutheran counterparts, reacted so negatively when the awakenings led by radical Pietist Theodore J. Frelinghuysen in New Jersey's Raritan Valley in the 1720s and '30s spilled over into the larger colony. Among other things, Frelinghuysen's promotion of an "experiential divinity," enforcement of stricter church discipline, and disregard for Old World church liturgy prompted stiff opposition from a group of pastors headed by New York City's dominie, Henricus Boel.[59] Efforts by this opposition group overshadowed the pietistic sympathies of other ministers, including Bernhardus Freeman (Schenectady; later Long Island) and Cornelius van Santvoort (Staten Island; later Schenectady). The group also kept Pietism from initially having much impact on the Dutch Reformed congregations of the Hudson Valley.[60]

In succeeding decades, these same clergy and their ministerial heirs continued to speak out against the proponents of revivalistic Pietism. Hence the cool reception afforded the evangelistic visits of Anglican Methodist George Whitefield in 1740 and 1747 by pastors Thomas Colgan and others. An SPG missionary in Queens County, Colgan branded Whitefield a "notorious" preacher and contended that his "false and erroneous opinions concerning the doctrine of Regeneration" tended toward the destruction of "true religion."[61] Many New Yorkers agreed with Colgan and flocked to Orthodox congregations (especially Anglican) that were resolutely opposed to the "excesses of revivalism."[62] But while antievangelical forces remained strong in the colony through the American Revolution, they did not succeed in preventing the growth of a sizable evangelical community that posed an ever-increasing threat to Orthodox Protestantism's hegemony over the colony's religious life.

Most colonial historians have paid little attention to the influence of evangelical religion in the province prior to the Revolution. Presumably, that is because they have been persuaded that this influence was relatively minor, particularly when compared with the experience of other colonies. Such a conclusion derives, no doubt, from the oft-repeated claim that the Great Awakening was "especially weak" in New York, due in large part, they say, to the strength of the antievangelical forces.[63] As a comment upon the lack of a concentrated wave of local revivals in the state occurring some time between the 1730s and 1760s, this conclusion is accurate. But in also leaving the broader impression that evangelicalism never made any significant inroad among New Yorkers during the pre-Revolutionary era, it distorts the actual religious situation.

As mentioned earlier, New Light or pietistic revivalism penetrated New York's borders for good by 1740. From the start, it was anything but monolithic. Among its proponents in the colony throughout the next generation were persons of vastly different theological and ecclesiastical backgrounds, ranging from the various traditions of Lutheran, Moravian, and Reformed Pietism exemplified by Henry Muhlenberg, Count Von Zinzendorf, Michael Schlatter, and Theodore J. Frelinghuysen to the British Calvinism of Anglican George Whitefield, Presbyterian John Rodgers, and Baptist John Gano and the Wesleyan Arminianism of Francis Asbury and Thomas Rankin.[64] Despite their contrasting heritages, however, they all agreed that Christianity did not consist simply of good morals and observance of the outward forms of religion. Nor, in their minds, were fallen human beings capable of living morally responsible lives by merely believing in God's revelation or intellectually assenting to the truths revealed.[65] Such were the misguided notions of the Orthodox Protestants. Instead, Christianity, they argued, was an "experiential religion" in which individuals were to be radically converted or transformed through God's grace to lives of moral holiness. Virtue was dependent on the reception of a "vital, indwelling principle" of righteousness, which was the gift of the Holy Spirit who brought regeneration to the believer.[66] This regeneration or "new birth" was understood by some revivalists, including Whitefield, as a dramatic, instantaneous experience in which the individual passed from spiritual death to life. Others, including Muhlenberg, spoke more often of conversion as a gradual process in which a person moved away from worldly and sinful pursuits toward a life that was more and more Christian.[67] In both interpretations, however, the new birth was at the center of what they thought it meant to be a Christian and was wedded in similar ways to such key doctrines as the covenant of grace, Christ's atonement, the work and power of the Holy Spirit, and the supreme authority of Scripture. On these grounds, therefore, Whitefield, Muhlenberg, and the others may be legitimately characterized together as "evangelicals."[68]

By such a characterization I do not intend to homogenize these religionists into a simplistic category. Nor is the characterization designed to cover up the real and important differences among them. The sacraments, church governance, hymnody, and divine election were all issues on which they held sharply variant views. Likewise, there was no unanimity on preaching techniques, ministerial qualifications, or the use of confessions of faith. In some cases, their differences even boiled over into open conflict, as in the hostile reaction of Muhlenberg and Presbyterian Gilbert Tennent to Zinzendorf and the Moravians.[69] Clearly, those I label evangelical did not always see eye to eye. Nevertheless, their common antipathy toward "dead Orthodoxy" and their mutual support for an experiential religion centered in the new birth linked them together in ways that both they and their opponents readily recognized. For modern historians to do the same, then, seems eminently reasonable.

New York's familiarity with the evangelical message rapidly increased during the 1740s owing to the large crowds attracted by Whitefield, the establishment of the New York Presbyterian Synod in 1745, the ministerial visits of Muhlenberg, the revivals led by Gilbert Tennent in lower New York, the itinerant evangelism of Moravian missionaries in the Hudson and Mohawk Valleys, and the rise to prominence of Frelinghuysen's disciples in the Dutch Reformed ministry. By 1750, several of Frelinghuysen's sons and a number of candidates tutored by his close colleague J. H. Goetschius were ready to enter the ministry. Their presence would shortly swing the balance of power among the Dutch Reformed clergy to the pietistic side.[70]

Once introduced, the evangelical impulse became progressively stronger in both urban and rural communities. Between 1750 and 1776 a growing number within virtually every denomination embraced it. Contributing to its growing influence were Whitefield's itinerant tours (1754, 1763–65, 1769–70), the training of evangelical ministers at the College of New Jersey (Presbyterian), and the introduction of Wesleyan Methodism. Even the colony's archetype of European traditionalism, Anglican Trinity Parish in New York City, developed an evangelical wing.[71] By the mid-1760s, the popularity of evangelicalism prompted one contemporary observer to remark that "a person who could not speak about the grace of God and the new birth was esteemed unfit for genteel company."[72] Methodist preacher Joseph Pilmore informed John Wesley in May 1770 that the "religion of Jesus" was a "favorite topic in New York." Many of the "gay and polite" spoke much about "grace and perserverance," and some were "alive to God."[73]

Evangelicalism's growth in New York did not result from a sudden wave of revivals. In the colony's back settlements, and even in New York City, the long and faithful service of local pastors and committed laypersons, rather than the momentary visit of an evangelist such as Whitefield, gradually infused evangelical vigor into old congregations or prompted the organization of new ones. Surely Whitefield helped spark relgious renewal (and strife) in numerous communities.[74] And in some instances, congregations responded immediately to the call for conversion. But more often, evangelical ministers were rewarded with a wide reception to their message only after years of patient preaching. Presbyterian Samuel Buell ministered in Easthampton, on eastern Long Island, for over a decade before mass conversions swept his and other nearby congregations in 1764.[75] The Baptist congregation in Paulings Precinct, Dutchess County, experienced slow but consistent growth under the teaching and pastoral care of Samuel Waldo from its organization in 1757 until 1775, when it added an amazing fifty-four new members.[76] Other clergymen succeeded in establishing a powerful evangelical tradition in their communities without ever witnessing a major revival in their own flocks. Examples of such an accomplishment included Congregationalist (later Presbyterian) John Smith's work in Rye and White Plains, Baptist Simon Deacon's service in Philip's Patent and Oblong, Dutchess County, and the ministries of Presbyterians David Bostwick and John Rodgers in New York City.[77] Still other pastors, including Theodore Frelinghuysen in Albany (son of Theodore J. Frelinghuysen), had to be content with making smaller pietistic inroads against the religious traditionalism and secular tendencies in their towns.[78] In communities that had no settled pastors, devoted laymen sometimes bore a continuing evangelical testimony that permanently affected their neighbors.[79] The net result of these diverse efforts was the progressive dissemination of an evangelical witness into virtually every part of the colony before the American Revolution began.

Some of the clearest evidence that this evangelical growth did, in fact, pose a serious challenge to the dominance of European Orthodoxy in provincial churches comes from New York City. Prior to the 1740s, virtually all of the city's churches adhered to Orthodox Protestantism. Protestant residents wishing to hear or practice a decidedly different brand of Christianity had only one place to turn, the meeting house of the Society of Friends. Thirty years later, however, of the eighteen Protestant congregations in Manhattan (eleven denominations), at least thirteen reflected the influence of either Anglo-American evangelicalism or Continental Pietism in their preaching or congregational activity. Members of the three congregations belonging to the Dutch Reformed Collegiate Church now heard evangelical sermons from two of their four ministers (Archibald Laidlie and John Livingston), as did Presbyterian churchgoers at their three fellowships from pastors John Rodgers, Joseph Treat, and John Mason.[80] The recently formed Moravian (1748), Baptist (1762), and Methodist (1766) congregations also preached their own varieties of evangelical faith and piety to rapidly increasing crowds.[81] The liturgies and constitutions of New York's two Lutheran churches reflected their control by the Pietist-dominated Pennsylvania Synod and its leader, Muhlenberg.[82] And Anglican sympathizers with the message of Whitefield enjoyed fellowship together while worshiping at St. George's Chapel.[83] An evangelical presence clearly pervaded the city's religious scene by 1770.

What happened in New York City was not unique. Parallel religious developments took place in numerous other congregations and communities throughout the colony in the third quarter of the eighteenth century. If by nothing else, this conclusion is suggested by the compulsion Orthodox Protestants felt to keep spewing forth a steady stream of attacks upon the revivalists' irrational "religion of the heart."[84] In their defense, it must be added that they were often merely responding to evangelical charges about "unregenerate clergy" and "legal Christianity."[85] Whatever the cause, however, it seems clear that they feared, with just cause, that their own style of faith was being supplanted in New York by the message and methods of evangelicals.

If the evangelicals were not enough to deal with, Orthodox proponents also had to contend in the 1750s and '60s with the rise of a small and generally intellectual group of New Yorkers who were gravitating toward what they thought was a more rational and liberal brand of Christianity. Influenced by the British Enlightenment, these intellectuals welcomed a latitudinarian disdain for dogma, forms, and creeds and wished that all Christians would emphasize their fundamental agreement rather than the minor issues that divided them.

Unlike the religious liberals in New England or in the Southern colonies, those in New York were not prominent clergymen; nor did they belong to only one major denomination. In fact, it is difficult to isolate even one congregation in which theological liberalism predominated. In light of the liberal doctrinal drift of many British Presbyterians, it is noteworthy that the colony's Presbyterian clergy were thoroughly evangelical in the mid-eighteenth century. And even though New York Anglican ministers espoused "rational" religion, they demonstrated their commitment to traditional Anglican dogma by flatly rejecting the liberal Arminianism of some of their English counterparts.[86]

Instead, the liberal theological perspective was limited in New York to laymen like Presbyterian William Livingston. From his perspective, neither the cold formalism of Old Side Presbyterianism nor the emotionalism of the New Side party provided a satisfying faith. He charged that "the lovely Simplicity of the Gospel" had been barbarized and perverted by both evangelicals and traditionalists, each of them claiming an exclusive hold on historic truth. Livingston's solution was to accept a noncreedal, latitudinarian Christianity, purposefully supradenominational in character so all Christians could embrace it.[87] In correspondence with other "pragmatic

Calvinists," including Samuel Cooper in Boston and Ezra Stiles in Newport, Livingston found support for his ideas.[88] Once secure in his "enlightened" faith, he disseminated to the public his "pure and simple" religion.

Another latitudinarian liberal in New York was Anglican Cadwallader Colden. A lifelong member of the colony's political elite, Colden went beyond Livingston's views and departed more radically from historic Christianity. He embraced a deistic view of God and saw the value of Christianity and the Bible as resting solely in providing moral guidance. Colden believed that all persons could benefit from learning the "Rules of Living well" taught by Jesus. Besides this ethical instruction, however, religion had little to offer and men were better off relying on the findings of science if they wished to be enlightened. In fact, in Colden's mind, Protestant and Catholic ministers alike were more often obstacles than avenues to true knowledge. For this reason he thought all education should be free from religious control.[89]

A more biblically oriented but nevertheless heterodox brand of liberal Christianity entered the colony with Englishman John Murray in 1770. A former Methodist, Murray had become a disciple of James Relly, who, though a trinitarian believer in divine election, preached universal salvation. Murray received a warm welcome in New York City and spoke a number of times to enthusiastic crowds at the First Baptist Church. That success, however, apparently was obtained by masking his universalist sentiments. When pastor John Gano detected Murray's true convictions, he closed his pulpit to him and joined with other ministers in the Middle Colonies in defaming Murray's moral and theological character. Murray eventually took refuge in New England, where he seemingly found a more receptive audience. Nevertheless, the seeds of universalism had been sown in New York and would be reaped in the postwar era by other preachers of general salvation.[90]

It was not just Protestants who felt the Enlightenment's liberalizing influence. Abigail Franks, wife of wealthy Jewish merchant Jacob Franks, found great appeal in the religious skepticism of Voltaire and other Enlightenment writers. Franks chose to practice her Judaism by observing holy days, keeping the dietary laws, and attending synagogue. But she was critical of the "superstitous obedience due religion," and her closest friends were Protestant members of the commercial elite, some of whom undoubtedly shared her critical views of organized religion, whether Christian or Jewish.[91]

Thus, from 1750 to 1775, the rationalist propositions of latitudinarianism, deism, universalism, and skepticism all made inroads into the religious thought of New Yorkers. Together their small number of liberal adherents constituted a third force on New York's religious scene, alongside the expanding evangelicals and the traditionally dominant Orthodox Protestants. Explaining precisely how and why the liberals and evangelicals diminished the dominance of the Orthodox goes beyond the scope of this work. Recognizing that this change did indeed take place, however, is crucial for understanding the impact of diversity in this era.

In evangelical circles, the issue of greatest religious significance was whether one had been regenerated and understood the centrality of that experience in scriptural teaching. Next to this question, one's particular church affiliation was comparatively inconsequential, for it had no "eternal" importance. Whitefield dramatically made this point in the 1740s when he proclaimed:

> Father Abraham, whom have you in heaven? Any Episcopalians? No! Any Presbyterians? No! Any Independents or Methodists? No, no, no! Whom have you there? We don't know those names here. All who are here are Christians. . . . Oh, is this the case! Then God help us to forget party names and to become Christians in deed and truth.[92]

Over the course of the next three decades, he and other evangelical proponents repeatedly told New Yorkers that the most important spiritual dividing line was not between one denomination and the others, but rather between the born again and the unregenerate. They proclaimed that the laity could find saving truth among members of any congregation who had an experiential knowledge of God's redeeming love. This suggested that any denomination which contained such reborn persons and at the same time upheld the other historic doctrines of the Christian faith could be considered one member of a larger group, the universal church of Christ. As Presbyterian revivalist Gilbert Tennent explained, "All Societies who profess Christianity and retain the foundational principles thereof, notwithstanding their different denominations and diversity of sentiments *in smaller things,* are in reality but one Church of Christ. . . ."[93] (Italics mine.) Similarly, Muhlenberg insisted that any religious body that maintained the classical Protestant emphases on word and sacrament alongside a stress on personal faith and Christian discipleship was a part of the true Christian church.[94]

Such views were not born of doctrinal indifference to denominational distinctions. On the contrary, most evangelicals in New York followed the lead of Tennent and Muhlenberg and remained convinced members of their own communions. Few would have disagreed with the Lutheran ministerium's proposal in 1760 that amid religious diversity preachers should occasionally explain in an unpolemical way what the major denominational differences were. In their minds, this type of doctrinal clarification could retard any tendency toward theological and ecclesiastical laxity without encouraging sectarian dogmatism.[95] Many evangelicals, in fact, discussed mutual differences and occasionally critiqued one another's theology or methods.[96] Furthermore, when they evangelized the unconverted, their hope was to bring new believers into the ranks of their own, rather than just any, evangelical congregation.

Even so, New Light rhetoric about various communions being part of the universal church of Christ was not simply idle talk. For after 1760 evangelicals backed up their rhetoric by exhibiting a growing willingness to associate and cooperate with those in other denominations who preached the necessity of the new birth. Ministers and laypersons began to disparage party labels and promote unity of faith. Evangelical pastors enthusiastically accepted opportunities to proclaim their revival message in congregations of other communions, and they welcomed the chance to have other "faithful" ministers preach from their own pulpits.[97] Hence, conservative Dutch Reformed minister John Ritzema complained that evangelical pastors preached willingly to religious gatherings of whatever variety and disparaged their rhetoric of unity: "All the sects in the country, even the Immersionists [Baptists] who, as the pretension is, differ in nothing except the mode of administration of Baptism, say that they are one with the Dutch."[98]

Evangelical bonds of friendship were thus forged across denominational lines, as when Francis Asbury preached side by side with several Presbyterian clergymen in Westchester County.[99] The Dutchess Presbytery demonstrated its approval of certain Dutch Reformed ministers when it advised the Presbyterian congregation in Sing Sing to ask the Dutch Coetus for a supply pastor in 1763–64.[100] Even the Anglican-dissenter rivalry receded in the face of evangelical unity in rural parts of New York and New Jersey. SPG missionary Harry Munro reported from his Yonkers parish in 1766 that "that spirit of contention and vain disputation about indifferent matters of religion" which had "greatly prevailed" among "the different sects and parties" on his arrival there had "now almost subsided."[101] Uzal Ogden, evangelical Episcopal catechist in Newtown, New Jersey, wrote in a similar vein to the SPG in 1771:

> I have had, & complied with, diverse invitations to read Prayers & a Sermon, on Week Days, in some of the Meeting Houses, & Dwellings, of the Dissenters; who of every Denomination attend Church in great Numbers, on Sundays, & behave very decently . . . prejudice wears off remarkably, & several of the most bigoted of 'em, are not only become constant attendants

at our public worship, but subscribe something towards our public Buildings,
& to my Salary.[102]

Presbyterian pastor Samson Occom published a hymnbook that contained
selections from authors of different denominations, hoping the volume
would assist all Christians in "their earthly pilgrimage."[103] Evangelicals also
gained a sense of oneness through interdenominational worship services,
joint prayer meetings, and reading common devotional literature, such as
Jonathan Edwards's edition of David Brainerd's diary.[104]

Virtually all of these ecumenical activities took place at an individual or
congregational level. It would be another generation before anyone would
seriously consider organizational cooperation, let alone union, at the denominational level. The fruit of these prewar efforts was nevertheless an
increasingly self-conscious evangelical community in New York whose development paralleled the emergence of an intercolonial evangelical party
in the late 1750s and early 1760s.[105]

Moreover, the cooperative ventures confirmed the notion that denominational distinctions were not supremely important. Along with the evangelical message itself, these ventures told New Yorkers that they, in contrast
with the settlers of previous generations, were not faced with choosing
between a multitude of groups in search of absolute truth. Rather, once
regenerated, a person was free to subscribe to any denominational creed
that both affirmed the doctrine of the new birth and sustained this doctrine
with the other main tenets of Christianity. Also contrary to what earlier
provincials had heard was evangelicalism's suggestion that there was little
virtue in taking pride in denominational exclusivity or sectarian competition. Loyalty to a denomination was to be expected and encouraged but it
was not to override an openness toward other believers or to obscure the
Christian's real foe. As the evangelical word spread in New York after 1750,
therefore, so too did the tendency for colonists to attribute far less spiritual
significance to their own religious diversity. In the process, fewer and fewer
of them had their religious interest or commitment strongly affected by the
mere reality of pluralism itself.

At the same time, many of evangelicalism's devotees were persuaded in
these decades to see pluralism in a far more favorable light than had
churchgoers of an earlier day. For even among those who had reveled in
the sectarian competition, there had been no real appreciation of diversity
as biblically acceptable, only a recognition that it was politically warranted
and might engender a greater determination to define the distinctions of
one's own group. Now, however, evangelicals had begun to discover that
they could accept Protestant pluralism as congruent with their basic under-

standing of Christianity. The presence of congregations belonging to a wide array of denominations could be reconciled with what the Bible taught about the nature of the church. As a result, diverse communions could be perceived less as a theological plague and more as a legitimate expression of the various members of Christ's one body. In moving toward this position, evangelicals of many persuasions (and the emerging denominational organizations they dominated) gave up exclusivistic claims for their group as "the Church" much earlier than Sidney Mead has suggested. In New York, at least, evangelicals theologically embraced denominationalism by the mid-eighteenth rather than in the nineteenth century.[106]

Although religious liberalism was initially attractive to only a small minority of colonists, it also offered a message that changed the meaning of diversity for provincials. In much the same way that the stress on the new birth and on the recovery of New Testament piety overshadowed denominational differences for evangelicals, the liberals' promotion of a religion based on the rational and most comprehensive denominators of Christianity made doctrinal diversity of little import. This form of theological simplification greatly eased the layperson's choice of belief and commitment. No longer need one decide on one's own which group was most trustworthy. Instead, one needed only to affirm the few basic theological or moral truths all Christians seemed to hold in common. Beyond that, liberals affirmed that individuals were at liberty to think as they wished, without having to fear the consequences. They reasoned that with their theological burden lightened, people could generate a new sense of Christian consensus. As they developed these ideas, liberals, like the evangelicals, came to see Protestant pluralism in a much more favorable light. It now signified the logical outgrowth of freedom of conscience and represented less a blight upon Christianity than a bulwark against coerced uniformity.

Between the 1740s and the outbreak of the American Revolution, then, the growth and spread of evangelicalism and rationalistic liberalism altered both diversity's impact on the quest for a satisfying religious faith and the way colonists understood pluralism. Given these trends set in motion by their opponents, it is not surprising that in the years preceding the War for Independence the Orthodox Protestants also began to speak less disparagingly of diversity and to fraternize more regularly with compatriots in other denominations. But they were clearly the followers and not the trend setters in these matters, and many of them never lost their deeply ingrained distrust or fear of diversity. As a result, they were forced to live in constant tension with one of the central realities of their religious culture.

More broadly speaking, it is now possible to see that during the first three-quarters of the eighteenth century, religious diversity's meaning and importance for the religious interest of New Yorkers changed significantly. While pluralism had relatively little impact in the seventeenth century, it came in the first few decades of the eighteenth century to exert a greater and greater influence over religious beliefs and practices, peaking in the 1740s. Not surprisingly, its effect on particular individuals and groups varied, so that on the whole it cannot be seen as either markedly improving or seriously undermining the colony's religious vitality before 1750. With the spread of evangelical religion and rationalistic liberalism in the next generation, diversity's impact gradually declined as denominational distinctions became less important and sectarian competition was replaced in part by interdenominational cooperation. In the process, growing numbers of New York Protestants began to see their own pluralism as acceptable and to entertain a more positive view of its moral and religious potential. Once they did, they were free to endorse and promote a restructuring of the colony's religious order.

III

"AN EQUAL FOOTING FOR ALL"
THE STRUGGLE FOR RELIGIOUS
EQUALITY

Adaptation and adjustment to the organizational demands and spiritual challenges of pluralism were difficult tasks for New Yorkers in the eighteenth century. No less difficult was making sense of a colonial religious order built on conflicting, if not contradictory, principles. For alongside free worship for a multitude of groups stood a partial establishment of one minority church (the Church of England), certain special privileges for another communion (the Dutch Reformed), and the total exclusion of Roman Catholics.

George Smith and John Pratt have demonstrated how New York arrived at this confused set of church-state relations by the early 1700s.[1] During most of the seventeenth century, virtually all New Yorkers enjoyed freedom of worship, due first to the decision of the Dutch West India Company directors to tolerate diversity and then to the benevolence of the Duke of York. From 1664 to 1689, the imperial administrators followed a policy of multiple establishments, requiring each village designated as a parish to build and sustain a public church for whichever communion represented the largest number of residents. In this way, English officials maintained a close relationship between church and state while transferring much of the initiative from the central administration to the towns.[2] After the Glorious Revolution in 1689, however, the Church of England was established in the four counties centering on New York City (New York, Queens, Westchester, and Richmond), and Roman Catholic worship was declared illegal. These changes challenged the long tradition of religious toleration in the colony. The establishment was accomplished principally through the Ministry Acts of 1693 and 1705 and the forced planting of Anglican churches in and around the city by missionaries of the Society for the Propagation of the Gospel during Lord Cornbury's governorship (1702–8). He and other Anglican political and religious leaders sought to transform the colony from a bastion of diversity to a Church of England stronghold.[3] Most non-Anglicans naturally objected to these designs and continued to prefer either multiple establishments, believing that freedom of worship could be linked with a state-supported clergy without any conflict between the two ideas, or voluntary subscription, believing that the freedom of all religious groups should extend to financial independence from the state.

By the early eighteenth century, then, New York's religious order was a complex mixture of conflicting elements aimed at religious uniformity on the one hand and religious freedom and pluralism on the other. That this situation seems often to have sparked confusion and discord among provincials comes as no great surprise. Take, for example, the case of Jamaica parish on Long Island. There, beginning in 1703 and continuing off and on through the 1760s, the Presbyterian majority squabbled with the Anglican minority over town tax support for Anglican clergymen and control of the town church building. At the root of this long contest was the latent conflict between the dissenter majority's traditional rights in the colony to worship as it chose and to control its own religious affairs and its opponents' desire to promote their church by whatever means necessary, including an imposed establishment.[4]

A similar struggle unfolded in Bedford, Westchester County. Its Presbyterians had worshiped in peace for twenty years when suddenly in 1704 Anglican authorities tried to impose missionary Thomas James on the church. While this tactic failed, the Anglicans succeeded in removing the dissenting pastor through other means. Between 1705 and 1720 the Presbyterians found it impossible to bear the expense of a minister of their own while also being taxed for the support of the Anglican priest at Rye. As a result, they had to be content with the monthly visits of SPG missionary George Muirson until a temporary lull in the collection of the tax in the early 1720s afforded them an opportunity to call Presbyterian William Tennent, Sr., as their own minister.[5]

Not all dissenters in New York felt the establishment so directly or so harshly. On Staten Island, for instance, the Ministry Acts were only loosely enforced and the non-Anglican majority retained great leeway in selecting its pastors. Moreover, nonconformists in the regions outside the four lower counties were free from the establishment altogether. Still, there were numerous occasions during the first half of the eighteenth century for dissenters throughout the colony to find reasons to label the Anglican Church as intolerant or financially burdensome. The trial of two Presbyterian ministers for preaching without licenses, the refusal of the provincial government to grant charters of incorporation to dissenting congregations, and Anglican monopolization of the colony's politics were all indicative of Anglican encroachment on religious freedom.[6] So, too, was the compelling of Quakers to violate their denomination's remonstrance against church taxes, although many Friends willingly paid their tithe in hope of retaining the right to vote (gained in 1702).[7] Jews lost that right temporarily in the 1730s and '40s, thanks to the Anglican-dominated colonial assembly.[8] Meanwhile, all dissenters disliked the efforts of SPG missionaries to proselytize members of other denominations and feared the consequences of Anglican schoolmasters training their children.[9] Their protests to London eventually led the Archbishop of Canterbury to suggest privately that no new Anglican missions be started where nonconformists already had congregations.[10] Dissenters also disputed the legal basis of the claim of the Church of England to be established anywhere in the colony, on the grounds that the wording of the law called only for the maintenance of a "Protestant" minister. They insisted the legislation did not exclude the appointment of non-Anglican clergymen to a parish.

Because these verbal and legal battles provoked widespread reflection about church-state relations, they served as a prelude to the much more intense debates over this issue that ensued between 1750 and 1775. The struggles in New York over King's College, the New York Society Library, and an American episcopate in these three decades have all been well documented. Yet they are worth reexamining in detail for two reasons. First, as others have shown, these controversies provide us with the clearest presentations of the conflicting opinions New Yorkers held on church-state issues. They are therefore the best means of finding out what these colonists actually thought about church establishments and religious liberty. Second, and more important for our purposes, they help reveal how religious diversity and attitudes toward it shaped provincial ideas about the type of religious order colonial governments and churches should promote. In so doing, they tell us about another important aspect of pluralism's impact on New York's religious life in the eighteenth century.

King's College was founded in New York City in the early 1750s.[11] For several years previously, a number of prominent citizens had advocated the establishment of a college in the colony. Funds were raised through a provincial lottery and a temporary board of trustees was appointed in 1751, seven of whose ten members were Anglicans. The board looked favorably, therefore, on the offer of the vestry of Trinity Church to contribute part of its land on Manhattan Island as a site for the school, on condition that the college use the Anglican liturgy and have an Anglican president.[12] Fearful that this scheme would result in Anglican domination of the college, a small group of dissenters launched a campaign in early 1753 to make the college nonsectarian.

The result was a literary battle with the colony's Anglican clergy that lasted for more than two years.[13] Commencing with the March 29, 1753, issue of their weekly newspaper, *The Independent Reflector,* Presbyterians William Livingston, John Morin Scott, and William Smith, Jr., argued against any one "party" having control over the colony's college. "Unless its Constitution and Government, be such as will admit Persons of all protestant Denominations, upon a perfect Parity as to Privileges," Livingston wrote, "it will itself be greatly prejudiced, and prove a Nursery of Animosity, Dissension, and Discord." If the direction of the college was to be monopolized by a single denomination, representing only a small minority, the three Presbyterian laymen asked, why should the whole province be made to support it?[14]

The Anglican clergy took the offensive in responding to this challenge. Encouraged by their outspoken colleague in Philadelphia, William Smith, they contributed articles to Hugh Gaine's New York *Mercury* urging adoption of the Trinity Church proposals.[15] And they privately advocated the appointment of Samuel Johnson, rector at Stamford, Connecticut, as president of the institution. Though Johnson at first was reluctant to take the job, he soon realized it afforded him a unique opportunity to advance the Anglican cause.[16]

The new president's views of religious liberty were a study in contradiction. In Connecticut, Johnson had attempted to relieve Anglican students from discriminatory treatment at Yale College. In a heated correspondence with President Thomas Clap, he contended that infringements on their freedom of worship deprived these studenets of their liberty of conscience.[17] Once in New York, Johnson continued to characterize Yale and other colleges as sectarian, while insisting, contradictorily, that King's College reflect the colony's Anglican establishment.[18] He denounced the prejudice of those "freethinkers" and dissenters who, though having three colleges of their own in the northern colonies, would deny Anglicans similar educational opportunities.[19] From his perspective, King's was to be "a seminary for the [Anglican] Church, though with a free and generous toleration for other denominations."[20] Johnson apparently believed that as long as the college protected the freedom of worship of all students, it could be Anglican and nonsectarian at the same time.[21] He published a message informing parents of prospective students that the institution had "no Intention to impose on the Scholars, the peculiar Tenets of any particular Sect of Christians" but aimed only "to inculcate upon their tender minds, the great Principles of Christianity and Morality, in which true Christians of each Denomination are generally agreed."[22]

Livingston and his associates retorted that the Anglican scheme would reproduce the worst features of other denominational colleges, and in addition set a dangerous political precedent. In their minds, as Milton Klein has explained, "concession to the Anglicans . . . would represent tacit acquiescence in the larger Episcopal contention that the Church [of England] deserved preferential treatment by law in the colony." Their essays in *The Independent Reflector* (1752–53) and in a series called "The Watch-Tower," published in the following two years, set forth a new concept: democratic control of higher learning. They proposed that the legislature incorporate and place under public management a college with a non-denominational constitution. All students would enjoy liberty of conscience. Supervision of the school would be exercised not by any private group, but by the community itself through its elected representatives, the New York Assembly, which would elect the college trustees.[23]

Part of Livingston's argument for a nonsectarian college was based on the assumption that sincere men of all denominations considered their own profession of faith the most accurate and scriptural. The resulting competition between the sects would be especially intense in a society characterized by great religious diversity and freedom of thought.[24] Such competition was beneficial, however, for it kept any one sect from securing political control and any one orthodoxy from gaining uncritical assent. "The Variety of Sects in the Nation," he wrote, "are a Guard against the Tyranny and Usurpation of one over another."[25] Pluralism, then, assured religious freedom because it provided a natural system of checks and balances.[26]

For this system to work well, however, all groups had to be on an equal plane before the government and the law. The Anglican minority's growing pretensions to political power, though, seemed to threaten liberty of conscience in New York. Denying that the Church of England was established, Livingston insisted that all Protestants in the colony enjoyed perfect equality of religious rights. The Anglican plan for the college, he charged, would establish a hierarchy of privileges among the different sects previously unknown.[27] He appealed to each denomination to protect liberty of conscience by defending its right not only to toleration but also to full legal parity.[28]

Livingston's appeal was only part of the effort each side made to gain popular support for its respective position. Both Anglicans and Presbyterians appealed directly to the Dutch Reformed.[29] The Anglican-dominated board of trustees outlined a plan to establish a Dutch professorship of divinity. Henry Barclay, rector at Trinity Church, persuaded pastor John

Ritzema, the Dutch Reformed board member, to endorse this proposal.[30] But Ritzema did so without bothering to gain the approval of either his ministerial colleagues or the church's consistory. The consistory thereupon censured him. They believed the plan represented no real advantage because the Dutch professor would be controlled by the board of trustees.[31] A more successful Anglican tactic was to offer a position on the college's board to one pastor in each of the city's Protestant communions. They correctly presumed that those who accepted such a position would develop both closer bonds with them and a vested interest in the college.[32]

The Presbyterians also realized they must have Dutch Reformed support if they were to stop the Anglican plan. In the preface to *The Independent Reflector* published in January 1754, Livingston pleaded with the Dutch to ignore the overtures of the Anglicans, and instead to adjust their policies to colonial realities. He denied his real intention was to unify the two Calvinist communions, however, and repeated his endorsement of religious pluralism:

> I am convinced nothing can tend so much to maintain our freedom and independency in religion as a division into a variety of sects. My sole aim is to make all Protestant denominations support a mutual harmony, and not prefer the certain ruin of one, to the fear of its union with another.[33]

The Dutch Reformed Coetus party, convinced that an established Anglican school would threaten their plans for a separate Dutch college in New York or New Jersey, overwhelmingly approved Livingston's views and allied themselves with the Presbyterians.[34] Their opinions appeared in several pamphlets probably written by Theodore Frelinghuysen but published pseudonymously in New York in 1754–55.[35] The pamphlets disapproved of Livingston's liberal Christianity and criticized his zealous anticlericalism, as had other Dutch Reformed and Presbyterian evangelicals. Indeed, one of them expressed the hope that Livingston might be truly converted.[36] They nonetheless supported his attacks on the Anglican plan on the grounds that it amounted to a Church of England establishment. Like Livingston, Smith, and Scott, the evangelicals in the Coetus party had embraced pluralism and were ready to defend its religious and political benefits. They praised New York for having several denominations of Protestants "whose religious liberties hang in Equilibrio, no one by Law established above the rest." They charged that Anglican ascendancy in the college would promote an alliance between one church and the state that would negate all these benefits. And they implored Dutch Reformed ministers and laymen to consider the dangers this Anglican plan presented to "the inestimable Blessing of Blessings . . . the Enjoyment of Liberty of Conscience in public Worship, and in Church Discipline."[37]

Despite the efforts of the Presbyterian "Triumvirate" of Livingston, Smith, and Scott and their evangelical supporters, in late 1754 the college was granted a royal charter providing for the appointment of twenty-nine Anglicans and only twelve dissenters to the board of governors, and Samuel Johnson assumed the presidency.[38] Livingston and his friends persisted, however, in their attacks on the "bigotry" of the Church of England in the series of essays called "The Watch-Tower," published in 1755. The Anglican clergy again responded quickly, first in the New York *Mercury* and then in an independent sheet entitled *John Englishman.* The excitement over the Seven Years' War gradually caused the public to lose interest in the college debate in the last months of 1755.[39] By then the board of governors had met several times, the first students were attending classes and chapel, and the Anglicans were clearly in control.

The sole concrete accomplishment of the dissenter opposition was to convince the New York Assembly to grant King's College only half the funds a provincial lottery had raised for education in the colony. Yet Livingston and his following had reasons to feel satisfied. They had pulled the ecclesiastical controversy into the public arena and made New York's citizens aware of the practical consequences of the two opposing concepts of religious order. The outcome of the debate had shown that Anglican leaders, committed to a religious system based on special privilege, were ready to assert their power to ensure dominance over public institutions, even at the expense of infringing upon the liberties dissenters were striving to protect. On the other hand, the controversy had given evangelical and liberal nonconformists an opportunity to affirm the colony's diversity and to promote a religious order based on an equality of rights among all groups.

A closely related controversy emerged over the establishment of the New York Society Library in 1754. The Presbyterian Triumvirate and a few friends founded the library to serve area residents and to aid King's College. The latter intention injected the campaign for the library into the struggle for control of the college. Although the library's first few years were filled with strife between religious groups competing to control it, the Presbyterians succeeded at least temporarily in having its facilities opened to all.[40]

The Seven Years' War with the French tended to unify Protestant New Yorkers in the late 1750s and early 1760s. All could join the fight to preserve "the true protestant religion and the laws and properties of

Englishmen" against the Catholic menace.[41] Anglican and Presbyterian agreed in calling King George II the "Father of his people," and in claiming that widespread unrighteousness had provoked God's judgment (the war) upon the colony.[42] Regardless of these shared perceptions, however, New York's religious factions continued to pursue their own interests during the war years. Anglicans repeated their long-standing plea for a resident bishop, while Presbyterian and other dissenting congregations renewed their petitions for charters of incorporation.

As suggested earlier, the colony's Anglican clergymen argued that without a bishop, their proper disciplinary and spiritual head, their communion could not compete on equal terms. During the King's College crisis, their arguments sounded remarkably like those dissenters advanced for a non-sectarian school. Echoing the sentiments of his adversary William Livingston, Samuel Johnson wrote Philadelphia's William Smith that Anglicans were entitled to the same privileges other Protestants enjoyed. America's peace and good government, Johnson reasoned, depended on Anglicans keeping pace with other denominations. The several communions provided a check on one another that prevented any one of them from exercising ecclesiastical oppression. The "very spirit of religion and the civil harmony of America," Johnson concluded, "seem to depend on laying the Church of England under the same advantages with other religious societies here."[43]

Other New York Anglicans quickly adopted Johnson's line of reasoning. In early 1755, two SPG missionaries, Isaac Brown and Thomas Chandler, informed the Archbishop of Canterbury they believed it fair that the Church of England should "be, at least, upon a Par with other Denominations, & have the Benefit of all her own Institutions."[44] Several months later, the Anglican clergy collectively complained that congregations that were "branches of the national establishment" were "deprived not only of the benefit of regular church government, but their children debarred the privilege of a liberal education."[45]

Such appeals continued throughout the 1760s.[46] The petitioners argued that an American episcopate would not threaten the liberties of dissenters. Samuel Johnson and others insisted they wanted a strictly spiritual leader whose office would have no impact on nonconformists or their privileges.[47] Their claims were probably sincere, for the desire for a bishop stemmed primarily from their religious perceptions. Most Anglican clergymen were unable or unwilling to accept Protestant pluralism as desirable or permanent. They continued to believe that their church's religion was true, orthodox, and necessary to salvation and that nonconformity was false, schismatic, and a danger to immortal souls.[48] They needed a bishop to maintain spiritual discipline, to confirm Anglican converts and restrain them from schism, and to establish their congregations as "true places of worship."[49]

In response, the Archbishop of Canterbury simply urged colonial Anglicans to continue their efforts to persuade dissenters that the plea for an American episcopate was no cause for alarm, since it aimed to give them equality with all other communions.[50] While New York's churchmen followed this strategy, they found it increasingly difficult to accept the idea that the established church of their mother country should have to endure even temporarily what they called "an inferior position to that of the sectaries."[51]

By arguing for a bishopric on the grounds of a desire for religious parity, Anglicans seemed to endorse pluralism. But that argument contradicted their continuing advocacy of their own establishment and their persisting belief that a balancing of sects was impossible. Indeed, they continued to predict that "dreadful convulsions" would result from a multiplicity of sects.[52] Apart from the rhetoric of their appeals for a bishop, the repeated use and defense of their privileged position demonstrated that equality was not all they desired.

That became clear when dissenting congregations attempted to obtain the charters necessary to give them legal status and the right to own property. Prior to 1760, the only corporate charters ever granted to non-Anglican churches were those of the four Dutch Reformed congregations whose right to them had been stipulated in the Articles of Capitulation of 1664.[53] Beginning in 1759 and through the next decade, Lutheran, Presbyterian, French Protestant, and Dutch Reformed congregations joined several Anglican ones in submitting petitions for incorporation to the provincial governor.[54] The political influence of the Church of England hierarchy on both sides of the Atlantic blocked all except the three Anglican petitions, from Jamaica, Schenectady, and Albany. Samuel Auchmuty's response to the 1766 Presbyterian request typified the exaggerated reactions of New York's Anglican clergy. "This Affair has fully imployed me," he wrote to Samuel Johnson; "I have left no Stone unturned . . . to render abortive the pernicious Scheme, replete with mischief—And I do not doubt of Success."[55]

Such reactions do not square with the contents of most of the petitions. Those from the Dutch Lutherans and French Protestants in New York City expressed full loyalty to the British government, declared their willing submission to an Anglican establishment, and explained that they existed primarily to meet the needs of immigrants who did not speak English.[56] Had charters been granted to these congregations, they would probably have become even more closely wedded to the existing order. Afraid, however, that concessions to any might set an irreversible precedent, Anglicans consistently urged both the New York Council and the imperial authorities to reject all dissenter petitions. Lieutenant Governor Cadwallader Colden wrote the Lords of Trade that since the dissenters in New York and in the neighboring colonies were "more numerous than those of the Church of England," their lordships should "judge how far it is consistent with good policy and the English Constitution" to grant them by charter "an equality with the Established Church." The King's Order in Council of 1767 declared it a "general policy" that all nonconformist petitions be denied and that they be granted no privileges or immunities beyond what the English Laws of Toleration specified.[57]

Most of New York's dissenters kept their disappointment to themselves. Several years later, however, Presbyterian minister John Rodgers wrote an anonymous pamphlet presenting his denomination's perspective on the charter controversy. He pointed out that the 1664 Articles of Capitulation directed that all provincial Protestant denominations were to enjoy legal parity and complete freedom of worship. On that basis, he argued that English ecclesiastical laws did not apply in New York and insisted that all groups were entitled to the protection and aid of the British Crown. He contrasted his own congregation's four futile attempts to acquire a charter with Trinity Parish's misuse of its privileges in acquiring properties with "a revenue fit for a Popish Abbey."[58] In light of these circumstances, he wrote, why should anyone marvel "that the project of erecting Episcopacy in America excites such general apprehensions in the rest of the American Churches!"[59]

The quest for an American episcopate was, of course, a source of great contention from the Treaty of Paris to the War for Independence. During the 1760s, the debate steadily intensified as both Anglican frustration and dissenter fears increased. After the French surrendered Canada to the British, the presence of a Catholic bishop in Quebec from 1766 on led Anglicans to consider their situation even more anomalous, especially when their English superiors responded to their repeated requests for a bishop with the word that the mother country's political climate made it inexpedient.[60] In 1763, Samuel Johnson had exclaimed, "Is there nothing more that can be done . . . for obtaining bishops?"[61] By the close of the Stamp Act crisis three years later, he was convinced the Anglicans in America could no longer realistically hope for assistance from British political authorities.[62]

The Anglican clergy in New York and New Jersey began meeting together voluntarily in annual conventions led by Thomas Chandler, Samuel

Seabury, Charles Inglis, and other ministers.[63] In 1766 these clergymen wrote the secretary of the SPG requesting the society to help them procure a bishop and to resist the efforts of Congregationalists and Presbyterians to undermine the Anglican Church. That very week eighty ministers from these communions were meeting in New York City in an attempt to draw up a Plan of Union against the episcopate scheme. New Yorkers actively involved included Presbyterian pastors John Rodgers and John Mason, Dutch Reformed minister Archibald Laidlie, and the Triumvirate.[64] Despite such actions, however, the Anglicans seemed still to believe that most moderate dissenters would approve an American episcopate if assured it posed no danger to their liberties. Inglis reiterated the old argument that it was only fair to allow his communion to complete its ecclesiastical organization as other denominations had.[65] Whether consciously or not, he and his colleagues divorced this "right" of all groups to full development of their discipline and government from the special ecclesiastical privileges the established church properly claimed. Most dissenters, however, could not accept this contradictory perception.

The enlargement of imperial control over the colonies in the 1760s heightened the nonconformists' concern to maintain their civil and religious liberties. Jonathan Mayhew and others depicted the desire for an episcopate as part of a conspiracy to undermine colonial freedoms.[66] Bishop advocates, they charged, did not want a bishop of the primitive Christian variety but a "modern, splendid, opulent, court-favored, law-dignified, superb, magnificent, powerful prelate."[67] Whether such an Anglican plot actually existed is not known, but many dissenters believed that it did, and that belief had important consequences.

Emphasizing the political danger of an episcopate was a new departure. As one historian has pointed out, prior to the mid-1760s most dissenters perceived the proposal in the context of competition between themselves and Anglicans for the spiritual allegiance of the colonial population. Consequently, they concentrated on biblical and theological arguments supporting the validity of Presbyterian government and ordination. After 1750, however, and especially in New York, these arguments were gradually exchanged for political ones.[68]

This change occurred in part because the chief opponents of Anglican dominance in the late 1760s included some who were less concerned with theology than with liberty. Influenced by the Enlightenment, liberal dissenters such as William Livingston and William Smith, Jr., cared less about conflicting views of ordination and church government than about civil and religious rights. They charged that bishops would endanger political freedoms, whether or not they obscured the way to salvation.[69] This reasoning was soon repeated by evangelicals in the Plan of Union conventions held between 1766 and 1775 and in New York City's Society of Dissenters.[70]

Despite its brief existence, the Society of Dissenters expressed well the shared convictions of liberals and evangelicals. The members declared that their opposition to a bishopric was not theologically motivated: "We are disaffected to no man, of any Christian persuasion on account of his religious sentiments. Nor are we prejudiced against any episcopalian for his religion."[71] Rather, they were apprehensive about the future of religious equality in the colony. "It is the politics of the Church," they wrote, "its power and its thirst of domination, a thirst not to be satiated but by our absolute destruction, that we are combined to oppose."[72] And if religious parity was in jeopardy, then religious liberty itself was at stake:

> No one who is properly sensible of the important Blessing [civil and religious liberty] can help being alarmed at the Attempts lately made by many of the Episcopal clergy and some of their Laity to introduce Bishops into America. . . . Should such be the Event, how Terrifying the prospect! We should be obliged to bid farewell to that religious Liberty, in which Christ has set us free; . . . for so extraordinary and dangerous an Innovation, would be attended with such Restraints, impositions and penalties on all Nonconformists as would make life itself intolerable.[73]

Their advocacy of common beliefs suggests that during the 1760s both liberal and evangelical dissenters had determined that doctrinal diversity was consonant with human reason and divine revelation. Given pluralism, then, each Protestant group was entitled to freedom of thought and a full exercise of its spiritual government, as long as neither privilege encroached on the liberties of others. Equal enjoyment of common rights would protect those freedoms and promote pluralistic harmony. While doctrinal differences were no longer considered a legitimate reason to oppose bishops, an episcopate could be protested on the grounds it threatened religious equality and liberty in the colony. At the same time, evangelicals retained their image of episcopacy as a traditional opponent of the revival and as a haven for the "unsaved" of other churches.[74]

The close ties between church and state in New York entwined questions of ecclesiastical domination and religious liberty with provincial politics. At no point was this more evident than in the Assembly elections and sessions of 1768–70. By this time, the main substantive difference between the colony's two political parties was religious affiliation. The Livingston party consisted completely of dissenters—Presbyterian, Dutch Reformed, Lutheran, and Quaker—while the DeLancey group was an unwieldy alliance of Anglicans and Dutch Reformed. Though both parties vacillated in their positions on imperial and constitutional problems, they were consistent on religious issues.[75]

All this was evident in the Assembly election campaign of 1769 in New York City. The four Livingston candidates urged the voters to elect men who would protect their liberties. They reasoned that the DeLanceys favored an American bishopric, which portended the extension of the English Test and Conformity Acts.[76] DeLancey supporters countered that it was the "Dissenting junto" and not the Anglicans who thirsted after domination and threatened liberty of conscience. In addition, they challenged the Livingston party's claim to represent better a broader range of interests by suggesting that they in fact represented the viewpoints of only one or two denominations, to the exclusion of all others.[77]

While the DeLancey candidates were elected, the Livingstons retained enough strength to secure passage of a number of bills aimed at equalizing religious privileges. Among them were statutes to incorporate all Protestant churches north of Westchester County, to enable non-Anglican churches to own land, and to exempt inhabitants of the four lower counties from taxes supporting ministers of churches to which they did not belong.[78] None of these became law, however, because the provincial Council remained firm in its defense of Anglican prerogatives and rejected them. On the other hand, whenever the DeLanceys tried to extend those prerogatives through legislation, their Dutch Reformed members bolted and voted with the Livingstons. That this stalemate in the politics of religion continued until the Revolution explains why the religious issue became less visible after 1770.[79]

By that time New Yorkers had witnessed twenty years of almost uninterrupted debate over ecclesiastical privileges, religious liberty, and church-state relations. Because two conflicting conceptions of the relationship of the churches to the state erupted in public disputes, members of all denominations realized the seriousness of the issues at stake. As religious differences blended thus with political ones, individuals and congregations were increasingly forced to embrace one view or the other.[80]

As suggested earlier, New York's Presbyterians led in affirming complete equality of ecclesiastical rights. They believed no group was entitled to legal prerogatives—especially not the Anglicans, who numbered at most only one-tenth of the province's inhabitants.[81] No less committed to this principle were the small but growing number of Baptists in the colony. Both New York's Regular and Separate Baptists identified with their faith tradition's long-standing attachment to religious liberty and considered their situation fortunate in comparison with the "ecclesiastical oppression" their brethren in New England and Virginia suffered.[82] Fearing that an expansion of Anglican power might bring them the same fate, they protested all measures they believed would undermine religious equality.

Analysis of the colony's other Protestant groups reveals that, in general, evangelical sympathizers within each denomination supported the Presbyterian and Baptist position, while many of the Orthodox Protestants lined up with the Anglican hierarchy. The Coetus wing of the Dutch Reformed Church repeatedly indicated its willingness to risk the denomination's special privilege of church charters to prevent the Anglicans from threatening religious freedom.[83] The Dutch evangelicals were, however, more reticent than others in political controversy, primarily because their church's internal struggles occupied most of their attention.[84] Pietists in the German Reformed, Lutheran, and Moravian churches were likewise reticent, though clearly committed to religious equality.

Meanwhile, the colony's Quakers promoted religious liberty through their committee on sufferings. Whenever bills likely to limit their freedoms arose in the Assembly, the committee was to endeavor "to Prevent the Ill Consequences which may Attend their being Passed into Laws Either by a Representation in Writing to the House of Assembly or by a Particular Conference with the Members thereof."[85]

Most religious liberals of all types, including those in the Church of England, stood with the evangelicals and Quakers on these issues. Minister Samuel Provoost had to leave Trinity Parish because of his theological liberalism and sympathy for the plight of dissenters.[86] Others were simply persuaded their communion would be more prosperous if disentangled from the state. Anglican assemblymen Lewis Morris and John Thomas introduced several prodissenter bills in 1769 because they feared other legislation might pass that would exempt all colonists but Anglicans from church taxation. Such circumstances would make it difficult for their church to attract members.[87] One group of discontented Anglicans tried to establish a congregation independent of Trinity Parish hoping it would obliterate the distinction between establishment and nonconformity.[88]

The views of liberals and evangelicals aimed logically at religious disestablishment. Some New Yorkers had adopted this position as early as the 1750s, agreeing with Livingston's argument that "among the many Instances of the Abuse of Government, there is none more immediately destructive of the natural Rights of Mankind, than the Interposition of the secular Arm in Matters purely religious."[89] Others were drawn to it by events of the following twenty years.

Though diverse in their view of nature, society and religion, both liberals and evangelicals in New York embraced disestablishment and the principle of religious equality only after confronting their theological meanings and implications. Surely, almost all had long agreed that toleration of diversity was far preferable to coerced uniformity. But they had to ask whether pluralism's effects on religion in general were salutary enough for those who took religion seriously to accept it as the permanent solution. Liberals and evangelicals eventually answered this question by giving Protestant diversity a positive religious significance through their acceptance of either an enlightened and latitudinarian Christianity on the one hand or a conversion-centered revivalistic message on the other. For evangelicals, the discovery that an essential harmony lay beneath their diversity eventually made their variety seem a blessing. Similarly, liberals could endorse pluralism once they perceived it would both reflect and protect their commitment to freedom of thought. Once they had agreed that diversity was acceptable, evangelicals and liberals could unite in insisting on a perfect equality of privileges for all groups, in the name of liberty of conscience. A specially privileged sect, they agreed, posed a constant threat to the survival of others and, therefore, to the pluralism that sustained the liberties of all. They found mere toleration of dissenters under a church establishment unacceptable. Religious liberty could only be secured through disestablishment and equal state protection of the religious rights of all.

To reach these conclusions, New York's evangelicals and liberals had to do precisely the kind of intellectual wrestling with pluralism that Sidney Mead has said was absent in the pre-Revolutionary period. Mead is correct in suggesting that practical necessity pushed colonial Christians toward accepting religious freedom and religious diversity. But he has underestimated or overlooked the thoughtful efforts of these Middle Colony religionists to interpret positively the theological significance of pluralism before embracing it. This is not to say that these provincials had figured out all that pluralism would mean for American religion or American society in the future. In fact, it is important to note that most of these evangelicals and liberals were thinking primarily in terms of religious liberty and equality for all *Protestant* bodies. Given the smallness of New York's non-Protestant minority, it is not surprising that few made mention or gave thought to the future civil and religious rights of Catholics, Jews, or others prior to the American Revolution. Those who did were almost all situated in New York City, where they were more accustomed than other colonists to rubbing shoulders with Jews and closet Catholics. Even so, it can be argued that collectively these New Yorkers had taken several major strides in the direction of making intellectual sense out of the principal reality of their religious environment. And as a result, they were in a good position in future years to help the state's citizenry as a whole decide whether to draw limits on religious liberty as well as make up its mind about the value of a pluralism broader than Protestantism.

Meanwhile, the colony's Anglican leadership stood firmly with traditionalists in other denominations in defending the historic establishment. For some Anglicans, this was purely a matter of protecting the self-interest of the Church of England. The political loyalties of theological liberal Cadwallader Colden to the British Empire, for example, made him a longtime supporter of Anglican privileges in the colony. Other Anglicans defended the established church on more ideological grounds. From their perspective, pluralism of any kind was a necessary evil, to be tolerated but not encouraged in the colony. While acknowledging that variety was a central aspect of God's creation, they thought that it was not a rationale for equality but an evidence that God intended hierarchy and subordination to characterize human relationships in the religious as well as in the political and social orders. Rather than threatening freedom of worship, an established church would protect it from the dangers inherent in sectarian strife.

Similarly, conservative Protestants of other denominations supported the Anglican establishment for both ideological and practical reasons. This group included the Dutch Reformed Conferentie party, Orthodox German Reformed and Lutherans, most French Protestants and Methodists, a minority of Quakers, and a handful of Presbyterians, Congregationalists, and Baptists. Methodism had the closest links to the Church of England and was in no position to question existing church-state relations. For many Reformed and Lutheran Protestants, attachment to the European state-church tradition made the alternative inconceivable. Some Dutch Reformed conservatives even argued that their communion, in light of the church charters it had received, was also "established" in the colony.[90] During the 1769 assemblymen campaign in New York City, a Dutch layman wrote a pamphlet urging fellow members to disavow those who portrayed the Church of England as desiring to subvert other communions. After briefly showing the historical ties between the Anglican and Dutch Reformed bodies, he wondered what more Anglican opponents expected to gain since they were fully tolerated. Unable to comprehend the quest for equality of rights, he concluded that the dissenters were the ones who sought dominion; they would never give up their demands until they had "swallowed up the Rights of every other Denomination."[91]

Others feared the loss of their churches' existing privileges. In particular, some Dutch Reformed colonists, along with their Amsterdam supervisors, feared that their church charters might be revoked if they helped undermine the established clergy, while currying their favor might even secure new benefits, as in the case of the theology professorship at King's College.[92] Quakers on Long Island supported the Anglican faction to retain their right to vote; French Protestants in the southern counties did so to get continued pastoral help from the city's Anglican clergy.[93]

Still other Protestants identified with the Anglican establishment for what could be gained personally. Nominal Presbyterian Archibald Kennedy, as a member of the colony's Council from 1726 to 1761, saw firsthand the political and social benefits that accompanied Anglican membership. He thus encouraged his son and other young men to give up religious dissent and join the English church for the sake of their careers.[94]

New Yorkers continued to debate these questions of ecclesiastical order and religious equality between 1770 and 1775. Anglican clergymen Inglis, Chandler, and Cooper maneuvered to secure an American bishopric through every available means.[95] As time went on, they became convinced their opponents aimed to destroy Anglicanism, and began to demand new privileges to prevent the further erosion of its position.[96] On the other hand, some nonconformists still sought to protect themselves from Anglican encroachment. Many reacted strongly against a petition calling for tax support of an Anglican clergyman in Yonkers, and others continued the long legal battle over the ministerial appointment to Jamaica, Long Island. In that court case, dissenter lawyer John Morin Scott repeated the claim that there existed in the province "a perfect legal Parity of religious Rights among the Denominations of Protestants," and that the parish's vestry was entitled therefore to call a Protestant minister of any denomination.[97]

These controversies took on added significance because of the close association of the Anglican Church with English imperial policies and practices. During the previous two decades, dissenters had learned that the struggles to maintain their civil liberties and their religious freedoms were inseparable, for the agents of Canterbury and Whitehall endangered both.[98] Distrust of bishops as agents of the British political ministry sprang from appeals of colonial Anglicans to British officials of state which stressed Anglicanism as a bulwark of loyalty to the Crown, a bulwark needing to be strengthened by a colonial episcopate. Non-Anglicans took such arguments at face value, and the reputation of Anglicanism among Americans suffered. As relations between England and America worsened, therefore, many colonists came to associate all forms of corruption with English politicians, the English church, and even English culture.[99] Meanwhile, New York's Anglican leaders regarded their efforts to secure an episcopate and to stave off political rebellion as two parts of a single campaign. Although the more moderate ones were unwilling to defend all the British

measures, they resisted the use of illegal tactics to oppose them.[100] Consequently, on the eve of the American Revolution, most New Yorkers recognized that the colony's political and religious fortunes were intertwined; in
their minds, the outcome depended on the decisions of the English ministry, the moral vision of the American people, and the grace of God. The
confluence of religious disputes with the imperial conflict intensified feel-
ings about both sorts of issues and certainly contributed to the outbreak of
war.

Before proceeding to examine the interplay between New York's religious diversity and the War for Independence, we should pause to recognize that New Yorkers lived through the events of the previous thirty years
without any awareness that a violent revolution was soon to occur. They
sought only to cope with their immediate problems and to construct religious institutions, systems of belief, and an ordered relationship between
church and state that would meet their needs. They would have done this
with or without the American Revolution. These efforts, and the controversies they generated, must be understood as the colonists understood
them, as a quest to mold a satisfying religious life in America rather than as
a prologue to the War for Independence.

Perceived in this light, what is noteworthy is the emergence between 1725
and 1775 of two ways of looking at the relationship of religion to society
and culture. The contrasting perspectives cut across denominational and
even congregational lines. Certainly there was a middle ground, which
some colonists felt most comfortable in holding. Nevertheless, at some
point during these years the majority gravitated to one side or the other.
Not surprisingly, the correlation of both political and religious sensibility
among those accepting and those rejecting the traditionalist position was
extremely high. Put more simply, what this means is that most of those who
opposed self-sufficient American denominations also defended Orthodox
Protestantism and sided with the Anglican establishment. Conversely, proponents of ecclesiastical independence were usually evangelical sympathizers who joined with most religious liberals in demanding religious
equality.

The touchstone of choice between these groups in New York seems to
have been the evaluation of pluralism made by each set of participants. On
one hand, the values and beliefs of traditionalists continued to be molded
by their understanding of, and preference for, European law and custom.
The effort to transplant that tradition to a radically different setting left
them frustrated and ready to defend with increasing fervor what was
familiar.[101] They came thus to live in continuing conflict with their actual

surroundings. On the other hand, the evangelicals and liberals who championed religious equality had shared the experience of becoming politically and theologically reconciled to a diverse environment. They had found a way to affirm religious pluralism, and especially Protestant diversity, as a social benefit, not simply as an unfortunate fact to which they must adjust. Their joining in the struggle to resist the Anglican establishment and to secure religious liberty in the 1770s and '80s therefore was more than the mere "coalition of convenience" posited by Sidney Mead. Rather, it was the product of deep-rooted agreement on the religious and political meaning of pluralism.

II

Plural Religion amid War and Peace, 1775–1800

IV

"A SHOCKEN TIME"
CHURCH LIFE DURING THE
REVOLUTIONARY WAR

Religious diversity in New York continued to influence religious developments there during the last quarter of the eighteenth century. During the
"shocken time" of the Revolutionary War from 1775 to 1783, pluralism
influenced the responses of the province's religious communions to the
imperial crisis, contributed to the political restructuring of the colony's
religious order, and affected the churches' efforts to maintain their institutional lives and spiritual interest amid the disruption of wartime.

New York's path to independence and eventual strategic military importance during the war have been described ably elsewhere.[1] My concern
here is not to retell those events but to examine, first of all, the way
provincial religious bodies responded to the mounting conflict with Great
Britain. By the spring of 1775, and particularly after the outbreak of
hostilities at Concord bridge, virtually all denominational leaders acknowledged "the gloomy aspect of . . . public affairs" and lamented their nation's
"present sad and perilous condition." They included such comments in
pleas for days of public repentance that interpreted the imperial conflict as
God's righteous judgment on a sinful America.[2] In October 1774, the
Dutchess Presbytery appointed a day of humiliation, fasting, and prayer on
account of the "heavy judgments God was placing on their guilty land and
nation," especially the invasion of their civil and religious rights.[3] The
following April the Dutch Reformed General Body recommended a similar
observance after "considering that our multiplied, aggravated, long-con-
tinued, and unlamented sins, have afforded reason to God to give up our
land to the most deplore[able] calamities. . . ."[4] After his congregation
participated in the day of fasting requested by the Continental Congress in
July 1775, French Protestant elder Jacques Buvelot wrote that colonial trials

resulted from "a lack of respect, and care for what we should have followed and [failure] to obey and perform the commandments of our God. . . ." He urged fellow believers to beseech God "to fogive our transgressions which are the cause of our distress, so that He may be propitious and favourable unto us, turning away from us the punishments that threaten us."[5] By October 1775, the Philadelphia Baptist Association established quarterly fast days, deploring "too much deadness among Christians," and the Presbyterian Synod of New York and Philadelphia encouraged its presbyteries to make the last Thursday in every month a special time of prayer.[6]

If prompted largely by political events, these calls for public fasting and prayer were still fundamentally spiritual responses to the colonial crisis and did not represent an endorsement of any specific course of political action. As such, they reflected the long-standing belief among most New Yorkers that neither denominational assemblies nor local congregations were proper organs of political expression. This conviction helps explain the relative silence of provincial church records about the momentous events of the prewar years. For instance, although the membership of New York City's Brick Presbyterian Church included such patriot leaders as John Morin Scott, Peter Van Brugh Livingston, Alexander McDougall, and John Broome, its session book for 1768 to 1775 contained only two significant references to current politics: an address of welcome in October 1770, when Lord Dunmore arrived from England to become governor, and another in July 1771, when Governor Tryon succeeded him. Both addresses unequivocally expressed loyalty to King George.[7]

The colony's religious leaders preferred their churches to be apolitical institutions because they could not afford the economic and spiritual risks of taking an official position on volatile political issues. Certainly within all denominations, and probably in every congregation, the strife with the mother country created split loyalties. Outright endorsement of either side would in many cases have produced irreparable internal division, thereby destroying not only their spiritual harmony but also the consensus they needed to keep their ministers paid and church buildings repaired. At the same time, it would have likely caused external friction with neighboring congregations. This was the price religious diversity exacted for political outspokenness.

For the same reasons, most provincial clergymen refrained from clearly expressing their political sentiments when preaching, at least until late 1774 or early 1775. As private citizens, many of them actively defended or attacked British policy. But in the pulpit they tried to avoid politicizing.[8] Hence, the sermons of such politically active ministers as John Rodgers (Presbyterian) and Archibald Laidlie (Dutch Reformed) between 1765 and

1774 dealt chiefly with personal piety, submission to God, and the divine provision of eternal life. In comparison with later sermons, they were noticeably free of references to imperial afflictions or America's place in God's plan for the future.[9]

As conflict intensified and imperial tensions rose, however, both the clergy and the laity found it more difficult to avoid expressing political opinions through ecclesiastical channels. Examination of events in New York City during one week in May 1775 reveals the growing pressure on members of all religious groups. At the annual meeting of the Presbyterian Synod held there from May 17 to 23, Rodgers and several other delegates composed a pastoral letter for distribution throughout America outlining the synod's perspective on the colonial crisis. The letter began by explaining their decision to speak out politically:

> It is well known . . . that we members of the Synod have not been instrumental in inflaming the minds of the people, or urging them to acts of violence and disorder. Perhaps no instance can be given on so interesting a subject, in which political sentiments have been so long and so fully kept from the pulpit . . . but things are now come to such a state, that we do not wish to conceal our opinions as men and citizens. . . .[10]

The epistle went on baldly to echo Whig thinking. It attributed responsibility for the crisis to the king's ministers and colonial administrators, discouraged luxury, advised private and public virtue, and insisted that "There is no example in history in which civil liberty was destroyed, and the rights of conscience preserved entire." It climaxed ominously: "Hostilities long feared, have now taken place"; if the British continued to enforce their claims by violence, "a lasting and bloody contest" would ensue, and the defenders of liberty must therefore "be prepared for death."[11] During the same weekend, Dutch pastor Laidlie identified the American cause as "good" and therefore the "cause of God"; it could not fail. He proclaimed to his congregation that because "the Glory of God and preservation of his Church, his Truths, our Civil and Religious Liberty" were at stake, they could with "fervent Confidence rely on God for help and deliverance."[12]

Meanwhile, outspoken Anglican minister Thomas B. Chandler, rector at Elizabethtown, New Jersey, had come to New York seeking protection, fearing the Sons of Liberty might do him harm. Forsaking both family and parish, Chandler was aboard a ship bound for Bristol, England, by May 25.[13] Apparently, Chandler's Anglican colleagues in New York City, Samuel Auchmuty, Charles Inglis, Benjamin Moore, and John Bowden, were less apprehensive about their personal safety. They joined ministers from the Baptist, Presbyterian, Dutch Reformed, and Scottish Presbyterian congregations in providing daily prayer for the sessions of the Provincial Congress, which met that week in New York.[14]

Participation on public committees like the Provincial Congress was ill-advised for Friends, according to the colony's Quaker leadership, because it was inconsistent with their "Religious Principles." The best means to maintain their "peaceable Testimony in these times of peril" was refusing to participate in political or military bodies.[15] Nevertheless, on May 25 a subcommittee of the New York Meeting for Sufferings reported little progress in persuading certain Quakers to that viewpoint. In fact, during this same week one of the committee's own members joined the Provincial Congress.[16] Retaining this Quaker distinction seemingly proved too much for him and others amid the counter examples of their pluralistic neighbors.

Political quietism was also the advice given to New York's Methodists. In two letters from John Wesley dated May 19, he encouraged them to serve as peacemakers by using every possible means to oppose party spirit ("the bane of all true religion") and suggested that all those who feared God on both sides of the Atlantic needed to pray that war might be avoided.[17]

Thus, in New York in late May 1775, members of the colony's various religious groups were busily defining their opinions, preparing strategies, and, in a few cases, taking decisive actions in response to the calamitous times. Their responses, though generally made in light of their religious values and beliefs, were conditioned as well by such new political realities as the Provincial Congress and such long-standing social realities as their own religious diversity.

Over the course of the following year, most of the colony's congregations were satisfied to carry on their normal work. A few, including the Baptists in Paulings Precinct and Goshen and the Dutch Reformed in Kinderhook, experienced considerable growth.[18] Others suffered the opposite. By February 1776, about forty Moravians had left their congregation in New York, primarily because of the presence of patriot troops in the city.[19] When a few Quakers took an "active part in the commotion of the times," including bearing arms, the New York Yearly Meeting recommended that each of its monthly meetings "keep a close watch over their members so that they do not join in practices inconsistent with their Christian Testimony."[20] French Reformed minister John Peter Tetrard and Presbyterian pastor Israel Evans were asked to leave their former duties to become chaplains for the state militia.[21] And Francis Asbury did not return to New York, or visit any other northern colonies, in part because of the growing public resentment of Methodist loyalty aroused by the publication of John Wesley's pamphlet *A Calm Address to our American Colonies*.[22] These limited disruptions, however, fade in significance when compared with the drastic upheavals that were soon to follow.

Between July and October 1776, developments occurred that determined the colony's political and religious course for much of the next decade. The new Declaration of Independence claimed that the colonies were politically free. From that point onward, it was impossible for a clergyman of any variety to avoid taking some kind of political stance. On July 11, the Provincial Convention adopted a resolution addressed to the Continental Congress requesting that prayers for the king be forbidden, since they interfered with American interests.[23] Even the most apolitical Anglican ministers either had to stop praying for the king as the Prayer Book required, or risk being considered enemies of the American cause by continuing to do so or by suspending all church services.[24] Pastors hardly had time to choose a course of action, though, before the British assaulted lower New York and captured Long Island and Manhattan. The British attack forced thousands of uncommitted New Yorkers to decide quickly which army they would support. As Washington's troops fled from Long Island and the city, so too did scores of other colonists of every religious persuasion: Presbyterians, Baptists, Dutch Reformed, German Reformed, Jews, Lutherans, French Protestants, Catholics, Quakers, Moravians, Methodists, and Anglicans. In virtually every case, however, they left behind coreligionists who, for whatever reasons, opted to stay at home, even at the cost of being identified with the British side.

As the war spread throughout the rest of the colony in the closing months of 1776, few New Yorkers found it possible to pursue the path a majority of them had earlier preferred—neutrality.[25] For by the year's end, public opinion had "palpably begun to categorize neutrality as an unacceptable option."[26] How and to what extent these Revolutionary decisions were conditioned by the religious values, ideas, or affiliations of the colonists are questions that have received growing scholarly attention in recent years. My research has convinced me that religious issues as such, specifically the episcopate issue, were not central in sparking the Revolution. While Americans cared deeply about them, ecclesiastical grievances were not sufficiently divisive to provoke war. Nor can the revolutionary struggle in New York be simplistically summarized as a conflict pitting Anglicans against dissenters.[27] If a majority of Anglicans were loyalists, a majority of loyalists were not Anglicans; and Anglicans played major roles in the leadership of the patriot cause. Members of all denominations were found on both sides of the conflict, though not always in equal proportions.[28] On the other hand, certain religious ideas seem to have possessed tremendous revolutionary potential, especially as they became politicized.[29] Gary Nash has argued that evangelical ideology played a central role in shaping the political radicalism of the lower elements in the urban social hierarchy.[30] Yet, he insists that the political preferences of laboring men were determined less by religion than by concern for their economic survival.[31]

While helpful in reaffirming the importance of religion to the colonists, the research of Nash and others raises more questions than it answers about religion's causative role in the Revolution. Perhaps a more fruitful line of inquiry is that of another group of historians who have noticed in the Middle Colonies striking parallels between the lines of division in the pre-Revolutionary religious debates over organizational, theological, and political issues and the choice of loyalties during the war.[32] Members of a particular denomination who had disagreed over religious matters in the 1750s and '60s usually took opposite sides in the Revolution. Furthermore, former conservatives or traditionalists generally became Tories, while their opponents almost invariably became patriots.

Study of the alignment of New Yorkers confirms these findings and also indicates that the division of colonists into the two distinctive religious perspectives described in the preceding chapters correlates closely with Revolutionary behavior. Only four of forty-one Dutch Reformed ministers in New York and New Jersey declared themselves Tories, but all four had supported the Conferentie party. The several pastors ambivalent toward the patriot cause also had favored the conservative wing of the church.[33] Studies of Dutch laypersons in the Hackensack and upper Hudson River valleys show that where the Conferentie influence had been powerful, a strong Tory minority emerged.[34] This same pattern is evident on Long Island, where the high incidence of loyalism in Kings and Queens counties paralleled a long tradition of conservative Dutch churchmanship. Conversely, on Staten Island, the ministers (Cornelius Van Santvoord, William Jackson) and congregation had been consistent evangelical supporters of the Coetus, and most Dutch residents became patriots.[35] In New York City, the split in the Collegiate congregation over English services apparently flowed into the Revolution; according to one Anglican minister, the supporters of Archibald Laidlie had "all proved violent Rebels," while "those who adhered to their ancient Institutions & Language . . . have been among the most loyal of the King's Subjects during this Rebellion."[36]

The political behavior of other religious groups has yet to be examined as thoroughly, but a quick survey points to the same conclusions. Among the colony's Anglican clergy, all became Tories except Samuel Provoost, who still demonstrated the same independent thinking that had forced him to leave Trinity Parish. The majority of Anglican laymen also became loyalists, but those who rebelled were often from the middle or lower classes (for example, John Lamb and Isaac Sears). Anglicans from these ranks had largely constituted the communion's small evangelical minority prior to the war and been apathetic about an American bishop.[37] Most Baptists in New York City and the Hudson Valley joined the Revolutionary cause, just as they had affirmed revival doctrines and the quest for ecclesiastical self-sufficiency.[38] Those in Queens County split more evenly into Whig and Tory, much as they had divided in the 1750s in Oyster Bay into New Light (Separate) and Regular Baptist churches.[39] Lutheran minister Bernard Houseal, not surprisingly, sided with the British; he had few ties to the Pietist branch of his own denomination and was strongly attached to the colony's Anglican hierarchy through membership on the King's College Board of Governors. In contrast, his colleague in the city, Frederick A.C. Muhlenberg, a son of Pietist Henry Muhlenberg, became so committed to the patriot fight he eventually left the ministry for a political career.[40] The split loyalties of these two clergymen were mirrored in the choice of lay Lutherans all over the colony.

Other denominations divided on the same terms. Earlier in the century, the French Protestants in New Rochelle had conformed to the Church of England, and now followed the loyalist bent of their Anglican clergymen and the locally powerful DeLancey family.[41] The French in New Paltz, however, had a close association with a Dutch Reformed congregation pastored by Coetus minister John M. Goetschius; they chose over-whelmingly to support the Revolution.[42] New York City's Moravian, Meth-odist, and Jewish congregations all saw parts of their membership flee during the Battle of Long Island. Within each group, the degree of religious and cultural attachment to Europe foreshadowed, if it did not shape, the choice of loyalties. For instance, the Toryism of Moravian pastor Oswald Shewkirk may be explained by his recent arrival (1774) from Europe, after a stay of several years in England.[43] On the other hand, Congregation Shearith Israel's hazzan, Gersham Mendez Seixas, was the first native-born Jewish precentor; he and other patriots in the congregation left the city for Connecticut and Philadelphia during the war.[44]

The denomination and clergy most associated with gaining ecclesiastical self-sufficiency, embracing evangelicalism, and opposing the Anglican establishment—Presbyterians—followed suit by supporting the Revolution in larger numbers than any other group in the colony. All but one of their pastors in New York became rebels. The lone exception was Mathias Burnet, pastor at Jamaica, Long Island, in predominantly Tory Queens County.[45] Even in Jamaica, however, 62 percent of Presbyterians were Whigs and only 12 percent were Tories on the eve of the Revolution.[46] Here and elsewhere in the province, the bulk of Presbyterian laypeople followed the lead of the overwhelming majority of their ministers and backed the patriot cause.

For Quakers, the war severely tested their peace testimony, especially since New York was the scene of so much military conflict. Within areas of British occupation, Friends naturally maintained the loyalism to British authority they had earlier displayed. In their minds, disrupting rightful government was grounds for disownment by the monthly meeting. Quakers living under American control were in a more difficult position. They had to decide whether to subscribe to the oath of allegiance required by the state's revolutionary government. To do so meant probable disownment. But refusal left Quakers under a cloud of political suspicion. Overall, despite these trying circumstances, most Friends kept their pacifism intact by declining to give active support to either side.[47]

Thus, this overview of Revolutionary attitudes shows that during the war, as in the mid-century religious debates, not only did Baptists oppose Anglicans, but Lutherans, Dutch Reformed, and Presbyterians took sides against their own spiritual kin. When portrayed in this way, the Revolution may be seen for what it was in New York: a painful experience that separated families, strained the consciences of sensitive men and women, and left congregations in a shambles. The tragedy of such an event deserves to be remembered.[48] That the respective positions adopted in the Revolution correlated closely with past religious differences, though, lends some credence to Robert Kelley's argument that religious and cultural attitudes were a major force in determining political loyalties in the province.[49]

Soon after declaring independence, New York's rebels began framing a new republican government and writing a state constitution. On August 2, 1776, the Convention of the Representatives of the State of New York (the former Provincial Congress) wasted no time in unanimously calling for "a day of fasting, humiliation, and prayer to Almighty God," for "his divine assistance in the organization and establishment of a form of government for the security and perpetuation of the civil and religious rights and liberties of mankind," and for "his further protection in the war which now rages throughout America." The convention asked to have three sermons preached before it that day, one each by pastors Martinus Schoonmaker (Dutch Reformed) of Harlem, Samuel Provoost (Anglican) of Albany County, and John Rodgers (Presbyterian) of New York City.[50] These resolutions show that the convention's members realized from the start that the new constitution must guarantee religious liberty through a restructuring of the church-state relationship. The arrangement of an interdenominational service suggests they also recognized that the state's religious diversity would be a prime consideration in determining the new system of religious order.

The committee of fourteen members appointed to prepare a plan of government reflected New York's Protestant pluralism by including Anglican, Presbyterian, Dutch Reformed, Lutheran, and Quaker members.[51] The drafting of the constitution took several months; not till the spring of 1777 did debate occur over its religious articles. That debate made clear the delegates' agreement on the merits of religious liberty and religious disestablishment. An article to exclude all ministers from civil and military offices aroused no serious opposition within the convention or the citizenry. Neither did the provision to disestablish Anglicanism and prevent any future establishments. The drafting committee as a whole was happy to put an end to an establishment whose Anglican exclusivity dissenters had denied all along and continued to deny in the article itself: "That all such parts of the said common law, and all such of the said statutes and acts aforesaid, or parts thereof, *as may be construed to establish or maintain any particular denomination of Christians or their ministers . . . be, and they hereby are, abrogated and rejected.*"[52] Likewise, the committee was united in rejecting a new system of multiple establishments, as was recommended by Presbyterian minister John Rodgers and adopted by six other states in the Revolutionary era. New York's long and bitter disputes over interpreting the Ministry Acts, along with the fact that much of the colony was already accustomed to voluntary support of religion, persuaded lawmakers to avoid altogether any kind of religious establishment. Because of the convention's consensus on these issues, New York substantially avoided the type of long-term debate over the church-state relationship that characterized Virginia and other states. A substantial minority in Virginia favored the retention of a single establishment or its replacement by a multiple system with state aid for all churches.[53]

Conflict did arise in the convention, however, over article 38's declaration that the free exercise and enjoyment of religious profession and worship be allowed without discrimination to all people in New York. Anti-Catholic sentiment, which had emerged periodically in eighteenth-century New York and most recently in reaction to the Quebec Act of 1774, reappeared briefly.[54] Anglican evangelical John Jay, fearing that Catholics with such unrestricted freedom would be politically dangerous, made several attempts to amend the article. He first suggested that the State Legislature be given large powers to determine what religious principles were "inconsistent with the safety of civil society"; when that failed, he proposed an amendment, also rejected, that would have forced Catholics to take an oath of allegiance declaring their ultimate loyalty to New York rather than the pope.[55] Apparently, Jay was unsuccessful in convincing other committee members that the very small number of native Catholics in New York posed a serious political threat. On the other hand, Protestant prejudices were strong enough so that the constitution eventually included a naturalization oath which, in effect, prevented Catholic newcomers from Europe from settling in the state. Few Catholic immigrants would be willing to settle in a place that forced them to affirm a higher loyalty to the state than to the head of their church. Nevertheless, the constitution adopted on April 20 provided a larger degree of religious freedom than most other constitutions in Revolutionary America.[56]

By granting all religious bodies a perfect parity of rights and by refusing to lay doctrinal restrictions upon civil freedoms, as did many other states, New York gave complete religious liberty to its residents, whether Protestant, Catholic, Jew, or other, and thereby ensured a religiously pluralistic future.[57] In fact, by implication the constitution provided for the civic legitimacy of irreligion or unbelief (though few New Yorkers would have agreed with such a notion or admitted that the constitution allowed for it). Why did New York go so far in its new religious order? As discussed earlier, many of the colony's evangelicals and liberals had advocated in the decade prior to the Revolution a new type of church-state relationship based on religious equality. But their endorsement of religious equality was founded largely on their acceptance of *Protestant* pluralism as consonant with both Scripture and human reason. The arguments they used to defend Protestant diversity and religious equality, therefore, had little to do with Catholics, Jews, or members of other religions and said virtually nothing about whether these other groups would be on a par with Protestant ones under the new religious order. So the question remains: Why did the new state constitution endorse religious liberty for all in 1777? And what accounts for the acceptance of this more extreme form of religious pluralism by most New Yorkers?

For the constitutional framers, the answer seems to lie partly in their belief that the state was responsible to protect and support equally all religious groups because each contributed to the stability and welfare of the republic. Among America's Revolutionary elite, there was a pervasive conviction, regardless of personal theological beliefs, that religion in general was a positive force within society and was to be valued highly.[58] From their republican ideology, as well as their Protestant backgrounds, the framers derived the belief that religion was the most effective promoter and ensurer of moral virtue, the key ingredient in the preservation of liberty and the republic's success. Since in their minds the churches represented in

New York (including Judaism) each, on balance, undergirded traditional morality, the state was well-advised to promote them all, rather than encouraging some and deterring others. Furthermore, history had taught that picking ecclesiastical favorites was ill-advised. Consequently, it was best to eliminate state interference on religious grounds into the rights of any person or group of whatever opinion. That meant not only prohibiting the government from meddling into the internal affairs of churches but eliminating any religious qualifications for the magistracy. New York's constitutional framers no doubt shared the conviction of other states' Revolutionary leaders that rulers needed to be virtuous. Yet they were persuaded that such virtue would be better ensured by a discriminating electoral process than by a constitutional provision. These views explain well, I think, why John Jay's efforts to limit Catholic rights proved futile.

At a more pragmatic level, New York received the kind of constitution it did because of the relative political weakness of those favoring a less generous allotment of religious liberty. Among patriot Protestants in the Middle Colonies, Presbyterians were probably the most avid supporters of religious restrictions on officeholding. They pushed for such restrictions less because they feared Catholics (as Jay did) and more because they believed that Protestants would make the best magistrates in a new republic.[59] Not surprisingly, then, Presbyterians were the ones largely responsible for getting this principle incorporated into the state constitutions of New Jersey and Pennsylvania. In the former state, Presbyterian ministers Jacob Green and John Witherspoon were prominent members of the provincial congress that framed a constitution in 1776 that included the stipulation that "no *Protestant* inhabitant of this Colony shall be denied the enjoyment of any civil right, merely on account of his religious principles" (italics mine). In Pennsylvania, Presbyterians Francis Alison and Judge George Bryan were active behind the scenes in producing a constitution that made state legislators profess faith in God and acknowledge the divine inspiration of the Old and New Testaments. While this article was less than some Presbyterians wanted, it was still a step in the right direction as far as they were concerned.

Within New York's convention, Presbyterians exerted far less control over the outcome. For one thing, the one Presbyterian minister in this body, Abraham Keteltas, attended only a few sessions. For another, Presbyterian proposals from outside the convention fell on deaf ears. John Mason, Scottish Presbyterian (Associate Reformed) minister in New York City, got nowhere in trying to convince convention-member George Clinton that the constitution should avow Christianity as the true religion and the surest base for civil government. Likewise, the recommendations of the convention chaplain, John Rodgers, that ministers be exempt from taxation and that all religious bodies receive state financial aid, garnered little support. Resistance to suggestions like these stemmed from the reluctance of the framers as a whole to consider anything that smacked of religious establishment or preferential treatment. In their minds, given New York's history and the prevailing sentiments of the dissenter majority, their most important task regarding church-state relations was eliminating all vestiges of the Anglican establishment and preventing any new establishment. Presbyterian members of the drafting committee very likely shared this conviction and were therefore less concerned than their colleagues in adjoining states (who had no establishment to overturn) with imposing religious tests on magistrates. Preoccupation with disestablishment and limited Presbyterian agitation for religious qualifications, then, also played roles in producing a constitution that extended religious liberty to all.

Beyond that, it could be argued that New York opted for a more liberal religious settlement than other states because most provincials were relatively unconcerned about the religious issue beyond wishing to ensure liberty of conscience and full civil rights for themselves. Since the only way to guarantee that they would enjoy such rights was to grant them to everyone, they willingly agreed to complete religious liberty.

While this perspective was surely the view of some New Yorkers, it was alien to those colonists who were concerned about the plight of "true religion" in their communities. For them, acceptance of a religious order that opened the door wide to persons of all religious beliefs (or none) may have come instead as a result of new notions about the nature of truth. Rooted in the Enlightenment's faith in human reason, and more specifically in the writings of John Locke on religious toleration, there was a growing belief in the late eighteenth-century Anglo-American world that "truth" would not suffer where all opinions had equal access to the public ear. Instead, in a free marketplace of ideas, "truth" would always win out because reasonable men through reasonable dialogue would naturally recognize it. In the religious or theological realm, this proposition meant that Christianity (and more specifically, Protestantism) would not be endangered by placing it on a plane with other religions. Rather, its innate truthfulness and superiority would always be evident to reasonable men (who were in the majority at most times), and they would see to it that Protestant values and ideals remained dominant in society.

Among those giving clear expression to these views in the Revolutionary era were English Dissenter Richard Price and Connecticut Congregationalist Ezra Stiles. Price was convinced that truth, including that of Christianity, would always triumph from a free exchange of ideas, for nothing reasonable could suffer from discussion or examination. The government's role in religion was to preserve an equal freedom for all sects to participate in an open forum for discussion.[60] Similarly, Stiles believed that if Christianity was "allowed to make its way through free inquiry, people would embrace it because of its self-evident excellence and superiority."[61]

How far this point of view had penetrated the minds of New Yorkers in the late 1770s and early 1780s is impossible to say. But there are certainly some grounds for suggesting that a portion of these provincials had embraced it. For one thing, many colonists were conversant with the writings of Locke, as well as with contemporaries like Stiles and Price who advocated this perspective. More significantly, Gordon Wood has persuasively demonstrated that this same understanding of the relationship between truth and the free circulation of ideas came to dominate American intellectual and political life shortly thereafter in the first years of the new republic. In fact, he says, many defended their confidence that truth would rise to the surface in the political realm by appealing to the successful example of religious pluralism.[62]

However many New Yorkers adopted this viewpoint, there is no doubt that it provided them with a convenient conceptual framework from which to accept wholeheartedly the state's new religious order. Among Protestant colonists, complete religious liberty (and therefore religious pluralism) could be enthusiastically endorsed when one was confident that it would help rather than hinder the public to recognize the truth of Christianity. To the extent that some colonists thought in these terms it is plausible to argue that eighteenth-century American Christians were trying to figure out the implications of genuine religious pluralism.

For New York's small body of non-Protestants, of course, complete religious liberty and the plural religion it assured could be welcomed for a variety of reasons, but none more salient than simple self-interest. The new constitution meant not only that Jews would be able to continue worshiping as they pleased but also that they would be free from church taxes and eligible for public office. The same benefits would accrue to those freethinking individuals who found little worth in organized religion of any sort. Meanwhile, the state's almost invisible Catholic minority could suddenly look forward to openly practicing their faith for the first time in almost a century.[63] With these bright prospects, it is clear that all non-Protestants had ample grounds for embracing the restructuring of church and state in New York.

Deciding to end any kind of religious establishment prompted provincials during the war and after to question how their new republican government should relate to religion. In the minds of most colonists, this disestablishment in no way implied a divorce of religion from public life. Very few supported the idea of a complete removal of religion from any relationship with civil authority. On the contrary, as John Pratt has pointed out, the citizens were convinced that "the state could promote religion by affording the congenial environment within which all sects might develop their full potential for good in the community, short of interfering directly in the affairs of any of them."[64]

But how, specifically, were the churches and government to support each other? During the constitutional debates in 1777, John H. Livingston, the Dutch Reformed pastor, wrote three times to committee member Robert R. Livingston, a relative, concerning the articles dealing with religion. Pastor Livingston applauded the articles for granting total liberty of conscience but criticized their reticence on how religion was to be encouraged. "The State has a right to interfere in the religion of the Subjects only in these two respects," he wrote, "first to promote religion in general and secondly defend it from all persecution." In promoting it, he continued, "the magistrate has no right to judge which is the true and which the false," or to "give exclusive civil privileges to any particular worship. . . ." It simply "judges the fear of God and his service to be of great importance to Society and therefore determines to encourage & help the Subjects in this affair. . . ." It may not properly grant "any tythes in the appropriation of a part of the public revenues" but only put all sects "upon an equal and proper footing for obtaining & holding Estates sufficient for their maintaining their public worship."[65] To accomplish the latter aim, he wanted the constitution to give all churches the right to incorporate. Committee member Livingston replied by questioning whether the easy mode of incorporation his relative suggested would not injure religion by dividing congregations into too many little sects. The pastor responded that he saw neither religious freedom nor a multitude of sects to be detrimental to Christianity:

> in a free country there name has always been Legion and where hearing is promoted & a spirit of enquiry prevails I am not apprehensive that the Christian religion can receive any essential injury from the greatest scope that can be given to religious freedom. . . . The Idea of forcing mankind into a union of sentiment by any machine of State is altogether preposterous & has done more harm to the cause of the gospel than the sword of persecution has ever effected.[66]

Provincials had read some of these same opinions in a political pamphlet printed and sold in New York during the previous year. In *Observations on the Reconciliation of Great-Britain and the Colonies,* New Jersey Presbyterian Jacob Green had argued that the government should not only protect freedom of thought but should foster it: "'Tis not enough to say every religious sect should be tolerated," he wrote; rather, "no one should be established; and religion in general should be encouraged, and everyman not only have right, but be encouraged to think and judge for himself."[67]

As mentioned earlier, Wall Street Presbyterian Church minister John Rodgers went one step further. He thought the state should assist religion financially. To that end, he endorsed the recommendation of fellow Presbyterian William Smith, Jr., that all denominations receive a common provision from the government for the general support of Christianity and the ministry. After the state constitution passed with no stipulation of this kind, Rodgers privately criticized Anglicans John Jay, James Duane, and Gouverneur Morris, "who under the Disguize of Liberty of Sentiment have made Beggars of all the Clergy. . . ."[68]

But Jay and company were not the only ones opposed to Rodgers's views. Among New York's patriots in general, and even among Presbyterians, there appears to have been little support for any direct state financing of religion. By the time of the Revolution, the earlier dissenter support for a system of multiple establishments had largely evaporated. Most groups had simply grown accustomed to maintaining themselves and valued the freedom from state interference that came with voluntarism.[69] Meanwhile, among Anglicans there was a growing sense that their church's establishment had "cost them more in public esteem and acceptance than it had earned them in financial aid."[70] Overall, the perspective of William Tennent, a Presbyterian pastor, seems much closer to expressing the will of New York's patriot majority. Calling the proposal that all denominations receive state funds proportionate to their size "absurd and impractical," Tennent insisted that voluntary lay support was the only plan compatible with religious equality. He nevertheless agreed that the state could promote religion in other ways, "by defending and protecting all denominations of Christians, who are inoffensive and useful," and by "good laws for the punishment of vice, and the encouragement of virtue." What the state had no right to do, according to Tennent, was declare which system of religious opinions was true and which false, nor impose hardships on the professors of any faith.[71]

One of the first denominational expressions on this subject appeared in 1780 when the Dutch Reformed General Body sent a letter to Governor George Clinton and the State Legislature. It argued that the government's efforts to suppress the "spirit of licentiousness" had proved ineffective for vice and immorality abounded "to the perversion of the good order of society and the discouragement and depression of holy religion." The letter urged Clinton and the legislators to take seriously their responsibility to

promote virtue and recommended that they "use their authority to investi-
gate and . . . determine the causes of the prevailing deficiency" and remove
it "either by framing such salutory laws as shall be judged necessary . . . or
putting those already in being into execution."[72] These Calvinists, like
colonial evangelicals elsewhere, believed that the government should pass
laws that would protect and nurture Christian ideals and values for the sake
of the whole society.[73]

Hence, though New Yorkers voiced differing views on how the state
might support religion, they were united in the conviction that the government, while remaining separate from all churches, should promote religion
in some way. That demonstrates that most did not want disestablishment to
eliminate religion from public life. The alliance between church and state
had always been considered by its opponents as detrimental to both. The
steps taken to secure religious liberty and disestablishment, therefore, were
prompted not only by political motives but also by a concern for the well-
being of religious communities. Given an opportunity for change, a new
system based on religious equality could be developed because they believed it would ensure a prosperous future for both church and state in
New York.

While the Revolution afforded the chance to restructure the state's religious order, it also forced New Yorkers to face the daily consequences of
war: physical destruction, economic deprivation, emotional depression,
and spiritual disillusionment. In the words of political and religious radical
Thomas Paine, these were "times that try men's souls." As the social institutions principally charged with soothing the tried souls of provincials, the
colony's religious bodies faced a formidable challenge of providing spiritual
nourishment and moral encouragement amid the pain and upheaval
caused by the revolutionary crisis.

In assessing the churches' performance over the course of the war, most
students of the Revolution have concluded, or at least assumed, that
churches and religion in general fared very poorly. Among the war's most
obvious effects were the destruction or damaging of church buildings and
the scattering of congregations. Equally devastating, however, was the
manner in which the conflict took ministerial and lay attention away from
spiritual affairs and focused it almost exclusively on more worldly concerns.
That, in turn, contributed to a "general moral laxity marked by corruption,
extravagance, acquisitiveness, and debauchery."[74]

While recent studies of the war years in New York have mostly ignored
religion, older works by Alexander Flick, W.C. Abbot, Oscar Barck, and
Thomas Wertenbaker shared the pessimistic assessment of Revolutionary

church life.[75] Collectively, they seemed to think that John Wesley was correct in saying that whenever war breaks out "God is forgotten, if He be not set at open defiance."[76] Interestingly, however, Wesley's American protégé, Francis Asbury, seems to have disagreed. Writing from the Middle Colonies in 1783, Asbury told his English superior that he feared "the prospects of peace and prosperity unnerve our zeal for God," and might retard the spiritual progress of previous years.[77] Does Asbury's letter suggest that historians have overlooked more positive signs of religious activity during the Revolution? We can find out by looking closely at the institutional and spiritual history of congregations and denominations in the province during the war.

To begin, it is impossible to deny that the armed conflict brought great destruction of life and property to the state's churches. In New York City alone, Anglican, Dutch Reformed, Presbyterian, French Protestant, Lutheran, Baptist, Quaker, and Moravian buildings were either destroyed or converted by the British troops into barracks, prisons, hospitals, or stables.[78] Because of their patriotic reputation, Presbyterian churches were special targets of violence. British soldiers wrecked the Huntington, Long Island, church and used its timber to construct barracks and blockhouses in the cemetery. Numerous other Presbyterian structures in the Hudson Valley were burned.[79] The Dutch Reformed hardly fared any better. Their General Body informed the Classis of Amsterdam in 1778 that support for the American side was made "easier" by the "unrighteous acts and unheard of cruelties committed by the English army everywhere," particularly their "malicious and God-provoking destruction of our churches."[80] Even loyalist congregations were not immune from the unruliness of the king's troops. SPG missionary John Sayre reported in 1782 on the treatment accorded Moravian missionaries, who were "a simple, inoffensive People, firmly attached to His Majesty's Government"; they had been cruelly attacked "by a number of Savages . . . commanded by British officers."[81] Likewise, Leonard Cutting, Anglican rector at Hempstead, Long Island, complained bitterly about the "various Acts of Violence and Oppression" committed by the British army in his town and equated its presence with tyrannous rule.[82]

The British side had no monopoly on violence, however. American rebels seemed to take particular delight in harassing the loyalist Anglican clergy. In a letter to the SPG secretary dated October 31, 1776, Charles Inglis described in vivid but probably exaggerated detail the sufferings of Anglican pastors and missionaries at the hands of New York's patriots: "Some have been carried prisoners by armed mobs into distant provinces. . . . Some have been flung into jails . . . for frivolous suspicions of plots. . . . Some have been pulled out of the reading desk because they prayed for the King, and that before independency was declared."[83] Rebels in Samuel Seabury's Westchester parish constantly threatened his life and eventually destroyed his farm and church.[84] Other Anglican missionaries, including James Sayre (Fredericksburgh Precinct), Epenetus Townsend (Cortland Manor), and John Beardsley (Poughkeepsie), lost their estates when they were exiled for failing to take the oath of allegiance to the American cause.[85] Among the non-Anglicans treated harshly were Quaker and Shaker pacifists. Their refusal to fight or even to comply with military requisitions occasionally brought them imprisonment or other forms of physical abuse.[86]

The war's toll in human lives varied from congregation to congregation. Few communities paid as high a price as the First Baptist Church of New York City, which by 1784 had suffered the deaths of at least thirty-four of its prewar members, about 20 percent of the membership it had in 1775.[87] The great cost of the Revolution for this congregation and others like it most likely came as a direct result of the large number of its men who served in the Continental Army.

While it is difficult to generalize, New York's religious congregations seem to have suffered most in areas where neither side was able to establish clear military control. Hardest hit, therefore, were those in Westchester and Orange Counties in the southern portion of the state and those north and west of Albany. In these regions, especially between 1776 and 1778, fighting was often intense but inconclusive; single towns found themselves more than once occupied by the troops first of one side, then of the other. That both colonial and British forces tried to administer loyalty oaths simply compounded the confusion. Under these conditions, religious bodies found it practically impossible to maintain any routine. In Rye, Westchester County, for example, hostilities were so severe that inhabitants scattered and congregations disbanded regardless of which army they supported.[88] In nearby Bedford, Presbyterian pastor Samuel Mills and part of his flock fled when British troops burned their church and parsonage, as well as much of the rest of the village, in July 1779. Two years passed before the church session was able to meet again.[89] Minister John Gros served the Dutch Reformed in Sand Hill and Canajoharie (Albany County) between 1779 and 1783, but he appears to have spent most of his time as a chaplain for the New York militia.[90] All four of the Anglican parishes in upper New York—Albany, Schenectady, Johnstown, and Fort Hunter—virtually disappeared, and their priests fled from the territory.[91] John Stuart, missionary at Fort Hunter in the Mohawk Valley, wrote just prior to leaving in 1778 that he had been deserted by almost all his congregation. "There remains only three families," he said, "the others having at different times, joined the King's forces. I have not preached within these last two years."[92]

The indecisiveness of the military conflict encouraged persons in other villages, however, to remain at home. As a result, some churches in the war zone tried to continue worshiping as united bodies despite the heterogeneous political views of their members. Such attempts generally proved futile. Divided into patriots, loyalists, and neutrals, the Anglican parish in Phillipsburgh found its worship and other activities severely disrupted during the war. The resulting disharmony among its members was one cause of its failure to obtain a minister between 1782 and 1789.[93] In June 1777, minister Ichabod Lewis asked the Dutchess Presbytery if he could be dismissed from his White Plains pastorate, pointing to the "melancholy and broken state" to which the war had brought the congregation. The Presbytery granted his request, "taking into Consideration the very unhappy & Ruined State of that Congregation and that that part of the Country is so Desolated that humanly speaking there is no prospect of the great Ends of the Gospel Ministry being answered."[94]

The war's devastating impact in these areas did not abate quickly. As late as 1783, the Dutchess Presbytery had to assign three ministers to visit periodically the lower parts of Westchester County because that region still lacked a "preached gospel."[95] With closed church doors came a rise in what contemporaries called infidelity and moral laxity. Persons in war-torn towns were repeatedly accused of pursuing with gusto both new and old forms of immorality. And the troops on the front lines were thought to be among the worst offenders.[96]

For the most part, religious conditions were not as bleak elsewhere in the state. Long Island, New York City, and the central Hudson River Valley were more consistently under the dominance of either the British army or the American patriots. Because of this control, they enjoyed a greater degree of social and political order and churches were able to carry on their work more normally. In addition, shared allegiances to either independence or the mother country in these areas bound colonists of various denominations together.

Initially, the British occupation of lower New York greatly disturbed religious life. As mentioned earlier, the invasion forced hundreds of colonists to evacuate and halted the activities of some congregations for the duration of the Revolution. In addition, many church buildings were either destroyed or badly damaged. At the height of the takeover in 1776, Moravian pastor Oswald Shewkirk attested that on Sunday, September 15, he conducted the only worship service in the entire city.[97] Yet within several months, the British consolidated their military hold and began a seven-year rule under which relative calm prevailed.[98] As conditions stabilized, congregations resumed their previous routines, but now with members whose outward political sentiments were far more homogeneous. This consensus freed each congregation from much of its internal haggling, and the knowledge that their loyalties were similar facilitated cooperation among different groups. The vestry of Trinity Parish allowed Gerrit Lydekker and his Dutch Reformed people to worship in St. George's Chapel for several months in 1779 and 1780, when their building was being used as a hospital for British troops.[99] While in England, Thomas Chandler oversaw the collection of a relief fund for the American Anglican clergy; when he distributed the money, he sent fifty pounds to Lutheran minister Bernard Houseal.[100] Loyalist Presbyterians in Hempstead, Long Island, flocked to the Anglican services conducted by Leonard Cutting because they had no minister of their own.[101] New York City's Methodists paid their war-time minister, Samuel Spraggs, a much higher salary than previous pastors had received; the larger offerings stemmed partly from the contributions of two groups of new hearers: persons whose own churches were closed, and British soldiers.[102] In all these instances, the area's religious diversity served more as a vehicle than a barrier to spiritual activity. At the same time, the Revolution helped obscure that diversity by providing a political goal around which all loyalists could rally regardless of past religious differences.[103]

Congregations in the central and upper Hudson River Valley, controlled by the patriots, likewise continued to function. Many directly benefited from the patriot evacuation of lower New York. Among the pastors who migrated north, several served as chaplains for the American forces, including Presbyterians John Rodgers, Joseph Treat, John Mason, and Nathan Kerr (Warwick, Orange County) and Baptist John Gano.[104] Others chose to settle in towns and pastored local congregations. Dutch Reformed minister Solomon Froeligh left Queens County and became the "stated supply" in Fishkill and Poughkeepsie from 1776 to 1780. John Gebhard, once minister to the German Reformed congregation in New York City, assumed the pastorate at the Claverack Dutch Reformed Church, where he remained until 1826. All four pastors from the Dutch Collegiate Church moved to different religious communities in the Hudson Valley, John Ritzema to Kinderhook, Archibald Laidlie to Red Hook, Lambertus De Ronde to Saugerties, and John Livingston to Kingston (1776), Albany (1776–79), Livingston Manor (1779–81), Poughkeepsie and Red Hook (1781–83).[105]

The success of these clergymen and others in keeping the churches of the Hudson Valley alive is revealed by the baptismal, marriage, and membership records of these years. Among thirteen Dutch Reformed and seven Lutheran congregations in the region from New Paltz to Albany and west to Schoharie, almost all maintained levels of activity equal to or greater than prewar efforts.[106] In only two cases is there evidence of a marked decline. At the Lutheran church in Red Hook, baptisms fell from 105 in 1775 to 43 in 1780, and at the Reformed church in Schoharie, from 65 in 1776 to 30 in 1782. But the number of baptisms rose significantly between 1775 and 1780 in the Reformed congregations of Hillsdale (from 9 to 28), Gallatin (from 23 to 44), Claverack (from 10 to 57), and Livingston (from 19 to 90) and at St. Paul's Lutheran Church (from 2 to 18) in West Camp. In addition, the average number of marriages at the Claverack fellowship increased from about 5 per year in the decade prior to the Revolution to 20 per year between 1778 and 1783. Perhaps even more telling is the fact that minister George Doll and the Reformed people in Kingston kept their congregation's activity at its prewar level despite the burning of their building by the British.

Among other communions the same story prevails. While Presbyterians in lower New York suffered greatly, those in such communities as Philip's Patent, Newburgh, and New Windsor managed to worship often and to retain the services of a minister.[107] Also, the Dutchess Presbytery, unlike others, maintained a fairly regular pattern of meetings during the war and carried out its basic duties.[108] Similarly, the Dutch Reformed Particular Assembly in Kingston met regularly between 1775 and 1778. It sent delegates to the first "war" meeting of the General Body in 1778, something the Albany and New York assemblies were not able to do, having not met since 1775.[109] The years from 1776 to 1783 witnessed the organization or reconstitution of seven Baptist congregations in Dutchess and Albany Counties, located at Fishkill, New Canaan, Great Nine Partners, Cambridge, New Britain, Bottskill, Granville, and Hartford.[110] The Quaker meetings in Oblong and Nine Partners gathered monthly throughout the Revolution, and the latter body experienced remarkable growth between 1775 and 1779 due to the large-scale westward migration of New England Friends.[111]

From this evidence it is fair to conclude that against heavy odds the churches in a wide portion of New York managed to withstand the pressures of war and to maintain some degree of corporate life. That was no small accomplishment in light of the time, money, and energy required to keep a congregation functioning. Few if any of these religious institutions would have survived save for the sacrificial giving of laypersons and the devoted service of ministers.

To illustrate this point further, it is worth examining in greater detail the experiences of two congregations in the Dutchess County community of Poughkeepsie. By the advent of the Revolution, the Reformed Church of Poughkeepsie had grown accustomed to trying times during its sixty-year history.[112] It had had to endure the dissolution of a long-standing union with its sister congregation in Fishkill and a decade-long split among its members over denominational policies. Now, just as hostilities with the British were commencing, minister Stephen Van Voorhees left the church for a similar post in Rhinebeck Flats. With no pastor, a reduced membership, and numerous political distractions, it would not have been surprising if Poughkeepsie's Dutch Reformed congregation had simply stopped operating or disbanded. Yet, through a resilient laity and what it considered to be the providence of God, the church survived both the immediate and long-term crises created in large part by the war.

Shortly after Van Voorhees departed, the congregation enlisted the ministerial services of Solomon Froeligh. An outspoken patriot, Froeligh had hastily fled his Queens County home and parish during the British takeover and arrived in the Poughkeepsie area with little more than the shirt on his back. Church members eagerly welcomed him nevertheless and were happy to supply his physical needs in return for a preached gospel and the administration of the sacraments. While foregoing official installation as pastor, Froeligh performed all normal ministerial duties for the Poughkeepsie church until late 1780.

His successor was John Livingston, another Dutch Reformed clergyman who had evacuated lower New York in 1776. Livingston was a familiar figure among Poughkeepsie's Dutch Reformed, for he had grown up in this very congregation before heading off to Yale College and the University of Utrecht. Lay enthusiasm for calling him was apparently great; it took less than a month in the summer of 1781 to gather financial pledges for his salary totaling fifty pounds and 350 bushels of wheat, a handsome annual compensation by wartime standards. Livingston immediately accepted the church's invitation and served until December 1783. He provided his flock with a steady stream of evangelical sermons and with administrative oversight that helped it avoid serious financial difficulties by the war's end.

Poughkeepsie's Anglican congregation was not so fortunate.[113] The parishioners of Christ Church not only suffered the arrest and exile of their minister, John Beardsley; they also lost three hundred pounds during the course of the war, leaving them unable for many years to repay a prewar debt. In addition, their church doors were closed throughout the war after the vestry suspended all services in July 1776 rather than compromising the liturgy by omitting prayers for the king. Revolutionary conditions also prompted some members, including prominent lawyer Bartholomew

Crannell, to leave Poughkeepsie on account of their loyalist sympathies, while those who remained often endured the suspicions and ridicule of the patriot majority because of the close identification of their denomination with the mother country. As if that was not enough, the congregation also had to fight a prolonged legal battle during the war to retain possession of its glebe.

Despite these dire circumstances, however, there are still signs of parish activity which suggest that even here religious apathy was not pervasive. For one thing, the congregation continued to elect its vestry annually, and between 1776 and 1783 twenty-one men served. Three served continuously: Richard Davis, William Emott, and Dr. Richard Noxon. Their commitment to the interests of the church was undoubtedly a key factor in helping it avert total disintegration. Likewise helpful were several visits to Poughkeepsie by other Church of England clergy. At least three times during the war years an Anglican priest came and performed baptisms, a sacrament rich with the promise of new life. It is not surprising, then, that when peace finally arrived, Poughkeepsie's Anglicans wasted little time in reopening the doors of Christ Church and calling a new rector.

While the experiences of these Dutchess County congregations point in another direction, existing scholarship forces us to ask whether this institutional perseverance in reality masked a deepening spiritual and moral depression in the colony. Were not clergymen and laypersons alike naturally distracted from religious matters by the more pressing political and military concerns of the day? And didn't this spiritual neglect contribute toward a loss of public and private virtue?

At first glance, the minutes of various denominational bodies definitely give that impression.[114] The Philadelphia Baptist Association renewed its call for fast days every year, both warning of spiritual decline and entreating religious revival. In 1780 alone, the association received letters from twenty-one churches complaining of a great declension in vital piety.[115] At repeated meetings between 1777 and 1780, the Presbyterian Synod of New York and Philadelphia passed resolutions lamenting the low state of religion, the prevalence of immorality, the degeneracy of manners, the want of public spirit, and the decay of pious living.[116] In 1779, John Rodgers published a sermon supporting his denomination's call for a renewal of practical holiness "in this day of degeneracy."[117] The Dutch Reformed General Body followed suit in 1778; it appointed a day for special prayer, prompted by the growing immorality of young people and the loss of religious zeal in ministers and members alike. Three years later, "seriously considering and taking to heart the profound declension of the church," the body recommended that each of the particular assemblies begin visitation programs to vacant congregations.[118] The New York Yearly Meeting of Friends, while less pessimistic, expressed numerous times its concern that the war was forcing some Quakers to compromise their religious principles.[119]

In light of such widespread evidence, it would be easy to accept as accurate a gloomy portrait of the spiritual condition of New York during the Revolution. Closer examination of the evidence paints a different picture, however. For one thing, the judgments of all these ecclesiastical bodies except the Quaker Yearly Meeting were based primarily on information received from congregations in New Jersey and Pennsylvania. Throughout the war years, the dangers associated with traveling through battle zones or crossing enemy lines often made it impossible for New Yorkers to attend the yearly meetings of their synod or association. Sometimes no representatives came from the state, as in 1779 when the Dutch Reformed General Body met at Pompton, New Jersey, and in 1780 when the Presbyterians met at Philadelphia.[120] War conditions also made it difficult to maintain even infrequent correspondence. In 1781, for example, the Baptist Association received a letter from only one New York congregation (Amenia Precinct).[121] The paucity of direct reports from ministers or laypersons in the state forced these assemblies to rely heavily on information drawn from military or printed sources, both of which were preoccupied with conditions in combat areas. Another factor that may have skewed their vision was the British takeover of lower New York. They perceived it as a religious disaster that had forced many of their congregations to disband, totally overlooking its impact on the churches that continued to worship there. Finally, as long as these bodies understood the war as God's judgment upon American sins, they were obligated to make calls for repentance and revival, and they were in no position to speak optimistically about spiritual conditions. Indeed, when awakenings had occurred in previous decades, the minutes of many ecclesiastical bodies made no mention of them.[122]

If the dreary outlook pervading the reports of denominational assemblies is suspect, the evidence of religious activism among many individual congregations further undermines it. Beyond the examples of institutional survival mentioned earlier, a number of remarkable accounts testify to the spiritual commitment of many New Yorkers during the war. Few were more resourceful than the Friends in Mamaroneck and Shopaqua (lower Westchester County) who, despite living in a military no-man's land, worshiped actively. As one Quaker explained

Their zeal and Diligence herein increased with their Sufferings, and as no other Societies kept up their Meetings in this rebellious place, many of other denominations who before knew but little of Friends, on observing their Stedfastness were led into an enquiry of our principles, and to attend our Meetings, and divers were added to each of these Meetings by Convincement during the War.[123]

Several hundred miles north, a new sect, known initially as the Shaking Quakers, suddenly emerged in the small village of New Lebanon in 1779 and 1780. Through the preaching of their founder, Mother Ann Lee, many were converted to the doctrines of the Shakers, including the local Baptist and Congregational ministers, Joseph Meacham and Samuel Johnson.[124] A more modest but no less dramatic effort to enhance religious faith took place in 1779 in New York City when six Scottish Presbyterian patriots formed a secret praying society. With their former congregation scattered, these laymen determined to defy strict British regulations against unlicensed religious meetings so as to "bring glory to God" and reap the benefits of spiritual fellowship.[125]

Other less extraordinary examples testifying to the spiritual commitment of many New Yorkers can also be cited. The Linlithgo Reformed congregation in Livingston suffered difficult years in 1776 and 1777, when only two members were added. Over the next five war years, however, it admitted seventy-six new members, most upon confession of faith.[126] The Methodist church in New York City not only boasted an enlarged attendance at worship on Sunday morning but also saw many of the newcomers involved in a Methodist class. Small groups of closely disciplined believers met regularly for times of personal confession, Bible study, and prayer; a layperson's participation usually indicated a strong interest in spiritual growth.[127] When Ann Moore visited Quaker meetings in the city and on Long Island in 1778 she found large and active groups everywhere. By 1782 New York Friends informed the Philadelphia meetings that despite the war, God had preserved a considerable number of their society in love and unity.[128] Although the state's Quaker leadership was not known for evangelistic efforts, the approach of peace prompted it to recommend the purchase and distribution of Dutch copies of Quaker doctrinal works and to proclaim its desire for the "prosperity of Zion [America], that she may become the beauty of Nations to the praise and exaltation . . . of our God."[129] The small Baptist congregations in both Amenia and Paulings Precincts found survival difficult during the war, but by 1782 signs of spiritual optimism appeared in their letters to the Philadelphia Association. Minister Samuel Waldo acknowledged that although the war had caused a "Shocken time" in his town, God had now "come in to his Garden and hath fed among the Lillies till the Day begins to break & the shadows begin to flee away & God has Blest us with some of the Divine Breathings of the

spirit of love and union. . . ."[130] Even more encouraging developments
appeared among Baptists farther north. In Stillwater, forty-one members
were added between June 1781 and September 1782, and the Bottskill
church grew from a handful to a hundred adherents during the same
period.[131]

In summary, though none of the individual examples recounted here
proves a similar growth in religious vitality in the state as a whole, what may
be inferred is that religious life in New York during the war was far less
consistently depressed than either the denominational assemblies implied
or modern historians have suggested. There were congregations, certainly,
and even whole communities that drifted far from their religious faith.
Many pastors could have repeated James Benedict's woeful complaint that
his Baptist flock in Warwick, Orange County, experienced little religious
growth and had a declining membership.[132] For such pastors, Wesley's
prophecy was fulfilled. But others would have agreed with Asbury's discovery that war sometimes quickened religious sensibilities, and that where a
congregation's institutional life was reasonably maintained, spiritual progress was as much a possibility as its opposite. The story of popular religion
in New York during the Revolutionary War, then, was hardly a uniform
one; it contained contrasting elements of tragedy and triumph, chaos and
order, infidelity and commitment. Any future assessment of America's
religious condition in these years will have to take this diversity into account.

With the war's conclusion and the signing of the Treaty of Paris in late
1783, a new era began in the religious history of New York. The previous
eight years had witnessed several key developments in which the colony's
religious pluralism once again had an important shaping influence. As the
imperial crisis mounted in the early 1770s, diversity had been one factor
encouraging religious bodies to remain apolitical institutions. But as the
conflict intensified, New York's pluralistic milieu put increasing pressure on
minority groups like the Quakers to conform to the model of their politically active neighbors. Then, once the Revolution began in earnest and
provincials were forced to choose sides, a person's assessment of pluralism
itself was apparently one of the factors molding individual decisions. At
least that is what is suggested by the close correlation between Revolutionary behavior and earlier attitudes toward diversity. In the framing of a new
republican government during the first part of the war, the colony's long
heritage of plural religion, as well as the heterogeneous makeup of the
constitutional convention, pushed lawmakers toward a new religious order
based on equality and liberty for all groups. Finally, as the war dragged on,

its ravages were ameliorated somewhat by the presence of diverse brethren willing to offer a helping hand to keep other churches active and religious faith alive.

As for the future, the Revolution left a legacy of both religious division and religious union. On the one hand, it split families, congregations, and denominations over political matters and thereby added to the host of more specifically religious issues that had long kept Protestant New Yorkers apart. On the other hand, the fight for or against independence provided political purposes around which members of many communions could close ranks and unite with like-minded religionists from other groups. In these ways, the Revolution served both to accent and blur New York's religious diversity.

Patriot military and political success meanwhile assured major changes in the state's postwar church life. A significant proportion of those who had chosen to remain loyal to Britain would leave America permanently. In his farewell sermon in 1783, Charles Inglis defended the loyalist position one last time, insisting that his removal was not willful but rather the result of necessity.[133] As he and other ministers departed, along with scores of laypersons, they left many congregations with no pastor and a vastly reduced membership. Both the Methodist and Moravian membership in New York City shrank from two hundred persons to about sixty by December 1783.[134] More important, the Tory exodus meant that much of the prewar opposition to ecclesiastical self-sufficiency, evangelical theology, and religious equality was removed, leaving advocates of these ideas with greater freedom to pursue their goals. And, as will be seen in the next chapter, their control over the state's church life in the years that followed relegated those conservatives who remained in America to a position of relative unimportance.

The corollary to all of that was the restructuring of the state's religious order. By the war's end, all churches knew their freedoms would be protected and their environment permanently pluralistic. They also knew they must be self-supporting, even though they believed the state would promote the cause of religion in general. The government had already shown its willingness to do that when in 1781 the legislature adopted a policy of reserving land in the state tracts then being opened for settlement for the support of the gospel and public schools.[135]

With these ideas in the back of their minds, then, and the opportunities of a new start before them, New York's Protestants approached the postwar period with a guarded but nevertheless real optimism. Not just for congregations that had been devastated during the war but also for those that had managed to maintain their institutional life and spiritual interest, an immense task of gathering and building lay ahead. Of the many pieces of advice they received, perhaps none reflected more wisdom than minister Azel Roe's suggestion that believers needed a "double Portion" of the spirit of Christian brotherhood; for only through union and harmony, he said, could they hope to meet the trials of the present and the challenges of the future.[136]

V

"AN UNCOMMON TRAIN OF PROVIDENCES"
RELIGIOUS RECOVERY IN THE 1780S

Shortly after Sir Guy Carleton, the British commander in chief, oversaw the evacuation of New York City by his own troops and departing loyalists in November 1783, George Washington entered the city with his army and the victory celebration began. Washington remained for only nine days, but his soldiers gathered at St. George's Chapel on December 11, the day the Continental Congress set aside for public thanksgiving for America's blessings. Their chaplain, Israel Evans, described the new nation as a retreat for the oppressed, the resting place of liberty, and the rising empire of the Western world. He predicted religion, learning, and commerce would recover and flourish in the next few years because God had given Americans "liberty, that charter of all the blessings of life."[1]

Numerous other observers proclaimed similar messages that day and in the months that followed. John Rodgers preached on Psalm 126:3, "The Lord hath done great things for us, whereof we are glad." He stressed among their blessings the state constitution that secured liberty of conscience and guaranteed that "no one denomination in the State, or in any of the States, have it in their power to oppress another." He also rejoiced that "The Jews also . . . have the liberty of worshipping God in that way they think most acceptable to him. No man is excluded from the rights of citizenship on account of his religious profession. Nor ought he to be."[2] New York City's Jewish patriots expressed their thankfulness for recent events and optimism about the future in a letter sent to Governor Clinton shortly after they returned to the city in January 1784:

> Though the society we belong to is but small . . . yet we flatter ourselves that none has manifested a more zealous attachment to the sacred cause of America in the late war with Great Britain . . . we now look forward with

pleasure to the happy days we expect to enjoy under a constitution wisely
framed to preserve the inestimable blessings of civil and religious liberty.3

That same month, Abraham Beach gave a thanksgiving discourse in Trinity
Church that offered the new nation a prescription for success: "Let us build
our hopes of future prosperity on the firm basis of Religion and Virtue—
against a Superstructure raised on this Foundation, the Storms of Adversity
may beat in Vain. . . ."4

These brief glimpses of the mood of New Yorkers immediately following
the Revolution convey both their sense of relief that independence had
been secured and their anticipation of what lay ahead. On the whole,
religious leaders seemed eager to undertake the tasks of reconstruction.
Such eagerness seems nothing short of remarkable in retrospect, given the
prodigious obstacles they faced. Some of their enthusiasm undoubtedly
wore off as the months passed and the thrill of victory gave way to the
agony of rebuilding. Nevertheless, New York's churchmen had at least one
cause for encouragement during the first peacetime year: the state legislature's decisive action to eliminate all vestiges of religious establishment in
the state.

To make certain all groups had equal opportunity to exercise the freedoms guaranteed by the 1777 constitution, the legislature passed a series of
laws in 1784. The first act, approved on April 6, enabled congregations of
all denominations to be incorporated. They were to elect trustees demo-
cratically to oversee their property and transact related business.5 By allowing congregations an annual income from rentals of up to twelve hundred
pounds, the government expressed its willingness to encourage religion.6
Eleven days later, the legislators passed a second bill that altered the charter
of Trinity Church in New York City. The act declared this charter as well as
the Ministry Act of 1693 "contradictory to that equality of religious rights
which is designed to be established by the constitution."7 Another act
repealed several colonial laws relating to the Anglican establishment, and a
fourth transferred control of King's College to a board of regents of the
newly created University of the State of New York. Board members were to
be drawn from all the major denominations and no religious restrictions
were to be placed on the faculty.8 Finally, the legislature repealed a 1700 bill
excluding Catholic priests and Jesuit missionaries from the province.9 New
York's lawmakers by these acts moved swiftly and virtually without debate
to ensure the basic principle of the state's new religious order—religious
equality.10 In the process, they once again demonstrated the great respect
New Yorkers had developed for their own religious diversity.

This legislation certainly helped quell any residual anxieties the state's various religious bodies may have had over their political or legal status in New York, for it settled many of the remaining political questions relating to New York's religious pluralism. As noted throughout this study, however, pluralism's importance for religion in New York always transcended the church-state issue, and that continued to be the case in the 1780s. Specifically, religious diversity made a difference in the nature of both the ecclesiastical problems faced and the responses made by the state's religious communions in the postwar period.

A place to worship was the most immediate requirement for those congregations whose buildings had either been destroyed or needed extensive repairs. Of the nineteen churches standing in New York City in 1776, for instance, only nine were fit for use when the British left.[11] Temporary solutions included meeting in private homes or sharing the facilities of other congregations. The long-term answer lay in the construction of new sanctuaries and the repair of existing ones, both of which were costly. Few congregations in the city (or state) were as fortunate as the Moravians, two of whose members died and left large legacies to the church.[12] Most had to rely instead on sacrificial offerings from their members over a span of several years.

That many of the state's congregations now had significantly fewer members made the financial burden even greater. The emigration of loyalists reduced the size of some and war-related deaths shrank others. In addition, many patriots who had fled their homes in 1776 did not return after 1783, deciding either to remain in their new localities or move to the western New York frontier. Just 45 of the 180 prewar members came back to John Gano's Baptist congregation, and only 10 returned to the Second Baptist Church in New York City.[13]

Furthermore, most groups considered their ministers' salaries a higher economic priority than the repair or construction of church buildings. The members of the John Street Methodist Church, reduced by the loyalist exodus, could afford to pay their new preacher, John Dickins, only ten pounds per quarter in 1784, as compared with the thirty-four pounds paid to Samuel Spraggs during the war.[14] Under even greater strain were the state's Anglican congregations, which could no longer rely on aid from church taxes or SPG funds to support their rectors. That presented little difficulty for wealthy Trinity Parish. But the parishioners of Christ Church in Poughkeepsie, trying to raise a subscription to call Henry Vandyck as their pastor in 1784, not only asked their sister congregation in Fishkill for help but also requested and received money from the local Presbyterian and Dutch Reformed congregations, who in fact were also without ministers.[15] Financial losses incurred during the Revolution decreased the ability of many congregations of the Dutchess Presbytery to retain pastors. Numerous ministers had to resign on account of inadequate salaries in the 1780s. The war had so impoverished their congregations, the Presbytery explained in 1791, that they had "Scarcely recovered to Such a State as to be able to support the preaching of the Gospel" and could only with some difficulty "raise Monies essential for their own Existence."[16]

Moreover, the ability to support a minister was no guarantee that a congregation would have one, for the demand steadily outran the number available. The Dutch Reformed General Body found in early 1784 that only fifteen of its ninety congregations in New York and New Jersey had their own ministers and that thirty-eight more shared their pastors with others. The situation was likely to get worse because several older clergymen were about to retire and the war had severely reduced the number of young men training for the ministry.[17] The scarcity of Presbyterian pastors prompted a motion at the May 1785 synod meeting to relax the requirement that those entering the ministry should be able to read Hebrew and Greek.[18] Though the resolution failed, the problem it sought to resolve was real. Many congregations in the New York, Dutchess, and Suffolk Presbyteries were without a preacher.[19] Loyalty to Britain and deaths had meanwhile reduced the sixteen Anglican clergymen in the colony in 1774 to six in 1785.[20] Following the war, the state's twenty Lutheran congregations had only seven ministers among them.[21]

Besides depriving believers of both preaching and the sacraments, some feared the shortage of ministers made parishioners more susceptible to unsound doctrines and moral laxity. Dutch Reformed clergy lamented that "suffering congregations daily find their danger and affliction increased," both from the lack of ministers and "the floods of error, infidelity, and all kinds of irreligion which are everywhere boasting upon our land."[22] The Presbyterian Synod declared that their pastorless fellowships were endangered by ordained and licensed ministers of "unsound principles" who came to the Middle Colonies to prey upon them.[23] New days of fasting and prayer were set aside, motivated not by war but by the scarcity of faithful shepherds able to exercise scriptural discipline and combat the numerous "horrible errors and corrupt forms of religion," including universalism and deism.[24]

To the tasks of financing building projects, paying ministers' salaries, finding adequate clergymen, and warding off false teachings was added the problem of molding unified congregations from members whose loyalties the war had divided. Within many churches, the patriot victors were not immediately ready to forgive their loyalist brothers; nor were former Tories eager to admit they had made a mistake. The Dutch Reformed

General Body in May 1784 deposed pastor Johannes Rubel for his misbehavior during the war, especially his publicly cursing ministers who opposed his Tory sentiments.[25] Rubel urged his congregation to disregard the decision on the grounds that it violated the Holland Church Order.[26] Reformed lay leaders in New York City and Brooklyn dismissed their former conservative ministers John Ritzema, Lambertus De Ronde, and Ulpianus Van Sinderen more subtly, guaranteeing them a lifetime income.[27] Among Anglicans, the selection of a new rector of Trinity Parish set off a power struggle between the Whig and Tory factions. The Whigs finally won out, electing former patriot Samuel Provoost.[28] The trustees' letter to him in January 1784 expressed bluntly the reason for his call: their "utmost Confidence" in his "political Principles" and their high estimate of his "learning, Virtue, and Piety."[29]

These problems were newer in degree than in kind for New York's churches. Never before had so many of the state's religious fellowships simultaneously faced such formidable barriers to fulfilling their missions. The already weakened New York congregations were now vulnerable to collapse because of the presence of other religious bodies anxious to absorb their members. Although few churches feasted on the adversity of others, there is little doubt that in hard times like these the competition for adherents became more intense. Thus, as it had done earlier in the century, pluralism magnified the difficulty for any one congregation to survive, let alone prosper.

Then, too, the churches' overall task was made tougher by the distractions of the postwar period. Popular attention naturally focused on political and constitutional developments, and the foremost concern of countless individuals was putting their own lives back together socially and economically. Not surprisingly, religious matters often took a backseat under these conditions.

These obstacles to postrevolutionary religious life in New York and elsewhere have led historians for more than a century, from Robert Baird to Sydney Ahlstrom, into believing that American society wallowed in a swamp of religious indifference and impoverishment in the postwar years.[30] Scholars have repeatedly described the epoch as one of "spiritual deadness." William Warren Sweet called it "the lowest ebb-tide of vitality in the history of American Christianity."[31] Citing church membership statistics and the testimony of later observers, especially Lyman Beecher, most students have argued that spiritual and moral recovery did not come until the beginnings of the Second Great Awakening in the late 1790s.[32]

As applied to New York, such an extreme characterization of religious life in this era does not square with how New York's religious communions stood up to their postwar circumstances. Close examination reveals that the ministerial and lay leaders of New York's seven principal Protestant denominations (Baptists, Dutch Reformed, Anglicans, Lutherans, Methodists, Presbyterians, and Quakers) responded energetically, rather than idly, to the religious problems of this decade. In fact, they reacted in remarkably parallel ways. They made no attempt to map out a comprehensive strategy; nor were they motivated by a belief that religious success could be manufactured. Yet each group of leaders, perceiving the extensive needs of their congregations, advocated and oversaw three policies aimed at recovery and advance: the reorganization of their own denominational structures, the establishment of schools and colleges and of home mission projects, and the cultivation of friendly and constructive relationships with other religious persuasions.

For Anglicans and Methodists, restructuring was mandated by the coming of independence. Continued subservience to the Church of England was obviously impractical. Both groups moved rapidly to gain ecclesiastical independence and to identify themselves with the new republic's political principles. The Anglicans established a representative national assembly, the General Convention of the Protestant Episcopal Church in the United States. In 1785 this body altered the church liturgy to make it consistent with the state constitutions, outlined plans to secure the consecration of bishops, and adopted a constitution proclaiming the freedom of Episcopalians from all foreign authority.[33] Soon thereafter, the New York parishes organized a state convention and nominated Samuel Provoost to be bishop. When he returned properly consecrated from England in June 1787, his colleague at Trinity Church, Abraham Beach, declared that local Episcopalians were finally "in such a situation, that a regular succession of the ministry may be continued to us and our posterity, without being reduced to the necessity of applying to a distant land!"[34] Provoost wasted little time in exercising his new powers. By the decade's end, he had ordained several new priests and confirmed hundreds of laypersons.[35]

Among Methodists, the "very uncommon train of providences" that made the colonies free caused John Wesley to ordain Francis Asbury and Thomas Coke and name them superintendents for America in September 1784. Wesley defended this action on the grounds that his transatlantic followers were often deprived of the sacraments. Moreover, he argued, "As our American brethren are now totally disentangled both from the State, and from the English hierarchy, we dare not entangle them again, either with the one or the other."[36] The formation of the Methodist Episcopal Church and the establishment of regional annual conferences resulted. The first annual conference, in New York City in October 1788, assigned twelve young native preachers to assist Freeborn Garrettson in forming new Methodist circuits in the Hudson River Valley north of Westchester County; they were the early fruit of ecclesiastical independence.[31]

A similar desire for better leadership and closer supervision prompted other denominations to make organizational changes as well. During these years the state's Baptists and Friends formed many new congregations and accordingly expanded the number of associations and monthly and quarterly meetings.[38] The burgeoning number of Presbyterians made it desirable to divide the New York and Philadelphia Synod. The Suffolk Presbytery requested to be dismissed from the synod in April 1787 because they considered their participation more inconvenient than beneficial.[39] Faced with such petitions, the synod approved in May 1788 the establishment of a national General Assembly with four subsidiary synods: New York and New Jersey, Philadelphia, Virginia, and the Carolinas.[40] In addition, the synod issued a new directory for worship services, made minor amendments in the political articles of the larger Westminster catechism, and ratified both the larger and smaller catechisms for use in the Presbyterian Church in America.[41]

Changes made by the Dutch Reformed and the Lutherans during the 1780s were less extensive. Beginning in October 1783, the General Body urged all independent Dutch Reformed congregations to affiliate with it. By the following May, only five of these congregations were listed as "outstanding": Kingston, Albany, Stissing, Rhinebeck, and Camp. All eventually joined the communion.[42] In October 1784, the General Body changed its name to the General Synod and that of each subsidiary particular assembly to classis, signifying that they considered the American church an ecclesiastical equal of the church in Holland.[43] Meanwhile, Lutherans resumed their efforts to establish an assembly on the model of the Pennsylvania Ministerium. Most of the state's congregations still belonged to the Pennsylvania body, the Revolution having interrupted the attempts of Frederick Muhlenberg to organize a separate one.[44] In 1784, Johann Christopher Kunze, pastor of the reunited Dutch and German Lutheran Church in New York City, revived Muhlenberg's plan. Under his guidance three ministers and two laymen met in 1786 to establish the Evangelical Lutheran Ministerium of the State of New York.[45]

To what extent did these changes improve the quality of religious life in New York? The answer varies from case to case. They helped Lutheran congregations very little, for after its initial meeting in 1786, the New York Ministerium did not meet again until 1792.[46] Presbyterians in New York and New Jersey found that having their own synod did not immediately resolve the shortage of ministers; thirty-five congregations were pastorless in 1789.[47] The outlook and institutional condition of the Methodists, Baptists, Quakers, and Episcopalians, however, were much improved. Whereas in 1785 there were only three Methodist circuits in New York and no classes or congregations north of Westchester County, by the decade's end nine additional circuits had been established: Columbia, New Britain, Cambridge, Albany, Saratoga, Dutchess, Otsego, Newburgh, and Wyoming.[48] From 1775 to 1787, Quaker meetings in the state grew from one to two quarterly and three to seven monthly meetings.[49] Baptist congregations grew from seventeen to sixty-four between 1784 and 1790. In the latter year, they reported four thousand members, served by one hundred ordained or licensed ministers.[50] And the Episcopalians, perhaps the most destitute sect in 1783, had twenty-six active parishes in 1789, the same number as in 1774; the six pastors present in 1785 had increased to eighteen, of whom fourteen were ordained priests.[51] Clearly, the reordering of denominational structures in the 1780s contributed to a marked recovery and expansion of Protestant religion.

Besides reorganizing themselves, the denominations adopted a second policy, to establish schools and promote home missions. While the specific measures varied, the goals of all groups were similar. First, each hoped to provide more adequately for the education of its youth. Throughout the colonial period, denominational schools had proved an effective instrument in preserving the religious and ethnic identity of young people.[52] Now, catechetical instruction and other forms of religious education were needed to provide children with the Christian knowledge necessary for them to become faithful believers and virtuous citizens of the republic. Within most denominations, meeting this goal was largely dependent on achieving a second objective: increasing the supply of trained clergymen. That dictated both reviving old and devising new schemes for recruiting and educating pastors. Until these schemes bore fruit, however, Protestant leaders had to set their sights on a third goal—providing at least occasional pastoral care for vacant congregations. Finally, the state's rapid population increase, especially in its interior parts, encouraged all groups to seek to provide a gospel witness for settlers on New York's frontier.

After the Presbyterians established the College of New Jersey (Princeton) in the 1740s, the other communions recognized the importance of founding their own colleges to train a native ministry. Prior to the Revolution, Anglicans, Lutherans, Baptists, and Dutch Reformed attempted to provide for the education of their prospective pastors by apprenticeship. However, by the 1780s, only one of these five denominations, the Baptists, was well-supplied with preachers, and that was attributable not to the success of Rhode Island College but to the Baptists' nonrestrictive view of the ministry.53 Likewise, Princeton did not graduate enough clergymen to fill all the Presbyterian pulpits; nor could Henry Muhlenberg personally instruct every Lutheran pastor. Episcopalians no longer controlled King's College, and the Dutch Reformed were still at the proposal stage with Queen's College.

Lacking sufficient pastors, Presbyterians continued to rely on Princeton but also looked elsewhere for aid. The New York Presbytery agreed to help raise funds for the college in 1784, though aware its impoverished congregations could give only modest contributions. Similarly, the presbytery implemented the General Assembly's order in 1789 that all churches ·take collections for the support of poor theology students.54 The Dutchess Presbytery endorsed this primitive scholarship program, but confessed its congregations were simply too poor to offer any help.55 On Long Island, the congregations of Suffolk Presbytery gained new ministers by attracting Yale graduates and licensed candidates of the Connecticut Congregationalist Associations. Between 1785 and 1787, seven new pastors arrived, giving the presbytery the highest percentage (75) of "congregations with pastors" in the General Assembly in 1789.56 Hoping to lead more young people into the ministry, the Synod of New York and Philadelphia encouraged its churches in 1785 to foster their youths' religious education through catechization and public education through the establishment of schools.57

The reduced influence of Episcopalians at King's, William and Mary, and the College of Philadelphia did not diminish their interest in education. While they helped found new colleges and Episcopal academies elsewhere, in New York they continued supporting Columbia (King's College) and were instrumental in electing their highly respected layman William Samuel Johnson to the college's presidency in 1787.58 Besides the pastors trained at Columbia, Bishop Provoost drew to the state prospective ministers educated at other American colleges. By 1791, eight of New York's twelve active priests had been ordained locally by either him or Samuel Seabury, bishop of Connecticut, and all but one were American born and trained.59

Because any sect could have a theology professorship in the college simply by endowing a chair, New York's Lutherans tried to use Columbia in their educational efforts during the 1780s. Minister Johann Kunze, appointed professor of Oriental languages and literature in 1784, hoped to use this post to teach theology to American Lutherans.60 While his plan had little immediate success, he did instruct some lay Lutherans, as well as clergymen of other persuasions, in Hebrew and Greek.61

The driving force for education among the Dutch Reformed was John

Livingston, minister of New York City's Collegiate Church. As the war ended, he favored the erection of a divinity school, rather than a college, at New Brunswick, New Jersey, to provide seminary education for Reformed pastors.[62] Although his idea was rejected, Livingston's persistence led the General Body within a year to vote to continue its support of Queen's College as a liberal arts institution, maintained at New Brunswick; to form a committee to assist the Consistory of Schenectady in founding another college in northern New York; and to appoint Livingston as professor of sacred theology in New York City and Hermanus Meyer, pastor at Pompton Plains, New Jersey, as instructor of ancient languages.[63] During the next three decades, Livingston taught numerous pastors, many of whom attended Columbia in the 1780s and '90s, including John Bassett, David Bogart, John Barent Johnson, Samuel Smith, and Cornelius Brower.[64] More immediately, these educational policies quickly increased the number preparing for the Dutch Reformed ministry.[65]

As part of the effort to reform the Society of Friends through "separatism" and renewal of the Quaker ideal of a carefully educated membership, the New York Yearly Meeting in 1780 urged its subordinate meetings to form schools for their children.[66] Lack of funds prevented Friends in the Hudson Valley from carrying out this recommendation, but both the Flushing and Westbury Monthly Meetings on Long Island established separate Quaker schools before 1790.[67]

Although Methodists were relatively idle in educational efforts, they spearheaded the spread of the gospel in New York.[68] Beginning in the mid-1780s, itinerants Francis Asbury, Thomas Ware, and Freeborn Garrettson toured the lower Hudson Valley and gradually extended Methodist influence northward on both sides of the river.[69] As previously mentioned, Garrettson organized numerous societies in the upper Hudson Valley as well as the first Methodist congregations in central New York. Many of these efforts prospered where churches of other persuasions already existed, indicating that mission outreach was not restricted to newly inhabited regions. Methodists did not ignore outlying settlements, however. By the early 1790s the state's conference had appointed a missionary for the whites and Indians along the New York–Canadian border and had collected voluntary offerings for relief of their preachers on New York's western frontier.[70]

In supporting missions through a voluntary fund, Methodists followed a pattern set by Baptists, Presbyterians, Episcopalians, and Dutch Reformed. The Philadelphia Baptist Association resumed its prewar practice of annually sending several ministers as itinerants to frontier areas and supporting them with the interest from congregational quarterly donations to the association. Their outreach extended even to Nova Scotia, where William Van Horne ministered for part of 1788 in response to a request from Canadian Baptists.[71] Besides these formally sponsored efforts, individual ministers often served informally as evangelists to surrounding communities. Stephen Gano not only pastored the Baptist churches at Hillsdale and Hudson but also preached often in other towns along the Hudson River. Between 1789 and 1792 he helped form new congregations at Warren, Coeymans, Duanesburg, Rensselaerville, and New Concord, New York.[72]

Nathan Kerr and Joshua Hart were the first two missionaries sent by the Presbyterian General Assembly to the frontier settlers in New York and Pennsylvania. They were to organize churches, administer ordinances, ordain elders, collect information on the religious condition of the area, and propose the best means to establish a permanent ministry.[73] When the New York and New Jersey Synod asked New York's existing congregations for contributions to aid these efforts, those in the city again responded favorably. The Dutchess Presbytery claimed its congregations could not afford to help, but resolved that one of its members serve as a missionary for six weeks every year, itinerating among the vacant congregations in Westchester and Dutchess counties.[74]

A like concern for parishes without pastors prompted the Episcopal Diocese of New York to solicit donations to support missionaries to visit them. Financing, however, would also be provided by income from the convention's possession of former SPG property in the state.[75]

The Dutch Reformed recognized the missionary challenge of New York's frontier as early as 1784. A report to the General Body in May suggested their number of congregations could be doubled by evangelizing the settlers in the northern and western portions of the state. This optimism stemmed partly from the belief that a high percentage of them were from Reformed backgrounds.[76] In May 1788, the synod recommended that all congregations take collections for the synod to use as remuneration for ministers sent to plant new churches and that each classis organize congregations in villages that had none.[77] Within a year, preaching and mission stations were established along the upper Delaware and Mohawk Rivers, setting the stage for the expansion of the communion that took place there during the 1790s.[78] These missions, along with English dominance of the emerging national culture, encouraged the introduction of English services in more Dutch Reformed congregations and the use of a revised English Psalmody.[79] The synod also translated the Articles of Church Government passed at the Synod of Dort in 1618–19 because most of their churches used English and because they desired to follow the lead of other denominations in making known to all Americans their doctrine and form of church government.[80]

In November 1788, the Presbyterian Synod called for a day of public fasting and prayer that God would "pour out his Spirit upon his churches of all denominations," bless their schools and academies, and smile on the attempts all were making to plant the gospel in frontier areas.[81] This call not only summarized the commitments of New Yorkers to education and evangelism; it also strikingly portrayed the third aspect of the reconstruction program: the cultivation of fraternal relations among Protestants and their mutual recognition as fully Christian.

Since the 1750s churchgoers had often been told that sectarian bigotry only hurt the cause of Christ, whereas mutual respect and cooperation among different communions enhanced spiritual progress. Well before the Revolution, evangelicals and liberals began stressing theological ideas that diminished the importance of denominational distinctions, and they sometimes found practical ways of working together in common projects. While the war divided political loyalties, the religious experience of these years seems to have encouraged compassion more than conflict. For instance, pastors who served as military chaplains, confronted by men of diverse religious backgrounds, carried on nonsectarian ministries; spiritual needs required sensitive shepherding, not doctrinal diatribes.[82] Also, when congregations received individuals of various persuasions dispersed on account of the war, they usually did so with Christian charity rather than sectarian exclusivism. In both situations, the Revolution encouraged a sense of common religious and political cause that overshadowed ethnic or doctrinal differences.

When the war ended, many of the state's church leaders paid attention once more to the religious significance of Protestant pluralism. Convinced that the 1777 constitution and subsequent legislation had settled the political questions relating to religious diversity, they resumed discussions about its theological legitimacy and spiritual consequences. A consensus began to emerge in the first postwar decade that Protestant pluralism would prove more of a help than a hindrance to the advance of Christianity in the state. It is not surprising that Presbyterian minister John Rodgers was a forthright proponent of this view considering his role in the prewar quest for religious equality and his service as a chaplain during the Revolution. In a sermon published in 1784, Rodgers told New Yorkers that religious differences reflected only the present human state of imperfection. "It is not to be expected, that we should all be united in opinion; and it is best, for the more general exercise of the Christian temper, that we should not." Theological uniformity was not possible, therefore, nor even preferable. But,

Rodgers added, "We may be all united in affection. And this is what I most devoutly recommend. And where we cannot agree to agree, let us agree to differ. Love is the peculiar characteristic of Jesus." If the state's Christians would add charity to their gifts of liberty, equality, and diversity, he concluded, God would continue to open "the way for the more general spread of the gospel" and, in due time, "the universal establishment of the Messiah's kingdom."[83]

During the next few years, numerous pastors and lay leaders echoed Rodgers's sentiments. The preface to the first draft of the Presbyterian Directory for Public Worship, written in 1787, stated that while naturally believing their own doctrines and modes of worship to be the most biblical, the denomination maintained a high respect for the other Protestant communions in America, especially the Congregationalists of New England, the Associate, Dutch, and German Reformed Churches, and the Lutherans and Episcopalians. And it urged those living in areas without Presbyterian congregations to attend these other denominations rather than refrain from public worship.[84]

New York's Episcopalians seem to have addressed the issue of sectarianism more than any other group in the 1780s. Perhaps their recent image as defenders of an established church and antagonists of the other communions prompted an effort to identify with religious diversity and to cultivate mutual love. Uzal Ogden, assistant minister of Trinity Church in New York City and later rector at Newark, New Jersey, communicated this message often. Writing to Presbyterian clergyman Hugh Knox in late 1783, Ogden declared there always had been and possibly always would be "a diversity of religious opinions among men." He noted "that we are enjoined to 'receive,' or to be kindly disposed towards 'those who are weak in the faith;' and that agreeable to the idea of an eminent English Philosopher, 'those are the real heretics who live lives of impiety.' "[85] Agreement on such matters as forms of church government and modes of worship was not necessary, Ogden said, for "the essence of religion doth not consist in these things." It was "uncharitable and erroneous" for anyone to conclude that any would be deprived of salvation "merely on account of their disagreement in these non-essentials."[86] On the contrary, he said, some of every denomination were regenerate. "If Christ himself receives into his kingdom, those who differ from us in religious opinions and mode of worship," Ogden concluded, "why should not We receive such into the arms of affection?"[87]

Other Episcopalians sounded variations on Ogden's theme. Thomas Moore, rector at Hempstead, Long Island, told the state convention in 1789 that, given existing divisions among Christians, his communion must remain unified to gain the respect and forbearance of "the orderly and sensible of other denominations."[88] The previous year Jeremiah Leaming reexamined the layman's traditional problem of finding truth amid the variety of Christian opinions. As others had argued earlier, Leaming insisted that because God's truth is unchangeable, it could be found through studying Scripture. Christians, therefore, must call one another back to a dependence on the Bible as their rule of faith and practice and away from a divisive reliance on the "inventions of men."[89]

Perhaps the clearest and most comprehensive expression of what recent historians have called the "denominational theory of the church" appeared in Jedediah Chapman's sermon at the last meeting of the Presbyterian New York and Philadelphia Synod in 1788.[90] Christ's church on earth was one body, Chapman asserted, and every denomination should be considered a particular branch of it. Within this body, the headship of Christ laid a "proper basis for the most perfect unity and peace, amidst all possible variety."[91] He then outlined ways Christians could preserve "the unity of the Spirit in the bond of peace." He rejected the notion that uniformity was necessary for unity. Instead, believers of different persuasions living under different forms of government must "forbear one another in love" and acknowledge their mutual dependence within the larger body of Christ. Only then could they grasp the spiritual union God intended for his church.[92]

Though no dramatic change took place immediately, Chapman, Ogden, Rodgers, and others acted upon their convictions as the 1780s progressed. Ogden became good friends with other evangelicals, including Hugh Knox and Francis Asbury, and supported Methodist efforts throughout the Middle Colonies.[93] The creation of an interdenominational religious society among students at Columbia College was one hopeful sign that the next generation would forge unity out of Christian diversity.[94] This organization sprang from the students' belief that "if Christians frequently convene, they will quicken each others zeal, and enliven one another, but if separated will grow torpid and lifeless."[95] At Columbia John Barent Johnson and other prospective pastors formed close friendships and attended worship services with classmates of other persuasions, gaining an appreciation for the faithful ministries of clergymen outside their own denominations.[96]

Increased goodwill in fact characterized many congregational relationships. For example, in contrast to the strained relations Trinity Church had with other groups in earlier years, it now became a harbinger of the new spirit of unity. Perhaps most telling were its contacts with the city's Presbyterians. Just as the war ended, the vestry voted to allow the Brick Presbyterian congregation to worship in St. George's and St. Paul's Chapels while its building was being restored from November 1783 to June 1784. Then, two years later, without solicitation, the vestry gave pieces of property to each of the city's Presbyterian congregations where parsonages could be built for their respective senior pastors.97 While few churches could match Trinity's generosity, many were able to follow its lead at least in extending the right hand of fellowship to other believers.

Similar efforts soon emerged at the denominational level. In 1789 the Philadelphia Baptist Association, the General Convention of the Protestant Episcopal Church, and the Presbyterian Synod of New York and New Jersey endorsed the plan of Isaac Collins to print a new edition of the Bible and appointed delegates to cooperate with other denominational representatives in promoting its publication and distribution.98 Between 1785 and 1789 committees from the Associate Reformed (Scottish Presbyterian), Dutch Reformed, and Presbyterian Synods held periodic conventions to familiarize one another with their doctrinal statements, spread harmony and brotherly love, and promote the general interest of the Protestant churches in America.99 Such collective efforts prompted President George Washington to write in August 1789:

> . . . it would ill become me to conceal the joy I have felt in perceiving the fraternal affection which appears to increase every day among the friends of genuine religion. It affords edifying prospects indeed, to see Christians of different denominations dwell together in more charity, and conduct themselves, in respect to each other, with a more Christian-like spirit than ever they have done in any former age, or in any other nation.100

Despite such strong evidence of positive attitudes, a complete account of Protestant interdenominational relations cannot overlook the animosity Methodists encountered in evangelizing the Hudson Valley. Both Asbury and Garrettson recorded that ministers of different denominations called them agents of the king or simply false prophets.101 Asbury noted that the Reformed background of most of the people accounted for their extreme reluctance to accept, or even hear, the Wesleyan message of free will and free grace.102

While political prejudice and obvious theological differences partially explain the hostile reaction to Methodism, the Methodist itinerants in fact represented a distinctive addition to the religious environment. Whereas almost all existing congregations had been organized by laypersons who had come to the Hudson Valley already attached to particular religious traditions, Methodist preachers set out to gather congregations through vigorous evangelism and proselytization. As with earlier Anglican and Moravian missionaries, other ministers opposed these efforts. They may have theoretically accepted the virtues of pluralism, but they found reason to oppose it in practice when their livelihoods were directly threatened. Because the encounter with Methodists was unique, therefore, the reaction cannot be interpreted as typical. Furthermore, despite much hostility, Asbury and Garrettson found numerous religious communities where a catholic spirit prevailed, notably the Presbyterian congregations in Canaan and Lebanon Springs, the Baptists in Bethlehem, and the Quakers in New Castle.[103] Indeed, as time passed the Methodists' conception that the church should be primarily a missionary organization rather than a preserver of traditional institutions gradually penetrated the thinking of most other denominations. This conception underlay the rapid spread of the gospel westward at the end of the century.[104] Thus, the tensions over Methodism on the whole substantiate the conclusion that more often than not the state's churchmen sought to work harmoniously with other "branches" of the body of Christ.

What is more, the spirit of cooperation, or at least peaceful coexistence, extended to Protestant relations with Jews and Catholics following the Revolution. The Jews had been on remarkably good terms with Christians in New York City throughout the eighteenth century. That was due in part to the unwillingness of Congregation Shearith Israel to accept Gentile converts into its ranks. Protestant churches therefore had few worries about Jewish proselytization and in fact gained adherents through intermarriages. Jews further legitimated themselves as good neighbors in Protestant eyes through their support of the Revolution and embrace of republican ideology. The respect and friendship Jews had earned in Protestant circles became evident in the 1780s. For instance, when King's College became Columbia College in 1787, the leader of the Jewish community, hazzan Gersham Mendez Seixas, was named one of its incorporators. An even more explicit example of interfaith goodwill occurred when the Jewish burial ground was threatened by soil erosion in 1789. One Protestant family donated land to the congregation on which to build a retaining wall and a group of Christian merchants raised over £120 to defray the cost of building it.[105]

The state's tiny Catholic minority was still suspect in the minds of most Protestants after the war. Nevertheless, no major outbreaks of Protestant-Catholic hostility took place in the 1780s and a Protestant congregation played a vital role in helping New York's fledgling Catholic Church gain a foothold in the nation's capital. The vestry of Trinity Church, whose ecumenism has already been noted, leased and eventually sold land on Barclay Street to the trustees of St. Peter's Catholic Church for their first building. Whatever the vestrymen's motives, their action signaled the arrival, however temporary, of a more tolerant attitude among Protestants toward Catholics.[106]

In retrospect, then, the 1780s saw New York's Protestant communions work out three broad policies to deal with the problems they faced at the conclusion of the war: attempts to reorganize or form new denominational structures, the creation of schools and extensive support of home missionary projects, and the establishment of cooperative relationships with other religious persuasions. Though not successful in every case, most groups took significant steps to carry out such policies.

But did these efforts actually help solve the problems confronting churches in the postwar period? I believe they did, both in the short and in the long run. Because of the character of these innovations in conception and policy, however, they did not bear fruit for another decade or more. For instance, the early attempts at formal interdenominational cooperation produced no immediate tangible results, but they certainly contributed to the scores of efforts at evangelical cooperation in the 1790s and thereafter. It took time for new schools to produce graduates, for denominations to collect sufficient funds to support full-time missionaries, and for congregations to grow large enough to provide for their own ministers. Yet, even by the 1790s, Baptist and Methodist membership had grown enormously, the Society of Friends showed new signs of vitality, and the vibrancy of Protestant Episcopal congregations matched that of the prewar years. Although Presbyterians, Lutherans, and Dutch Reformed showed smaller gains, sampling of extant congregational records indicates that just as many flourished as faltered in these years.[107]

Furthermore, similar signs of success were noticeable among other groups outside mainstream Protestantism. Various forms of theological radicalism, for example, found greater expression in New York in the 1780s. Most prominent among them were universalism and Shakerism. Universalist devotees apparently purchased a church building in New York City in 1785 and no doubt supported the publication two years later of physician William Pitt Smith's *The Universalist,* a three-hundred-page treatise promoting the doctrine of general salvation.[108] Meanwhile, the original Shaker community at Niskeyuna not only grew but also served as an effective instrument of evangelism throughout New England. For, rather than using itinerants to spread their faith, the Shakers of Niskeyuna community moved from town to town as a whole, "living with converts for considerable periods and initiating them firsthand into the detailed practice of their new faith." The 1780s also saw the Shakers build their first meetinghouse (at New Lebanon) and develop distinctive institutions under the leadership of Joseph Meacham. From 1787 to 1792, he oversaw a series of creative organizational reforms that provided order and identity for this communitarian movement.[109]

On the whole, non-Protestants also fared well. With their religious freedoms restored, provincial Catholics organized into a formal congregation for the first time since the days of James II. St. Peter's Roman Catholic Church in New York City was incorporated in 1785 and by late 1786 was worshiping in its own new building. Although the congregation's first few years were rent with controversies over who was its rightful priest and its relationship to the Catholic hierarchy, its establishment nevertheless represented a major step forward in the quest of Catholicism to have an institutional presence in New York.[110] All was not well among Jews either in the postwar decade. The congregation was plagued with a growing laxity in religious observance and financial debts to its hazzan, shohet, shammash, and ribbi. Yet here, too, the dominant story was one of institutional revitalization. Former patriots and loyalists united in reorganizing Shearith Israel in 1784 and having it incorporated in 1785. During the next five years, they oversaw the writing of a new congregational constitution, repairs on the synagogue and cemetery, the creation of a benevolent aid society, and the reorganization of a congregational school.[111]

Such rapid recovery and expansion among various religious faiths bears witness to a religious dynamism that historians have tended either to deny or ignore. Far from being idle or indifferent, New York's churches revealed a spiritual energy at both the congregational and the denominational levels that generated not only institutional growth but numerous revivals. A notable series of such awakenings at New York City's First Baptist Church yielded 125 baptisms between 1784 and 1787. Samuel Buell's Presbyterian congregation in Easthampton added over 100 new members during three months in 1785. The Methodist Society in New Rochelle grew from a small group to over 700 by 1789. And the Baptist church in Warwick received 142 new members in 1788.[112]

These examples indicate that suggestions that the years following independence were "unfavorable to the promotion of religion" or were characterized by either "suspended animation" or widespread religious declension are inaccurate descriptions of New York's experience in the 1780s.[113] Instead, the state's religious groups demonstrated consistent vitality, in both institutional reconstruction and membership growth. As a result, they moved into the 1790s with confidence in God's faithfulness and their own mission, and with a better understanding of how to prosper in a pluralistic religious environment.

VI

"A GLORIOUS ENTERPRIZE"
RELIGIOUS COOPERATION IN THE
1790s

Decisions made during the 1780s set the agenda for New York's churches in the next decade. For, although significant progress had been made, the task of reconstruction was far from completed. Many policies aimed at institutional expansion or ecclesiastical self-sufficiency were not carried out until the 1790s. Meanwhile, the state's Protestant leaders continued to ponder the consequences of religious disestablishment and to discern more clearly how faith might thrive in a diverse milieu. Their combined efforts gave New York in 1800 a religious culture that both reflected the experience of the previous half century and presaged the shape American Protestantism would take in the following fifty years.

Contemporary accounts agreed that among the most noteworthy religious developments in New York during the 1790s and early 1800s was an emerging wave of cooperative religious ventures of which mission societies, religious periodicals, prayer concerts, and book publications were outstanding examples. Although some traditionalist Protestants participated, evangelicals dominated these activities and used them to enhance their hold over the state's religious life. By 1803, the New York Baptist Association found that other American evangelicals "drank into the same spirit with their brethren in New York," so that "the dear people of God in different parts and among different denominations are pursuing the same precious cause with increasing zeal. Prejudice and party spirit are on the margin of oblivion, and christianity has now more generally become a common cause."[1] Presbyterian minister Alexander MacWhorter told the New York Missionary Society that events in Great Britain and America showed that a "harmony, unparalleled, perhaps, in the modern history of the church, reigns among those who in every denomination, love the unadulterated gospel."[2]

What explains this unprecedented surge of cooperative evangelism? And what can be learned from it about the place of religious pluralism in New York at the beginning of the nineteenth century?

Past historians have generally associated the unifying and organizing activities of New Yorkers in the late eighteenth century with what has been called the Second Great Awakening.[3] This awakening, or at least its Northeastern phase, has been traditionally interpreted as the New England clergy's strategy to counteract the tide of infidelity and immorality that swept America following the Revolution.[4] Depicted as the Calvinist reaction to political, moral, and theological trends on both sides of the Atlantic, it is credited with rescuing this area's churches from the religious depression of the late eighteenth century.[5] While examination of New York's religious communities between 1776 and 1790 has already shown that declension was far less universal and uniform than scholars have thought, this view of the era's religious history seems to be confirmed by the plethora of complaints about the prevalence of infidelity voiced by the state's denominations in the 1790s.

Though outcries against irreligion sounded throughout the decade, they may have reached their highest pitch in 1796. The Presbyterian General Assembly urged its members to initiate whatever biblical measures they thought would most effectively counteract such evils as the prevailing impiety, widespread contempt for the institutions and laws of religion, profanation of the Sabbath, and the corruption of morals.[6] The Philadelphia Baptist Association devoted its 1796 circular letter to the theme of infidelity, suggesting that Baptists avoid vain arguments with Deists and instead demonstrate the truth of orthodox Christianity through their actions.[7] Their New York brethren similarly lamented the "strange indifference and inattention to divine things among the professors of religion," while the Methodist Conference complained of the growing carelessness and contempt for the Bible.[8]

The state's churchmen blamed themselves for these conditions. Both the Associated Westchester Presbytery (Associate Reformed Church) and the Hudson Presbytery (Presbyterian Church in the United States of America) attributed the low state of their churches to the lack of zeal among believers in discharging their Christian duties.[9] John Mitchell Mason, an Associate Reformed pastor in New York City, outlined in great detail how the insincerity, pride, obstinacy, and hypocrisy of Americans, and especially Christians, provoked God's judgment. The War for Independence, the conflict over the Federal Constitution, the plague of the Hessian fly, the Indian wars, and the yellow fever epidemic all seemed to him manifestations of the

Lord's wrath sent to awaken churchgoers out of their spiritual apathy and moral transgressions.[10]

Amid this self-condemnation, some groups saw at least one positive outcome of the spread of infidelity: Christians of various Protestant persuasions could concentrate on the struggle against their common adversary, lessening their preoccupation with doctrinal differences among themselves. According to its directors, the New York Missionary Society was formed partly because "the prevalence of infidelity pushes Christians to action."[11] Uzal Ogden endorsed the plan for a national concert of prayer since it would "silence the objection of infidelity, that Christians cannot agree among themselves."[12] One Baptist likened Protestant denominations to the tribes of Israel. When at peace with surrounding nations they contended among themselves, but "when a foreign foe drew near to battle," they were united "in one great bond, as the people of God," and "marched to contest and victory."[13]

If the threat of infidelity could unite Protestants, then it was easy for ministers to exaggerate that threat so as to produce a quick, and concerted response. Though not admitting it, clergymen realized their cause might be served by orchestrating religious renewal and harmony by magnifying the discord and threatened chaos of irreligion.[14]

That is not to suggest, however, that ministerial fears were either unreal or completely unwarranted. Members of the state's evangelical leadership sincerely believed that the cause of Christ in America was being weakened by the nation's intellectual preoccupation with political rather than religious matters, the proliferation of blatantly anti-Christian writings, and the rise of an intense political factionalism.[15] Furthermore, they were correct in noting that heterodox religious views were becoming more prevalent in the state in the 1790s. Evangelicals could point, for example, to the deistic leanings of many of the young men who belonged to such intellectual discussion groups as the Calliopean Society and the Schaghticoke Polemic Society in upstate New York and the Friendly Society of New York City.[16] Even more explicit evidence could be found in the publication of a universalist periodical, Abel Sargent's *Free Universal Magazine,* in New York City in 1793 and the organization in 1796 of the United Christian Friends, a religious society composed of disaffected Methodists who were committed to the doctrine of universal salvation.[17]

Thus the two components many historians have identified as principally causing the Second Great Awakening in the Northeast—the ministerial outcry against infidelity and the perception that this outcry could reinvigorate religion—were present in New York in the 1790s. Such rhetoric and perception, if they convinced the state's residents to participate in a vast religious mobilization, explain what happened. But did they actually do so? The existence of the rhetoric does not prove its persuasive effect.

Several reasons may explain why the jeremiads about infidelity were relatively unconvincing. For one thing, warnings of the immorality that it would produce were certainly not new. Study of ministerial laments reveals that their content changed very little between 1776 and 1796, although those sounded during the Revolution were naturally preoccupied with the war.[18] How then can it be argued that those uttered later provoked a sudden outburst of religious zeal after having been apparently ineffectual in the previous twenty years?

Based on the evidence for continued religious vitality in New York both during and after the war, one answer may be that this clerical "strategy" had been, in fact, responsible since the eve of the Revolution for generating spiritual interest and devotion. Such a view, of course, undermines the premise that the awakening began only in the late 1790s to pull America (including New York) out of the religious doldrums. Its plausibility is also suspect in light of the religious interest colonists demonstrated in the twenty-five years preceding the war. An alternative explanation is that while the content of these outcries had not changed, the social context in which they were heard had changed sufficiently to assure a widespread response. But that also discredits the original interpretation, for it argues that the awakening was not planned or launched by the message of ministers but was the spontaneous result of underlying social, economic, and political changes.[19] It seems untenable, then, to conclude that the threat of infidelity in itself produced the awakening, or that these oft-repeated ministerial complaints made much popular impression.

Furthermore, wherever the vitality of religion and the position of churches remained strong, the jeremiads would not have been persuasive. In many instances a minister or layman lamented the spread of false religion or immorality but in the next breath praised God for blessing his particular congregation. Members of the First Baptist Church of New York wrote in 1787 that they regretted the prevalence of "Deism, Arminianism, and numberless other errors," but added, "yet blessed be God, the Gospel hath not been preached among us without effect, nor has the labors of our worthy pastor been in vain—we have within the year past had 31 members added to us. . . ."[20] During the next decade, Stephen Van Voorhees preached about the world's growing impiety and irreligion to various Dutch Reformed and Presbyterian audiences in the central Hudson Valley, yet he rejoiced with his colleague Stephen Goetschius, Dutch Reformed pastor at

New Paltz, over the formation of nine new congregations in this region.[21] In February 1800, John Bowen related to his former pastor in England, Baptist John Rippon, that vice and infidelity had spread among New York's young and middle aged in the previous seven or eight years; nevertheless, some in various denominations were "enquireing their way to Zion with their faces thether ward, so that we are not left wholly without Witnesses for God. . . ."[22] Such positive views of religious life in their own communities seem in fact to have shaped the attitudes and actions of churchgoers, despite the grim warnings of growing irreligion.

Since it seems unreasonable then to argue that ministers manufactured an awakening in New York by magnifying the spread of infidelity, the religious events of these years need an alternative explanation.[23] Any new view must abandon the traditional interpretation's assumption that changes in the religious piety of the popular classes of the late eighteenth century must have been the result of manipulation by an enlightened religious elite. Such a two-tiered model of religious change overlooks the internal dynamism of popular religion and exaggerates the cleavage between the religious experience of the elite and the masses in the early republic. A new perspective must also be rooted in a proper understanding of religious and social events between 1750 and 1795. Perceived in the context of evidence for continued religious interest rather than declension in New York during the 1770s and '80s, the religious developments of the late eighteenth and early nineteenth centuries do not appear to have constituted a new "boom period" or dramatic turning point in a cyclical scheme of religious activity. Instead, what happened was the logical outgrowth of the spiritual energy and theological consensus generated and sustained during the previous half century by the evangelical impulse in New York.

To understand the emergence of the united efforts of the 1790s, three factors seem important: the growth of spiritual fervor in local congregations throughout the state; the perception that events in Britain, France, and around the world indicated the approach of the "last days"; and the maturation of a biblically based understanding of religious diversity. An examination of these factors will show their role in shaping public attitudes and actions.

Wherever one looks in New York during the 1790s, clear signs of religious vibrancy abound. Notwithstanding the persisting jeremiads, numerous congregations demonstrated a fervor that infected both the pulpit and the pew. This fervor refreshed old members and attracted new converts in urban areas as well as rural, old settlements as well as new, lower New York as well as upper, small congregations as well as large. The contemporary designation of 1800 as "the year of the revivals" in New York, then, was less a comment on past times than a tribute to current vitality.

Historians have confused matters by labeling any discovery of strong religious interest in a congregation or a community as a revival. As Donald Mathews has pointed out, a revival is a revitalizing or resurgence of spiritual intensity. Rather than introducing religion into a region, it is a "repeat performance" and normally does not take place apart from a church.[24] Implicit in the definition is the assumption that something needs to be revived. Historians readily believe, therefore, that spiritual deadness always precedes a revival. They tend, on that account, to depict religious history as a series of valleys and peaks and to neglect the less dramatic ways in which religious fervor is expressed.

In the 1790s, some places in New York experienced "typical" revivals. After years of what ministers called spiritual dryness, a renewal of interest took place, large numbers of new members were brought into the churches, and whole towns displayed a heightened religious and moral sensibility. Presbyterian pastor Aaron Woolworth described the awakening of Bridgehampton, Long Island, in 1799 and 1800 in these terms. Following a long period of seeming lack of interest, news of Connecticut revivals sparked a revival in his own congregation, and others in Middletown, Huntington, and Southold.[25] Eliphalet Nott, Presbyterian minister in Albany, gave a smilar account of a revival in the Albany County town of Bern. Late in 1797, renewed spiritual concern among a few villagers prompted the Methodist, Baptist, Dutch Reformed, and Presbyterian ministers to combine labors that led to the conversion of three hundred persons, the establishment of three new congregations, and the revitalization of the Dutch Reformed church.[26] Between 1795 and 1800, the New York Baptist Association, the Presbyterian General Assembly, and other denominational gatherings reported in similar fashion such events in many places; God had brought spiritual refreshment after periods of prolonged indifference.[27]

While these times of "refreshing" within a church or a community should definitely be called revivals, it is important to differentiate them from the nineteenth-century revivalism associated with frontier camp meetings and the evangelism of Charles G. Finney in western New York. What occurred at Bridgehampton or Bern was deemed a revival only in retrospect and did not flow from the kind of planned revival meetings that later became a dominant feature of antebellum Protestantism. These New Yorkers, following their eighteenth-century predecessors, thought of a revival as a spontaneous divine miracle that was solely the work of God. They had no conception of revivals as the predictable ends of the right means used by a minister.

These revivals must also be differentiated from the kind of religious experience that characterized many other churches in New York in the 1790s. The presence of intense fervor within these other bodies points up an essential but rarely mentioned feature of the life cycle of congregations. Over a span of years, virtually all congregations have short periods of great spiritual prosperity and severe depression. But scholars often do not understand that in most years the majority of them proceed on an even keel, neither grounded nor at high tide. Most of the time they carry on their routine of religious activities in a climate of modest assurance that their worship and work are pleasing to God. Within this context, a revival, understood as a dramatic upswing in spiritual and moral concern, is clearly an extraordinary occurrence. Consequently, its absence in a church or town at any one moment is to be expected and by no means predicates spiritual decay or institutional stagnation. This fact is borne out by the experience of numerous New York congregations in the 1790s in which the presence of religious fervor was not a sudden departure from the past but a persistent, ongoing reality that reflected the continued spiritual and moral commitment of pastors and laity alike. That many of these churches enjoyed spurts of great prosperity for a few months at different points in the decade only demonstrates that awakenings sprang as often from spiritual health as from spiritual lethargy.

During the 1791 revival in Samuel Buell's Easthampton Presbyterian congregation, fewer converts were added than in 1764 or 1785. But this "work of God" was nevertheless special: "for a universal visitation and fresh anointings of the Lord's people and their increasing light and comfort," Buell wrote, "I never know [sic] a revival of religion among us equal thereto since I have been your pastor." He rejoiced that his laity had been renewed, and explained that throughout his Easthampton ministry even when no revival was occurring, there had always been signs of God's working in the lives of old and new believers.[28]

The steady growth of New York City's John Street Methodist Church from about 60 members to 360 in the 1780s necessitated the erection of a second church building in 1789. Religious interest grew even more sharply in the early 1790s. In eight weeks 400 were converted, most of whom joined the society and became closely disciplined participants.[29] Four years later pastor Thomas Morrell reported that "very few of them fell away; most of them continue faithful unto this day."[30] This thriving religious community of 750 members and hundreds of other listeners experienced another "glorious work" in February–March 1797. A hundred more people were admitted as members, and a third Methodist church was built later that year.[31]

The story is similar with upstate Baptists. In rural Saratoga County, north of Albany, Baptists from various small villages had begun holding services in 1762 at Stillwater and worshiped there in the 1770s and '80s despite the war's devastation. Their steadfastness was rewarded between 1789 and 1793 under the ministry of Lemuel Powers and David Irish. Not only did the congregation increase eightfold, from about fifty to over four hundred, but it inspired the formation of numerous other Baptist fellowships. The small groups or "colonies" who attended the Stillwater church from different settlements now grew large enough to form their own congregations. In one five-year span, seven new churches were organized.[32] In addition, when David Irish migrated two hundred miles west in 1794, some of the Stillwater members joined him; soon Baptist multiplication began in that area.[33] The tremendous spiritual momentum generated in Stillwater and similar Baptist communities mounted throughout the decade, culminating in mass revivals in upper New York and western Vermont in 1799 and 1800.[34]

What happened at Easthampton, John Street, and Stillwater typified the experience of numerous other congregations in the state during the 1790s. The steady growth of the Associate Reformed congregation in New York City dictated the construction of a second church in 1797.[35] The Baptists in Battenskill gradually increased in the 1780s to number one hundred, then doubled their size in one year (1791); they later withstood the trauma of excluding their pastor Nathan Turner.[36] Between 1777 and 1787 the Dutch Reformed Church in Kinderhook added 42 members under the ministry of John Ritzema, and then from 1789 to 1799, 134 were received by pastor Isaac Labagh.[37] And the Methodist society in Saratoga, organized in 1790, progressively grew from 100 to 444 adherents by 1800.[38] Not all of these congregations were blessed with an awakening, but each showed a consistent vitality that reflected the ongoing religious commitment of its members and shaped the life of its local community.

The state's expanding frontier likewise witnessed growing spiritual fervor during the 1790s. Except for the rare visit of a missionary or traveling preacher, laypersons there at first had to rely on themselves for spiritual and moral discipline and the religious instruction of their children. While some remote towns gained a reputation for vice and infidelity, a surprising number demonstrated the opposite. When missionaries arrived, they often found pious individuals and families already worshiping on their own or in small groups and eager to be organized into congregations. After visiting more than twenty-five settlements in central and western New York, Presbyterians Nathan Kerr and Joshua Hart reported that although only a few places had churches, "in most there appeared a great attention to the preaching of the gospel. . . . Your missionaries found in many places serious, well-instructed, and apparently pious people."[39]

Such discoveries were not limited to evangelical preachers. Three Episcopal missionaries of mixed sympathies toward evangelicalism, Ammi Rogers, Robert Wetmore, and Philader Chase, told of hamlets where "the principles of the primitive Church had taken deep root in the hearts of several families," thereby allowing them to institute regular parishes quickly.[40] In some communities, including Ballston, Morris, Duanesburgh, and Hobart, lay initiative alone organized and sustained congregations committed to a sacramental theology. These efforts contributed to the remarkable expansion of the Episcopal Church in northern and western New York between 1790 and 1810. While in 1790 only one Episcopal parish in upper New York had resumed functioning, twenty years later, twenty-five parishes or mission stations existed, served by fourteen priests. In addition, ten new buildings had been completed, and others were under construction.[41]

Similarly, the missionaries of the Dutch Reformed Classis of Albany planted many new churches in northern New York and Canada. Among the laypeople they banded together was a minority for whom European Orthodoxy continued to hold greater attraction than revivalistic pietism. These persons coexisted with evangelicals in a denomination experiencing another burst of growth, witnessed by the formation in 1800 of several new classes: the Classis of Albany was split into three, Albany, Rennsalaer, and Montgomery, and that of Kingston into two, Poughkeepsie and Ulster.[42]

Elsewhere on the frontier, zealous laypersons sometimes secured the conversion of their neighbors. During 1792 in Austerlitz, a small village southeast of Albany, several laymen sparked an awakening that saw forty saved and a Congregational church organized.[43] Along the state's southern tier, Baptist Asher Wickham, writing in 1797 from Chenango to his former pastor in Dutchess County, explained that "there is no Church here nor much meeting only a Number of professors meet on the Lords day." Nevertheless, he reported that "God is a going through this part of the wilderness in displays of his Boundless Love to poor Sinners there is much crying out I have hear from down this River [Susquehanna] what they shall dew to be Saved and a great Reformation at the Caraque Lake."[44] Two years later Wickham wrote again:

> God has Begun his Blessed work in this place where I live my Eyes and Ears is a witness somes a mourning there awfull Situation while out of Christ while

others is a giving glory to God I see hapy seasons in this part of the Land as to matters of Religion we have no preaching hardly Ever But we hold up the worship of God on the Sabbaths with Exortation and Singing and praying. . . .45

The testimony of such laymen and numerous missionaries makes plain that many frontier settlements were alive with religious interest. Pious frontiersmen of both evangelical and traditionalist convictions welcomed the arrival of an itinerant preacher able to enhance their faith and bind them into a congregation. Such an event brought a sense of community and common purpose and produced social and spiritual satisfactions that were highly attractive to their neighbors. It was this type of organizing evangelism that New Yorkers labeled a revival in the interior parts of the state in the 1790s.46

The pervasiveness of religious devotion in these several forms was the organizing impulse that persuaded individuals to maintain or form congregations that were eager for both denominational and interdenominational leadership. Spiritual commitment provided the will and energy for action. It stemmed more often from hopes of enlarging God's kingdom than from mortal fear of Satan triumphing.

The perception by New York Protestants of two European developments, the French Revolution and the emergence of an evangelical ecumenism in Great Britain, reinforced their energy and gave them a blueprint for action.

Like most other Americans in the early 1790s, the state's evangelicals initially hailed the French Revolution as a sign that history was following America in the direction of republicanism.47 Dutch Reformed minister William Linn called the revolution "astonishing" and "glorious" because it promised the expansion of civil and religious liberty.48 He also thought, as many others did, that liberty and spiritual progress went hand in hand. Like the New England clergymen Nathan Hatch has studied, those in New York understood the destruction of political and ecclesiastical tyranny to be opening the way for the spread of the gospel and ultimately the start of Christ's millennial reign.49 Baptists in particular identified established religion as a "hated monster of iniquity" and the "principal agent in the havock which Satan has made among mankind." They believed that its existence in Europe presented "an insurmountable barrier to the spiritual reign of Christ in that quarter."50 They could endure the political excesses and irreligious character of the French Revolution, therefore, because it was liberating the oppressed and attacking at its head the "mystical Babylon," the papal Antichrist:

> We cannot but admire with all the attentive Israel of God the awful and
> astonishing dispensations of Jehovah's government. King Jesus . . . is terribly
> shaking the nations and Babylon is falling. The emancipation of twenty four
> Millions of people from a nation under the reign of popish and royal
> despotism, and the raised expectation that millions more will be thus liber-
> ated . . . are Events of awful power and how awful soever will terminate in his
> own glory and the enlargement of the Redeemers kingdom.[51]

Such Protestant believers also thought that the "fall of Babylon," America's successful revolution, and other European developments were signs of
the approach of Christ's millennial reign. "If we consider what great things
the Lord has done, in this American land and in the European world of
late," one wrote, "who can but prophesy? Who can but conclude Christ is on
his way? Let us, with one heart, and with one voice, cry 'come, Lord Jesus,
come quickly.' "[52] Apocalyptical interest grew in 1794 when a rumor spread
among the state's evangelicals that a group of Jewish leaders was to meet
shortly in Amsterdam to consider whether Jesus Christ was the true messiah.[53] Encouraged that this congress might be the first step in the restoration of the Jews to Israel, which students of prophecy believed depended
upon their conversion to Christianity, Baptists once again marveled at what
God was bringing to pass:

> Surely if . . . the result of their deliberations should be in the Affirmative,
> Zion will arise and shine—The elect Gentiles from the ends of the earth will
> come in with his ancient people the Jews. Will not these events lead on to the
> reestablishment of Christianity in its primitive purity in Doctrine Discipline
> and ordinances, and pure and undefiled religion of heart prevail Let us
> anticipate these desirable events—pray for their accomplishment— . . . and
> be prepared for this coming of the Lord Jesus in the hearts of Jews and
> Gentiles.[54]

Reformed pastor Linn echoed this Baptist anticipation of the unfolding
of the divine plan. His book, *Discourses on the Signs of the Times,* saw recent
events as the historical fulfillment of the prophecies in Daniel and Revelation and predicted that the millennium would arrive by A.D. 2000. For that
to come to pass, however, believers must obey two salient biblical commands for the last days: to unite on the fundamental doctrines of faith and
to cooperate in spreading the gospel to the whole world.[55]

While Linn aimed his remarks at Protestants in America, within a year he
discovered British evangelicals doing precisely what he had recommended.
Anglican and Dissenter evangelicals united in 1795 to form the London
Missionary Society. Its ecumenical membership and commitment to evangelism quickly spawned similar organizations throughout the British Isles,
and the news impressed New Yorkers. With this model for action, Linn

helped draw together ministers and laymen from different communions in forming the New York Missionary Society, America's first nondenominational mission organization. At its initial meeting in November 1796, the officers explained that the founding of similar societies in London, Glasgow, Edinburgh, and other British cities and their immediate success in spreading the gospel had inspired Americans to act. "It was impossible," they wrote, "on receiving religious intelligence like this, that Christians here should not feel their hearts warmed, and their emulation excited." Although "their means are scanty in proportion to those of their brethren over the ocean, they could not help asking themselves, and one another, what can we do in the same glorious enterprize?"[56] Within another three months, evangelicals of various persuasions in upstate New York created the Northern Missionary Society and likewise credited the British and European organizations with setting the example.[57] This flurry of missionary activity on both sides of the Atlantic prompted the editor of *The Theological Magazine* (published in New York City) to call those times the greatest era in the world's history since the apostolic age.[58]

Once evangelicals in New York and other states became aware of other cooperative endeavors being undertaken by British evangelicals, they emulated those also. The directors of the New York Missionary Society outlined a plan for monthly interdenominational prayer meetings to be held in various city churches whose ministers were society members. To those who suggested this scheme might be too liberal they answered: "Our brethren in Britain, of different denominations, have united in their prayers, on a more catholic plan than what is proposed here. . . . Ought not we to imbibe their spirit, and imitate their example?"[59] Connecticut evangelicals carefully imitated British examples in the formation of their Bible and tract societies and modeled the *Connecticut Evangelical Magazine* after the *Evangelical Magazine* published in London.[60] Similarly, the *New York Missionary Magazine*, which began publication in 1800, closely resembled the *Edinburgh Missionary Magazine*.

Thus, during the 1790s the political and social upheaval caused by the French Revolution and the rise of a broadly cooperative evangelical movement in Britain significantly affected the initiatives of New York's evangelical Protestants. By the turn of the century, the decline of the Roman Catholic hold on France, together with the nascent missionary spirit, seemed to indicate that some of the hopes they drew from scriptural prophecy were about to be fulfilled. These hopes included the extermination of popish superstition, the universal spread of the gospel, and possibly the restoration of the Jews to the Holy Land.[61] Persuaded therefore that the millennium could not be far away, many American evangelicals became firm postmillennialists, a viewpoint that reinforced their determination to act and provided a clearer vision of a prospective worldwide Christian union.[62]

The further development of evangelical appreciation for religious diversity is the third and final factor that contributed to the wave of cooperative activity in the late 1700s.

Because of their long experience with pluralism, New Yorkers shared a broader consensus on its meaning and value than most other Americans. Both religious and irreligious persons viewed diversity as politically, socially, intellectually, and spiritually beneficial. Protestant, Catholic, and Jew alike endorsed it as the cornerstone of the state's religious order. A large majority within the state's overwhelmingly dominant Protestant community had come to see their own internal pluralism as a biblically acceptable expression of the various parts of Christ's one body. And they had accepted the small Jewish and Catholic minorities as full partners in the state's liberties since neither posed a threat to Protestant hegemony. Despite these relatively advanced views, New York evangelicals in particular isolated two directions for further progress over the course of the 1790s: a more complete reconciliation of their denominational divisions with the scriptural mandate for Christian unity and a fuller recognition that in a pluralistic society the churches must assume moral and social responsibilities previously belonging to the state.

In June 1790 New England Congregationalist minister Samuel Austin preached to a New York City audience on "disinterested love." Austin proclaimed that benevolence and Christian charity should characterize all relationships among believers, as well as the church's relationship with the world.[63] His discourse was in fact one of many efforts in the last quarter of the eighteenth century to define how Christians were to treat one another.[64] William Linn published a more rigorous discussion in 1794. The New Testament, he wrote, revealed that Jesus and the apostles urged unity upon their followers. Modern Christians were, therefore, under a "solemn obligation" to seek it also. While the Bible indicated that union would grow amid variety rather than uniformity, no biblical basis existed to justify the argument that believers in different persuasions should remain separate in order to watch over and provoke one another to greater zeal and fidelity. Linn believed such a view failed to recognize that disunity was sin and that all advantages of diversity could be attained through unity. Furthermore, he insisted, Christians must testify visibly to their harmony through cooperative action.[65]

What was to be the basis for this active union? Linn answered, "the essential doctrines of religion." But he admitted that determining what these were and how they related to existing creeds was difficult. He defined the essentials as what a person needed to believe and practice in order to be saved.[66] Christianity rested fundamentally on the affirmation that Jesus was God's son and humanity's messiah. From this tenet flowed the doctrines which Linn believed could fix a ground for union, while not preventing individuals from holding what they thought right in matters of lesser importance. These doctrines were the innate sinfulness of human beings, the gracious character of God's gift of salvation, the substitutionary atonement of Christ, the sanctifying power of the Holy Spirit, individual acceptance of Christ as personal savior, and holy obedience to his commands. Calvinist and Arminian evangelicals differed in their interpretations of some of these doctrines, but they both affirmed all of them. Thus, in Linn's mind, Christians of various persuasions, committed to this common core of beliefs, could unite to perform God's work without sacrificing denominational distinctions or their own liberty of conscience.[67]

In outlining these specific precepts, Linn sought to draw the bounds of Christian union and hoped to be as inclusive as possible. But Linn, writing at a time and from a city in which religious challenges to historic orthodoxy were on the rise, was careful to make it clear that certain doctrines could not be surrendered or altered without overturning the Christian religion. Rather than attacking any local person or group, however, he chose to condemn British liberal Gilbert Wakefield's attack on Tom Paine as more pernicious to Christianity than Paine's book *The Age of Reason*.[68] Linn would likely have agreed with Francis Asbury's judgment that real schism occurred when true Christians separated from one another, not when they stood apart from hypocrites and nominal professors.[69] In addition, Linn contended that the abuse rather than the use of creeds was to be condemned. Every voluntary religious society, he wrote, whether an individual congregation or a denominational or interdenominational organization, had the "undoubted right to demand of its members an explicit declaration of faith." Those who refused to comply could not "with reason complain of any imposition, being at liberty to withdraw and connect themselves elsewhere."[70]

Linn found most of these ideas already at work in the recently established New York Society for Promoting Christian Knowledge and Piety.[71] Founded in 1794 to distribute Bibles and tracts to the poor, to assist missionaries in the state, and to encourage the creation of schools on the frontier, the society began with sixty-four members (including fourteen ministers) from seven denominations: Presbyterian, Lutheran, Episcopalian, Dutch Reformed, Moravian, Methodist, and Associate Reformed. Its constitution forbade the distribution of any books of a "controversial nature" or any that breathed the "spirit of party," and welcomed to membership persons of all Protestant communions. While the constitution contained no formal doctrinal statement, it indicated that the society's efforts were intended to inculcate biblical principles. These included five of the doctrines Linn had delineated (the exception was personal acceptance of Christ as Savior) plus the doctrine of the Trinity, the efficacy of the sacraments, and the certainty of a future state of eternal happiness or misery.[72] As one of its first acts, the society initiated contact with both denominational and interdenominational tract societies in Europe and America. The officers expressed the hope that such correspondence would "remove prejudices" and "more closely unite those of different denominations" who were "of one mind relative to the leading and saving doctrines of the Gospel."[73]

A host of other formal and informal attempts were made in New York to identify the theological basis upon which to build active Christian harmony. David Austin edited and printed four volumes of previously unpublished sermons of evangelical ministers from Presbyterian, Congregational, Episcopal, and Dutch Reformed churches under the title *The American Preacher*. He wished thus to unite "the several most important religious denominations in one work," he wrote, and to open "the door for the more extensive exercise of CHRISTIAN CHARITY . . . upon principles acknowledged and understood."[74] One paragraph in John Livingston's sermon "Growth in Grace" encapsulated well the thrust of evangelical religion in these volumes:

> As to you who profess the religion of Christ, and receive the Bible as the standard of your faith and practice . . . will mere orthodoxy in doctrines, will regularity in your conduct, or punctuality in worship, render you truly religious? Will these produce pardon for your sins, or make you meet for glory? Alas! in all these you may abound, and yet have no love to God, or sincere submission to the Lord Jesus. To constitute vital piety, and make you a real disciple of the Redeemer, you must obtain a new heart, and by faith become united to Christ.[75]

Methodists showed their interest in Protestant cooperation by publishing the *Experienced Christian's Magazine* and the *Methodist Magazine*. The former journal, edited by William Phoebus, related the testimonies of dying Christians of various persuasions to show that all believers shared equally in God's faithfulness. As one response to the editor put it, "Religion in theory and form, has been more or less different in all denominations, in all ages; but the religion of the heart has been the same in every age, and denomination of orthodox Christians."[76] In contrast to an earlier Methodist periodical, the *Arminian Magazine,* whose purpose had been to present Arminian theological viewpoints to counter America's long tradition of Calvinism, the *Methodist Magazine* sought to disseminate religious knowledge beneficial to Christians of all denominations. To that end, the lead article in the initial issue was John Wesley's essay "The Character of a Methodist," in which he boldly declared to all believers: "For opinions, or terms, let us not destroy the work of God. Dost thou love and fear God? It is enough. I give thee the right hand of fellowship."[77]

Several events in the Baptist congregation in Stanford (Dutchess County) during the 1790s illustrate how one local group confronted the issue of Christian unity. At its annual meeting in October 1791, the congregation voted not to object if a member's home was used for meetings by another denomination. Later in the decade, however, the fellowship rebuked several members for partaking of the Lord's Supper in a Methodist church.[78] Then in 1799 it had to decide whether to admit as members a group of laymen led by Robert Scott who frankly admitted that some of their Wesleyan ideas made it impossible for them to subscribe to every article of the church's covenant.[79] A church council composed of area Baptist ministers convened in September and momentously recommended that although they disagreed with Scott's belief in the possibilities of man's either falling from grace or attaining a state of sinless perfection, since "the Church had thus far admitted them and . . . the Candidates agreed with the Baptist Church in Fundamental points and that those that they Differed in were Som wat Disputable points with some . . . this Church shoul[d] Receive them. . . ."[80] This remarkable action demonstrated how much diversity Stanford Baptists were willing to tolerate within one congregation.

Far more explicit declarations of the grounds for Christian union appeared in the constitutions of the state's two interdenominational mission agencies. The confession of faith required for membership in both the New York and the Northern Missionary societies were virtually identical except for the inclusion in the latter of an article on the importance of Sabbath observance. Both statements closely resembled the confessions laid out earlier by Linn and by the Society for Promoting Christian Knowledge and Piety. They affirmed the Trinity, original sin, Christ's incarnation and atonement, the Holy Spirit's sanctifying power, the importance of the sacraments, and the necessity of a holy life. Their stronger language on total depravity and imputed righteousness, however, helped limit their membership to believers from Reformed communions—Presbyterian, Dutch Reformed, Associate Reformed, and Baptist.[81]

This sampling of attempts to formulate a theological basis for Protestant union demonstrates the wide range of contexts in which such discussions took place as well as the variety of their conclusions. William Linn's statement seems, then, to have both reflected and contributed to a pervasive trend. New York's ministers and lay leaders were realizing that diversity was beneficial and division was not, and that the respect of evangelicals for denominational differences still left a great deal of room for them to unite around shared experiences and doctrines. That Christians from a wide variety of Protestant traditions found it possible to participate in joint endeavors during the 1790s affirms the emergence by 1800 of an informal coalition that was both respectful of differences and thoroughly evangelical. To be sure, there were nonevangelical Episcopalians, Dutch Reformed, Lutherans, and Quakers who took part in or at least sympathized with these cooperative efforts. But their role was overshadowed by the evangelical leadership and opposed by other Orthodox Protestants who were leery of associating across denominational lines.

At the same time they were discovering these foundations for Christian unity, the state's evangelical leaders began to recognize more fully the long-term implications of religious disestablishment. Under most religious establishments, the civil magistrates had performed certain functions intended to enhance the people's spiritual and moral character. In Connecticut, for instance, the colonial government had originally required that every new town have an orthodox church and every home own a Bible, and had legislated against any seeming infringement of religious values. As church and state gradually separated there, the government abandoned these responsibilities, and evangelicals created voluntary societies to shoulder them.[82] In New York, however, though the Church of England had been established in four counties, the colonial government had done very little to encourage religion beyond promoting Anglican interests. When the 1777 constitution formally dissolved the civil establishment, therefore, the state government had neither a heritage of active support for religion nor clear guidelines on what its future role should be.

Evangelicals argued at the time of the adoption of the new constitution and throughout the next two decades that the state retained the duty to assist religion, but now must do so without discrimination. Defining specific ways the state could do that posed a problem for both churchmen and the government. Before 1790, the reluctance of New York's politicians to confront this problem and the failure of churchgoers to press them to do so allowed the legislature for the most part to ignore the issue. Only gradually did evangelicals realize that the state would not discover on its own how it could help sustain religion and morality. In the late 1790s, they determined to take the initiative in persuading the government to act.

At that point, they moved in two directions to accomplish this goal. First, they urged Christians to lobby for legislation designed to encourage a virtuous society. For example, the Washington Presbytery of the Associate Reformed Church in 1796 petitioned New York's State Legislature for a revision and extension of the existing Sabbath laws. However, the New York Presbytery of the same communion soon pointed out the limitations of this method. While agreeing with the petition's intent, the Presbytery declared that it was not the "proper season" for bringing the subject to the legislature. The original Sabbath laws had been approved only over great opposition several years earlier. Political and social developments since then had produced an even less favorable climate now:

> At present Infidelity is the fashion & infidels are men of consequence. Too many of them fill places of public responsibility; the Holy Sabbath reckons implacable enemies among Judges, Legislators, interpretors of the law and executive officers. The probability, therefore in our judgment is that if the law for the suppression of immoralities on the Sabbath should be now submitted to revision, instead of being improved, it would be abolished altogether. . . .

They argued further that since much of the problem lay in the "extreme backwardness & negligence of magistrates in enforcing the requisitions & exacting the penalties" of the present law, amending it would do little good.[83]

The state's reluctance to perform its duties to encourage religion and virtue prompted the Presbyterian Synod of New York and New Jersey to recommend in 1798 an alternative approach: local congregations should form voluntary committees or societies to help civil magistrates suppress vice and immorality.[84] If the state was going to shirk its responsibilities, then the churches would have to fill the void.[85] All three of the synod's New York presbyteries quickly adopted the recommendation, and within six months one reported that most of its congregations had established these committees.[86] Before 1800, then, the synod had recognized that in practice disestablishment meant the churches must assume the primary role as the moral guardian of society. By such reasoning, New York's evangelicals, who had never enjoyed active government support as those in New England had, reached the same conclusions as their Connecticut brethren: Christians acting through voluntary and perhaps interdenominational religious associations must take responsibility to promote moral reformation and social justice in a pluralistic society, regardless of what the state did or did not do.

Thus both the conviction that they must give the scriptural mandate for Christian union more serious attention and the realization that the churches must play an increasing role in promoting a righteous society deepened evangelical understanding of the implications of religious diversity and pushed the evangelicals toward interdenominational efforts. These new perceptions accompanied the renewal of moral will that flowed from the increasingly pervasive spiritual fervor. The model for action and the millennialist idealism Englishmen provided, and to a lesser extent the fear of infidelity that some ministers aroused, catalyzed perception and motivation as well. These factors explain why the 1790s witnessed an unprecedented wave of cooperative evangelistic enterprise among New York's Protestants.

Numerous other instances of Protestant interaction and cooperation fit well into the explanation I have set forth and reveal that Christian unity took a variety of forms in the late eighteenth century.[87] After a lapse of several years, the representatives of the Dutch Reformed, Presbyterian, and Associate Reformed Churches began meeting again in periodic conventions in the mid 1790s.[88] The Dutch Reformed also started corresponding with the German Reformed Church in Pennsylvania, and the Presbyterians progressed toward the Plan of Union they sealed with the New England Congregationalists in 1801.[89] Lutherans and Episcopalians discussed the possibility of formal merger, and prominent members in the Methodist and Episcopal Churches proposed a restoration of their original union.[90] Ministers from many religious bodies endorsed and participated in a national concert of prayer and jointly sponsored the publication of such books as William Linn's *Sermons* and Englishman John Brown's *Introduction to the Right Understanding of the Oracles of God.*[91] Theological dialogue was conducted more congenially than in the past, as evidenced by the warm but charitable debate between nonevangelical Episcopal rector Benjamin Moore and William Linn on the doctrine of baptismal regeneration.[92] The diaries and memoirs of such ministers as John Barent Johnson, John Rodgers, John Stanford, and John Livingston reveal levels of interaction and friendship with pastors and laymen of other communions that few clergymen had enjoyed at the close of the War for Independence.[93]

Evangelical Protestants in New York thus exhibited a substantial degree of ecumenicity in the last decade of the eighteenth century. Their efforts certainly demonstrate that if the Second Great Awakening is to be considered as an organizing movement, this state's evangelicals were its vanguard, both in forming new congregations and creating voluntary societies to meet specific needs. The Baptists and Dutch Reformed alone established between them over one hundred new congregations in the decade. And leading ministers and laypersons in all denominations eagerly joined others in supporting missionaries, distributing Bibles and tracts, organizing schools, contributing to religious periodicals, publishing evangelical books, conducting prayer meetings, and corresponding with European believers.

This flowering of evangelical activity was deeply rooted in the religious experience of the previous half century. Religious diversity was a central factor shaping this experience. Prior to the Revolution, the state's religious bodies were absorbed in the tasks of adjusting organizationally, theologically, and politically to the realities of their heterogeneous environment. From these efforts to cope with pluralism emerged a pervasive commitment to ecclesiastical self-suffciency, evangelical theology, and religious equality. This commitment first weathered a stormy war for independence and then conditioned a substantial reconstruction and expansion program. Far from lapsing into idleness or indifference in the postwar period, most communions experienced significant institutional growth and displayed strong spiritual interest. In the process, they came more clearly to see how best to survive in a religious and political milieu they realized would be permanently pluralistic. When they finally concluded that Scripture demanded that their diversity be defined as variety within Christian union, New York's evangelical groups closed ranks and embraced the vision of establishing God's kingdom on earth without the aid of any temporal power. By 1800, therefore, a Protestant evangelical religious order in New York was based squarely on equality for all groups. It was sustained by a spiritual movement and a set of shared doctrines that would become characteristic of much of Protestant America in the nineteenth century, bringing widespread moral reformation, social change, and spiritual regeneration.

CONCLUSION

By the beginning of the nineteenth century, New York was no longer set apart by its religious diversity. Over the course of the previous hundred years, and particularly since the Revolution, all areas of the new republic had become religiously pluralistic. New Yorkers nevertheless could take a certain pride in the fact that what had only recently become commonplace in the nation as a whole had long been the case in most of their communities. Nineteenth-century state residents thus inherited from their forebears a rich tradition of experience with plural religion.

That tradition, carried on in the next half century by the likes of Joseph Smith and William Miller, included the conviction that self-sufficiency was a prerequisite for ecclesiastical survival in the New World. Early in the eighteenth century, certain churchmen had begun to realize the practical difficulties of relying on mother churches three thousand miles away for ministers and mission funds. Both concern over the problem and efforts to find a solution were intensified by having to compete in a diverse environment. The presence of other religious communions eager to absorb the members of any floundering church lent an urgency to the situation that otherwise might have been absent. Hence, those who favored such measures as American trained and ordained ministers and English worship services spoke in terms of life and death not only for single congregations but for whole denominations. Whether continued reliance on Europe would have had such a deleterious effect cannot be known; what is certain is that the advocates of ecclesiastical home rule won out as definitively in the Revolutionary era as their political counterparts. That they did says as much about the shaping influence of their pluralistic milieu as it does about the appeal of independence.

The pressures of pluralism were felt individually as well as corporately during the eighteenth century. Faced with increasing religious options and competing claims to "orthodoxy," colonists had the luxury as well as the burden of personally choosing which spiritual food, if any, to swallow.

Some reveled in this freedom, others despaired. Whatever the reaction, the choice itself became less monumental after mid-century with the spread of evangelical religion on the one hand and liberal rationalism on the other. For both these understandings of the Christian faith served to de-emphasize denominational distinctions and to draw the spiritual dividing line elsewhere. In the process, they broke down much of the theological hostility to the mere fact of institutional diversity and even encouraged positive assessments of Protestant pluralism's religious and social consequences.

As a result, among the first fruits of evangelical and liberal gains in New York was a growing commitment to the principle of religious equality. While European traditionalists remained attached to the notion of church establishment, other provincials now claimed that all groups in a pluralistic setting should be entitled to the same privileges. In their minds, that could only be accomplished through a formal separation of church and state. When the new state's constitutional framers took this step in 1777, it marked the triumph of a religious order predicated upon something more than a temporary coalition of pietists and rationalists aiming to ensure their own religious liberties; rather, it sprang largely from the similar conclusions each group had reached regarding diversity's religious and political meaning.

But how well did these eighteenth-century Protestants understand pluralism? Opting for complete religious liberty meant that New York, even more than other states, opened its doors wide to the possibilities of an almost unlimited variety of religious beliefs and unbeliefs on the one hand and the unhampered growth of particular non-Protestant groups on the other. Since both of these possibilities did, in fact, materialize in the nineteenth and twentieth centuries, profoundly reducing the Protestant majority's hold over American culture (and perhaps especially in New York), it is tempting to conclude that Protestant Christians in the Revolutionary era had not thought very much or very hard about pluralism. That is the conclusion Sidney Mead reached regarding the vast preponderance of American religionists in the 1780s. Yet the evidence in New York seems to warrant another interpretation. Too many provincials there both before and after independence were struggling to understand religious diversity to suggest that the Enlightenment-influenced rationalists were the only ones wrestling with this issue. Even more important, too many of them believed they understood clearly the long-term implications of pluralism. Perfect freedom of conscience and an open exchange of ideas would inevitably point up the truth of Protestant Christianity, as well as help combat political and ecclesiastical tyranny. Far from boding ill for their cause, then, religious liberty, and the pluralism it allowed for, promised to aid the spread of the gospel and quicken the millennium's advent. While from a late twentieth-century vantage point these presumptions seem overly optimistic at best and hopelessly delusive at worst, they were grounded in concrete reality: the overwhelming religious dominance, in all ways, of Protestantism and the most progressive thinking of the day, the Enlightenment's idea of truth triumphing in the marketplace of ideas. Who is to say that our own "enlightened" notions about the future will seem any less fanciful to our descendants two hundred years hence?

Were New York's Protestants unique in their views of pluralism's promise? For a short time in the late eighteenth century, I believe they were. It was only natural that their longer experience with diversity should bring them to more "advanced" opinions than those held by their counterparts in New England or the South. They had had to wrestle with the consequences of plural religion throughout the colony's history. That had meant finding ways to reconcile their ecclesiastical organization, theology, and relations to the state with the fact of multiple religious groups. By the post-Revolutionary era, New Yorkers had largely accomplished these tasks and were therefore confident that their embrace of religious pluralism was not only well-founded but conducive to the religious and political success of the republic. While this confidence was shared by many Americans in states with long traditions of religious diversity (Pennsylvania, New Jersey, Rhode Island), it was foreign to large numbers of religionists in most other states, so that religious establishments of one type or another and limitations on religious liberty remained common at the state level well into the nineteenth century. And unfortunately, the confidence of Protestant New Yorkers themselves failed to hold up in the mid-1800s in the face of heavy Catholic immigration to the state. What these Protestants had been able to affirm about pluralism in theory in the 1790s when their overwhelming dominance seemed unshakable became much more difficult to believe or defend fifty years later when practical reality threatened their hegemony. The religious struggles and failures of the nineteenth century, however, should not blind us to the convictions and attitudes of those who went before.

On the other hand, we must be careful not to ascribe twentieth-century notions about pluralism to these eighteenth-century New York minds. In particular, the philosophical relativism that has accompanied the growth of pluralism in this century would have been anathema to the vast preponderance of provincials. The evangelical Protestant majority accepted denominational diversity, complete religious liberty, and religious disestablishment. But none of these principles involved for them an acceptance or an acknowledgment of the validity of contrasting religious beliefs, whether Catholic, Jewish, deist, or other. Instead, this majority remained solidly convinced that it alone held the truth and all other claims to the contrary were pernicious falsehoods. In this respect, evangelicals were not unique, for proponents of other faiths were equally absolutist in their perspective.

To modern ears, such views sound extremely exclusivist. Yet it must be remembered that to be able to speak in 1800 of an evangelical Protestant majority as a collective entity united in attitude and (occasionally) in action was itself a relatively new phenomenon that constituted a move away from exclusivism. Before the evangelical surge at mid-century, little sense of a mutual partnership in the body of Christ had emerged among the colony's various Protestant communions. Thereafter, a growing ecumenical spirit gradually evolved, reaching fruition in the wave of interdenominational endeavors begun in the 1790s. While the limits of this ecumenism were drawn rather tightly along evangelical lines, it nonetheless marked a substantial shift away from the sectarian exclusivism of earlier days. That sectarianism reappeared in New York in various forms during the nineteenth century only indicates that while circumstances change, human nature does not.

The nineteenth century saw not only the reemergence of a vital Roman Catholic community in New York but also the influx of a large Jewish population. Both served to change the qualitative and quantitative character of pluralism in the state. This trend toward greater diversity accelerated after 1900 as New York became home for members of virtually every religious and ethnic minority. Today's radical pluralism would no doubt come as a shock even to those seventeenth- and eighteenth-century New Yorkers accustomed to rubbing shoulders with neighbors of different backgrounds and beliefs. Still, despite these changes, one cannot help but sense that colonial New Yorkers lived in a world somewhat closer to our own than did their counterparts in Massachusetts or Virginia. Their experience with plural religion forced them to confront questions of freedom, tolerance, equality, and truth in ways that set them apart in their own day and presaged modern efforts to resolve the tensions inherent in a pluralistic milieu.

NOTES

Preface

1. Andrew Burnaby, *Travels Through the Middle Settlements in North America in the Years 1759 and 1760*, 2d ed. (London: T. Payne, 1775), 113.

2. Robert Kelley, *The Cultural Pattern in American Politics* (New York: Alfred A. Knopf, 1979); Henry F. May, *The Enlightenment in America* (New York: Oxford University Press, 1976).

3. Stephanie G. Wolf, *Urban Village: Population, Community, and Family Structure in Germantown, Pennsylvania, 1683–1800* (Princeton, N.J.: Princeton University Press, 1976).

4. Milton M. Klein, *Politics of Diversity: Essays in the History of Colonial New York* (Port Washington, N.Y.: Kennikat Press, 1974); Patricia U. Bonomi, *A Factious People: Politics and Society in Colonial New York* (New York: Columbia University Press, 1971); Alice P. Kenney, *Stubborn for Liberty: The Dutch in New York* (Syracuse, N.Y.: Syracuse University Press, 1975); Ronald W. Howard, "Education and Ethnicity in Colonial New York, 1664–1763: A Study in the Transmission of Culture in Early America" (Ph.D. diss., University of Tennessee, 1978); Joyce D. Goodfriend, " 'Too Great a Mixture of Nations': The Development of New York City Society in the Seventeenth Century" (Ph.D. diss., University of California, Los Angeles, 1975).

5. Milton M. Klein, "New York in the American Colonies: A New Look," *New York History* 53 (1972): 132–56.

6. Michael Zuckerman, Introduction, in *Friends and Neighbors: Group Life in America's First Plural Society,* ed. Michael Zuckerman (Philadelphia: Temple University Press, 1982), 13. The essays in this volume add to our understanding of the influence of cultural pluralism on colonial life, esp. familial and economic patterns in local communities.

7. John W. Pratt, *Religion, Politics, and Diversity: The Church-State Theme in New York History* (Ithaca, N.Y.: Cornell University Press, 1967), 64.

8. Another reason for studying New York is that most of the recent scholarship discussing cultural pluralism and religion has focused on Pennsylvania. Among many works, see those by Zuckerman and Wolf cited above, along with Martin E. Lodge, "The Crisis of the Churches in the Middle Colonies, 1720–1750," *Pennsylvania Magazine of History and Biography* 95 (1971): 195–220; Jon Butler, "A Spiritual Tower of Babel: Shifting Structures of Religious Diversity in Colonial Pennsylvania, 1680–1760," paper presented to the Newberry Library Early American history seminar, January 1983; Patricia U. Bonomi, " 'Watchful against the Sects': Religious Renewal in Pennsylvania's German Congregations, 1720–1750," paper presented to the Organization of American Historians, April 1983; and the dissertations done at the University of Pennsylvania between 1976 and 1979 by Barry Levy, Deborah Mathias Gough, and Laura Becker.

9. Sidney Mead, *The Lively Experiment* (New York: Harper & Row, 1963), esp. chaps. 2 through 4; Sidney Mead, "The Fact of Pluralism and the Persistence of Sectarianism," in *The Religion of the Republic,* ed. Elwyn Smith (Philadelphia: Fortress Press, 1971), 247–66; Sidney Mead, "Christendom, Enlightenment, and the Revolution," in *Religion and the American Revolution.* ed. Jerald C. Brauer (Philadelphia: Fortress Press, 1976), 29–54.

Introduction

1. George L. Smith, *Religion and Trade in New Netherland* (Ithaca, N.Y.: Cornell University Press, 1973). An older work stressing religious persecution in New Netherland is Frederick J. Zwierlein, *Religion in New Netherland, 1623–1664* (Rochester, N.Y.: John P. Smith, 1910).

2. Howard, "Education and Ethnicity in Colonial New York," 72.

3. Michael Kammen, *Colonial New York: A History* (New York: Charles Scribner's Sons, 1975), 118–19. Other works treating New York's religious and ethnic diversity between 1664 and 1700 include Thomas Archdeacon, *New York City, 1664–1710: Conquest and Change* (Ithaca, N.Y.: Cornell University Press, 1976); T. F. O'Connor, "Religious Toleration in New York, 1664–1700," *New York History* 17 (1936): 391–410; and Goodfriend, "'Too Great a Mixture of Nations'."

4. To compare New York's religious diversity with Philadelphia's, see Carl Bridenbaugh and Jessica Bridenbaugh, *Rebels and Gentlemen: Philadelphia in the Age of Franklin* (New York: Oxford University Press, 1965), 17–22.

5. J. Hector St. John de Crèvecoeur, *Letters from an American Farmer* (London: J.M. Dent & Sons, 1926), 49–51.

6. The figures are derived principally from Edwin S. Gaustad, *Historical Atlas of Religion in America*, rev. ed. (New York: Harper & Row, 1976), 1–28, 175; Peter Vandenberge, *Historical Directory of the Reformed Church in America 1628–1978* (Grand Rapids, Mich.: Wm. B. Eerdmans, 1978), 368–70; Robert H. Nichols, *Presbyterianism in New York State* (Philadelphia: Westminster Press, 1963), frontispiece; Harry J. Kreider, *Lutheranism in Colonial New York* (New York: Edwards Brothers, Inc., 1942), 141–47; Rufus M. Jones, *The Quakers in the American Colonies* (London: Macmillan and Co., Ltd., 1923), 250–51; Lester J. Cappon et al., eds., *The Atlas of Early American History: The Revolutionary Era, 1760–1790* (Princeton, N.J.: Princeton University Press, 1976); and Frederick L. Weis, *The Colonial Clergy of the Middle Colonies* (Worcester, Mass.: American Antiquarian Society, 1957).

7. See Jon Butler, "Magic, Astrology, and the Early American Religious Heritage, 1600–1760," *American Historical Review* 84 (1979): 317–46.

8. Douglas Greenberg, "The Middle Colonies in Recent American Historiography," *William and Mary Quarterly* 3d. Ser., 36 (1979): 396–427, identifies many of the distinctive characteristics of each middle colony.

9. While estimates vary, it is likely that Anglicanism claimed 5 to 10 percent of New York's population between 1720 and 1775.

One. "A Spirit of Independence"

1. Rev. Michael Christian Knoll to the Lutheran Consistory at Rothenberg on the Tauber, Germany, Dec. 21, 1749, in *Protocol of the Lutheran Church in New York City, 1702–1750*, trans. Simon Hart and Harry J. Kreider (New York: United Lutheran Synod of New York and New England, 1958), 463–67.

2. Jacob R. Marcus, *Early American Jewry: The Jews of New York, New England, and Canada 1649–1794*, 2 vols. (Philadelphia: The Jewish Publication Society of America, 1951–53), 1: 83; Frank Baker, "Early American Methodism: A Key Document," *Methodist History* 2 (1965): 3–15.

3. On how this was true of colonial congregations in general, see Timothy L. Smith, "Congregation, State, and Denomination: The Forming of the American Religious Structure," *William and Mary Quarterly* 3d. Ser., 25 (1968): 155–76.

4. Lodge, "Crisis of the Churches," 197–200.

5. Gerald F. De Jong, *The Dutch Reformed Church in the American Colonies* (Grand Rapids, Mich.: Wm. B. Eerdmans, 1978), 190; *Lutheran Church in New York and New Jersey 1722–1960: Lutheran Records in the Ministerial Archives of the Staatsarchiv, Hamburg, Germany*, trans. Simon Hart and Harry J. Kreider (New York: United

Lutheran Synod of New York and New England, 1962), 380–81, 390–93, 396–97; Kreider, *Lutheranism in New York*, 11–12; Deborah Mathias Gough, "The Roots of Episcopalian Authority Structures: The Church of England in Colonial Philadelphia," in Zuckerman, ed., *Friends and Neighbors*, 92–103, 108–09.

6. A.D. Gillette, ed., *Minutes of the Philadelphia Baptist Association from 1707 to 1807* (Philadelphia: American Baptist Publication Society, 1851), 28–30, 81–84; New York Yearly Meeting MS Minutes 1750, 1754, 1759, Haviland Records Room of the New York Yearly Meeting, New York City.

7. Quoted in Kreider, *Lutheranism in New York*, 22–23.

8. Mary Babcock, "Difficulties and Dangers of Pre-Revolutionary Ordinations," *Historical Magazine of the Protestant Episcopal Church* 12 (1943): 233.

9. J. Potter, "The Growth of Population in America, 1700–1860," in D.V. Glass and D.E.C. Eversley, eds., *Population in History: Essays in Historical Demography* (Chicago: Aldine Publishing Co., 1965), 638, 652–54.

10. Based on Weis, *Colonial Clergy of the Middle Colonies*, there were sixty to seventy ministers in New York in 1750. A general impression of the congregations they were responsible for may be gained from Weis and the following sources: "Names of the Ministers of the Dutch Reformed Churches in New York and New Jersey [1758]," in E.B. O'Callaghan, ed., *The Documentary History of the State of New York*, 4 vols. (Albany, N.Y.: Weed, Parsons & Co., 1850), 1: 625; "Records of the Coetus of the Low Dutch Reformed Preachers and Elders," in *The Acts and Proceedings of the General Synod of the Reformed Protestant Dutch Church in North America, 1771–1812* (New York: Board of Publication of the Reformed Protestant Dutch Church, 1859), vii–xci; Gillette, ed., *Minutes of the Philadelphia Baptist Association*, 28–50; and Guy S. Klett, ed., *Minutes of the Presbyterian Church in America 1706–1788* (Philadelphia: Presbyterian Historical Society, 1976), 275–95. Leonard Trinterud, *The Forming of an American Tradition: A Reexamination of Colonial Presbyterianism* (Philadelphia: Westminster Press, 1948), 71–72, discusses the problems of ministerial vacancy and itinerancy in rural areas.

11. Kreider, *Lutheranism in New York*, 33–48.

12. Martin E. Lodge, "The Great Awakening in the Middle Colonies" (Ph.D. diss., University of California, Berkeley, 1964), 8–70; id., "Crisis of the Churches," 195–210.

13. Lodge, "Crisis of the Churches," 198.

14. Kammen, *Colonial New York*, 216–19. Historian John B. Frantz, "The Awakening of Religion among the German Settlers in the Middle Colonies," *William and Mary Quarterly* 3d. Ser., 33 (1976): 266–72, shares this assessment.

15. Baker, "Early American Methodism," 14.

16. For population estimates, see Evarts B. Greene and Virginia D. Harrington, *American Population before the Federal Census of 1790* (New York: Columbia University Press, 1932), 89, 95–105.

17. This growth was concentrated in the Dutch Reformed, Presbyterian, and Lutheran communions, and may be noted in Kreider, *Lutheranism in New York*, 141–47; Vandenberge, *Historical Directory*, 368–69; and Nichols, *Presbyterianism in New York State*, frontispiece.

18. Introduction, in John P. Dern, ed., *The Albany Protocol: Wilhelm Christoph Berkenmeyer's Chronicle of Lutheran Affairs in New York Colony, 1731–1750*, trans. Simon Hart and Sibrandina Geertruid Hart-Tuneman (Ann Arbor, Mich.: By the Editor, 1971), xliv–xlv; Kreider, *Lutheranism in New York*, 43–48.

19. About a third of this growth took place among the Dutch Reformed, as they organized twenty-eight new congregations. Vandenberge, *Historical Directory*, 369.

20. Rev. Johannes Hartwig [John Hartwick] to the Rev. Dr. Friedrich Wagner, Manor of Livingston, Albany County, N.Y., Feb. 19, 1754, in *Lutheran Church: Records in Hamburg*, 371.

21. Lodge, "Crisis of the Churches," 201. These debates, in one form or another, affected New York's major communions—Lutheran, Reformed, Presbyterian, Anglican—as well as some of its smaller bodies. The debate involved persons from various colonies, since important denominational issues were at stake. My discussion focuses on New York's contributors to these debates and interprets their participation in light of their colony's religious circumstances.

22. I have chosen the terms *traditionalist* and *accommodationist* because they reflect the basic theme of each side. The terms *assimilationist* and *Americanizing* connote a cultural process that was in a number of ways distinct from the religious developments discussed here.

23. De Jong, *Dutch Reformed Church in Colonies,* 106; John Beardslee III, "The Reformed Church and the American Revolution," in James W. Van Hoeven, ed., *Piety and Patriotism: Bicentennial Studies of the Reformed Church in America, 1776–1976* (Grand Rapids, Mich.: Wm. B. Eerdmans, 1976), 19.

24. De Jong, *Dutch Reformed Church in Colonies,* 106. One indication of these trends was that between 1772 and 1775 the newly formed General Synod licensed six new ministers, all born and trained in America. See *Acts and Proceedings of the General Synod,* 5–65.

25. Of the sixteen ministers known to have tutored others in the colonies, twelve were clearly of the Frelinghuysen wing, and of the twenty-five native ministers active in 1775, all but perhaps three had studied under either a Dutch Reformed or Presbyterian evangelical pastor. These figures are derived from De Jong, *Dutch Reformed Church in Colonies,* 111, and biographical information in Edwin T. Corwin, *A Manual of the Reformed Protestant Dutch Church in North America,* 3d and 4th eds. (New York: Reformed Protestant Dutch Church, 1879, 1902); William Sprague, *Annals of the American Pulpit,* 9 vols. (New York: Robert Carter & Bros., 1869), vol. 9; and Vandenberge, *Historical Directory.*

26. Hugh Hastings and E.T. Corwin, eds., *Ecclesiastical Records of the State of New York* [hereinafter cited as *ERNY*], 7 vols. (Albany: J.E. Lyon Co., 1901–6), 5: 3553–54, lists Coetus members; for their educational experiences, see biographical information in Corwin, *Manual of Dutch Reformed Church;* Sprague, *American Pulpit,* vol. 9; and Vandenberge, *Historical Directory.* Conferentie members are listed in *ERNY* 6: 3927–30; biographical information is provided by De Jong, *Dutch Reformed Church in Colonies,* 203; Corwin, *Manual of Dutch Reformed Church;* Sprague, *American Pulpit,* vol. 9; and Vandenberge, *Historical Directory.*

27. Johannis J. Mol, "Theology and Americanization: The Effects of Pietism and Orthodoxy on Adjustment to a New Culture" (Ph.D. diss., Columbia University, 1960).

28. Elizabeth Nybakken, "New Light on the Old Side: Irish Influences on Colonial Presbyterianism," *Journal of American History* 68 (1982): 817.

29. Frederick V. Mills, Sr., *Bishops by Ballot: An Eighteenth-Century Ecclesiastical Revolution* (New York: Oxford University Press, 1978), 37–53, 137.

30. Rev. John Frelinghuysen to the Rev. Classis of Amsterdam, Apr. 4, 1753, *ERNY,* 5: 3351–54.

31. *The Records in the Lutheran Church at Amsterdam, Holland, relating to Lutheranism in Colonial New York,* trans. Arnold J.F. Van Laer (New York: The United Lutheran Synod of New York, 1942), 457–60. For the general point, see Theodore G. Tappert, "The Influence of Pietism in Colonial American Lutheranism," in F. Ernest Stoeffler, ed., *Continental Pietism and Early American Christianity* (Grand Rapids, Mich.: Wm. B. Eerdmans, 1976), 14.

32. John A.F. Maynard, *The Huguenot Church of New York: A History of the Church of Saint-Esprit* (New York: By the Church, 1938), 189, 197.

33. Baker, "Early American Methodism," 14; Samuel Johnson to Dr. Burton, Nov. 10, 1766, in Herbert Schneider and Carol Schneider, eds., *Samuel Johnson,*

President of King's College, His Career and Writings, 4 vols. (New York: Columbia University Press, 1929), 1:276–77.

34. John Gano, *Biographical Memoirs of the late Rev. John Gano* (New York: Southwick & Hardcastle, 1806), 88–89.

35. *ERNY,* 4: 3053, 3087; 5: 3119, 3148–49, 3157–60, 3177–81.

36. Introduction in Dern, ed., *Albany Protocol,* xliv; *Lutheran Church Records in Hamburg,* 394.

37. Klett, ed., *Minutes of the Presbyterian Church,* 516–20, 530. Also see Trinterud, *Forming of an American Tradition,* 164. For the attitude of one New York Presbyterian minister to the influx of heterodox preachers from Europe see John Rodgers to _____, Apr. 30, 1773, John Rodgers MSS, Presbyterian Historical Society, Philadelphia.

38. Henry M. Muhlenberg, *The Journals of Henry Melchior Muhlenberg,* trans. Theodore G. Tappert and John W. Doberstein, 3 vols. (Philadelphia: Evangelical Lutheran Ministerium of Pennsylvania and Muhlenberg Press, 1942–1958), 2: 290.

39. *Lutheran Church: Records in Hamburg,* 371. Another source of discouragement for Hartwick was his running feud with fellow Lutheran pastor William Berkenmeyer. Ironically, both men had traditionalist sympathies concerning the colonial-European relationship. In this case, Hartwick went against the typical Pietist pattern.

40. Schneider and Schneider, eds., *Samuel Johnson,* 3: 248–49.

41. *Protocol of Lutheran Church,* 360, 421–22; Jon Butler, *Huguenots in America: A Refugee People in New World Society* (Cambridge, Mass.: Harvard University Press, 1983), 189–96.

42. Alexander Wall, "The Controversy in the Dutch Church in New York concerning Preaching in English, 1754–1768," *New-York Historical Society Quarterly Bulletin,* 12 (1928): 39–58. Cf. *ERNY,* 6: 3826–27, 3853–56, 3898–99, 4008–9, 4071–73; O'Callaghan, ed., *Documentary History of New York,* 3: 510–21. Many of the original manuscripts relating to this debate are in the New York Historical Society Manuscript Division, New York City.

43. *ERNY,* 6: 3853–56.

44. John H. Livingston to _____, June 26, 1772, Emmett Collection, New York Public Library Manuscript Room, New York City.

45. *ERNY,* 5: 3459.

46. In some congregations American-born ministers were preferred for their multilingual abilities, which allowed them to communicate with both younger and older members of the church.

47. Lodge, "Crisis of the Churches," 208.

48. Klett, ed., *Minutes of the Presbyterian Church,* 344.

49. Muhlenberg, *Journals,* 1: 360, 363; Lodge, "Crisis of the Churches," 209.

50. Harvey L. Nelson, "A Critical Study of Henry Melchior Muhlenberg's Means of Maintaining His Lutheranism" (Ph.D. diss., Drew University, 1980), 90, 112, 116–18.

51. Introduction, in Dern, ed., *Albany Protocol,* xlv.

52. Smith, "Congregation, State, and Denomination," 174.

53. This pastor, Abraham Keteltas, had ministered in Presbyterian and Dutch Reformed congregations; Maynard, *Huguenot Church of New York,* 180–88, 299–300. On Keteltas, see Franklin B. Dexter, *Biographical Sketches of the Graduates of Yale College,* 6 vols. (New York: Henry Holt & Co., 1896), 2: 289–91.

54. Francis Asbury, *The Journal and Letters of Francis Asbury,* ed. Elmer T. Clark, 3 vols. (London: Epworth Press, 1958), 1: 10, 41–42, 82–85, 122; John Wesley, *The Letters of the Rev. John Wesley, A.M.,* ed. John Telford, 8 vols. (London: Epworth Press, 1931), 5: 231–32.

55. Coetus to Amsterdam Classis, Oct. 4, 1757, *ERNY,* 5: 3708–10.

56. Harry E. Stocker, *A History of the Moravian Church in New York City* (New York: By the Author, 1922), 111.

57. Gillette, ed., *Minutes of the Philadelphia Baptist Association,* 64–154; Klett, ed., *Minutes of the Presbyterian Church,* 275–525. The Presbyterian Old Side had certainly been influential in creating these denominational structures and, on this issue and others, many members of the Old Side held views more akin to the accommodationist position than to the traditionalist one. Nybakken, "New Light on the Old Side," 816–32.

58. Klett, ed., *Minutes of the Presbyterian Church,* 1–50.

59. Nybakken, "New Light on the Old Side," 821–25.

60. Presbyterian congregations in the colony overwhelmingly supported the New Side and enthusiastically endorsed the College of New Jersey.

61. *ERNY,* 6: 3965.

62. Muhlenberg, *Journals,* 2: 181.

63. On the gradual loss of Dutch cultural dominance, see Archdeacon, *New York City, 1664–1710,* 64–195; Kenney, *Stubborn for Liberty;* and Thomas J. Wertenbaker, *The Founding of American Civilization: The Middle Colonies* (New York: Charles Scribner's Sons, 1938), 346–49. On the denominational division, see De Jong, *Dutch Reformed Churches in Colonies,* 194: "Records of the Coetus," lxxxix–xcii (see n. 10 above); and Randall H. Balmer, "The Dutch Church in an English World: Political Upheaval and Ethnic Conflict in the Middle Colonies" (Ph.D. diss., Princeton University, 1985), chap. 7.

64. In the process of becoming ecclesiastically self-sufficient through the establishment of synods, associations, etc., colonial religionists often followed Old World examples or patterns of organization and leadership. See Jon Butler, *Power, Authority, and the Origins of American Denominational Order: The English Churches in the Delaware Valley 1680–1730* (Philadelphia: American Philosophical Society, 1978).

65. *ERNY,* 5: 3648–49.

66. "Records of the Coetus," xcii (see n. 10 above).

67. Muhlenberg, *Journals,* 2: 390. Cf. Kreider, *Lutheranism in New York,* 91, on the need of Lutheran congregations for constant supervision.

68. *ERNY,* 5: 3499–3500, 3561–65; De Jong, *Dutch Reformed Church in Colonies,* 197; Trinterud, *Forming of an American Tradition,* 63–65.

69. *ERNY,* 6: 4013–14.

70. *ERNY,* 5: 3499–3500, 3561–65, 3636–41.

71. *Lutheran Church: Records in Hamburg,* 384.

72. John Christopher Hartwick to Rev. Master Pieters, June 25, 1754, John Christopher Hartwick MSS., New York Historical Society.

73. *ERNY,* 5: 3499–3500.

74. Ibid., 3582–85.

75. Mills, *Bishops by Ballot,* 35–61.

76. Schneider and Schneider, eds., *Samuel Johnson,* 3: 248–53, 4: 39–41; Howard, "Education and Ethnicity in Colonial New York," 492.

77. Mills, *Bishops by Ballot,* 53–59. For a fuller treatment see Frederick V. Mills, Sr., "Anglican Resistance to an American Episcopate 1761–1789" (Ph.D. diss., University of Pennsylvania, 1967).

78. *ERNY,* 5: 3499–3500.

79. Nybakken, "New Light on the Old Side," 822–30.

80. *ERNY,* 6: 4013–14.

81. Ibid., 3898–99.

82. De Jong, *Dutch Reformed Church in Colonies,* 197.

83. *Lutheran Church: Records in Hamburg,* 382–83.

84. See, for example, the correspondence between Samuel Johnson and Arch-

bishop Secker between 1758 and 1766 in Schneider and Schneider, eds., *Samuel Johnson*, 3: 256–63, 269–71, 286–88.

85. Stocker, *Moravian Church in New York City*, 147. According to Stocker, in 1782 the synod stripped American Moravians of what little power they possessed and placed their congregations and stations under the immediate control of the Unity Elders' Conference in Germany.

86. *ERNY*, 6: 4120–25.

87. The Dutch Reformed Coetus made this point in a letter to the Classis of Amsterdam, Oct. 13, 1764. See *ERNY*, 6: 3963–67.

88. De Jong, *Dutch Reformed Church in Colonies*, 206. Several years earlier, coetus minister John Leydt had written a pamphlet in which he argued that the colonial Dutch church was not subordinate to its European counterpart but rather enjoyed equal rights and powers. See *ERNY*, 5: 3762–92.

89. Schneider and Schneider, *Samuel Johnson*, 1: 355–57; Bruce E. Steiner, *Samuel Seabury 1729–1796: A Study in High Church Tradition* (Oberlin: Ohio University Press, 1971), 107, 127.

Two. "The Vital Part of Religion"

1. Sydney E. Ahlstrom, *A Religious History of the American People*, 2 vols. (Garden City, N.Y.: Doubleday and Co., Inc., Image Books, 1975), 1: 259.

2. Rev. Gualterus Du Bois to the Rev. Classis of Amsterdam, May 14, 1741, *ERNY*, 4: 2756.

3. John Miller, *A description of the province and city of New York*, ed. John Gilmary Shea (New York: W. Gowans, 1862), 38–39. Miller's pessimistic characterization was undoubtedly colored by his own desire to be appointed the leading Anglican official, or perhaps even bishop, in the colonies.

4. Patricia U. Bonomi and Peter R. Eisenstadt, "Church Adherence in the Eighteenth-Century British American Colonies," *William and Mary Quarterly* 3d Ser., 39 (1982): 245–86. Quotations are from 273. Also see Patricia U. Bonomi, *Under the Cope of Heaven: Religion, Society, and Politics in Colonial America* (New York: Oxford University Press, 1986).

5. Population estimates are based on Potter, "The Growth of Population in America," 638. For the number of persons per family I have used the 5.98 figure employed by Bonomi and Eisenstadt. My conservative estimate of congregations relates principally to the Dutch Reformed. Michael Kammen has estimated that the Dutch Reformed had twenty-nine congregations in 1701 and sixty-five in 1740 (*Colonial New York*, 85). He may have been including places where services were held but no congregation was actually organized by a Dutch Reformed classis. The specific comparison of my data with Bonomi and Eisenstadt's is as follows: for the Middle Colonies in 1750 (the only year for which they make this judgment), their ratio of churches to population is 1:467; their church adherence levels are 80 percent for 1700, 75.1 percent for 1750, and 59 percent for 1780 (no estimate for 1775).

6. Not all accounts of colonial New York have dismissed religion as unimportant to provincials. Two works that emphasize the importance of religion in the colony in the seventeenth century are Alice P. Kenney, *The Gansevoorts of Albany: Dutch Patricians in the Upper Hudson Valley* (Syracuse, N.Y.: Syracuse University Press, 1969), 15–16, 43–45, and Howard, "Education and Ethnicity in Colonial New York," 208.

7. For the relationship between toleration and diversity, see Pratt, *Religion, Politics, and Diversity*, 5–6, 27, 110, and Smith, *Religion and Trade in New Netherland*, 179–246.

8. Jessica Kross, *The Evolution of an American Town: Newtown, New York, 1642–1775* (Philadelphia: Temple University Press, 1983), 111–13.

9. The most intense interdenominational conflict in the 1600s was between the Dutch Reformed and the Lutherans in New York City and the Hudson Valley. See Charles Wooley, *A Two Years Journal in New York,* in *Historic Chronicles of New Amsterdam, Colonial New York and Early Long Island,* ed. Cornell Jaray, 1st series (1860; reprint ed., Port Washington, N.Y.: Ira J. Friedman, Inc., 1968), 55–56, for a primary source account from the 1670s of Reformed–Lutheran hostility.

10. Kammen, *Colonial New York,* 87.

11. Kreider, *Lutheranism in New York,* 66.

12. Ibid., 66–68. This type of borrowing by the Lutherans is ironic in light of the antagonism between the two groups. Kreider discusses Lutheran relations with the Dutch Reformed Church on 69–74.

13. Mills, "Anglican Resistance," 61–62.

14. Kross, *Evolution of an American Town,* 168–76.

15. Vandenberge, *Historical Directory,* 369. The Lutheran congregation had been founded in 1711; Kreider, *Lutheranism in New York,* 141. Thea Lawrence, "Unity without Uniformity: An Exploration into the History of the Churches of Rhinebeck, N.Y.," *The Hudson Valley Regional Review* 1 (1984) 100–05, describes the religious options open to Dutch and German settlers in this part of the central Hudson Valley.

16. *Anglicization* here refers to the process in which colonial cultural, social, and political life was intentionally modeled on that of Great Britain. It does not refer to, or imply, the religious process of Anglicanization, although several historians have argued that the establisment of the Anglican Church in lower New York reflected both processes. For the wider impact of Anglicization, see Jack P. Greene, "Search for Identity: An Interpretation of the Meaning of Selected Patterns of Social Response in Eighteenth-Century America," *Journal of Social History* 3 (1970): 189–220; and id., "Political Mimesis: A Consideration of the Historical and Cultural Roots of Legislative Behavior in the British Colonies in the Eighteenth Century," *American Historical Review* 75 (1969): 337–60. Cf. discussions of this process in New York in Kammen, *Colonial New York,* 128–60; Jean Paul Jordan, "The Anglican Establishment in Colonial New York, 1693–1783" (Ph.D. diss., Columbia University, 1971), 61–67; Stefan Bielinski, "The Refounding and Anglicization of Albany, New York, under English Rule," paper presented to the Social Science History Association, November 1980; Balmer, "The Dutch Church in an English World," 59–76, 134–66; Douglas Greenberg, *Crime and Law Enforcement in the Colony of New York, 1691–1776* (Ithaca, N.Y.: Cornell University Press, 1976), 224–28.

17. *Protocol of Lutheran Church,* 421–22; Butler, *Huguenots in America,* 144–98; Nelson R. Burr, "The Episcopal Church and the Dutch in Colonial New York and New Jersey—1664–1787," *Historical Magazine of the Protestant Episcopal Church* 19 (1950): 102–6.

18. On the religious dimensions of Leisler's rebellion, see Balmer, "The Dutch Church in an English World," 55–96. David S. Lovejoy, *The Glorious Revolution in America* (New York: Harper & Row, 1972), is the best general work on this era.

19. Mead, *The Lively Experiment,* 20–27.

20. Edward J. Cody, "Church and State in the Middle Colonies, 1689–1763" (Ph.D. diss., Lehigh University, 1970), 26–43.

21. Rev. Mr. Colgan to the Secretary, 1735, *ERNY,* 4: 2668–69. I do not intend to suggest that interdenominatioal tensions existed in every community. Some New York villages were similar to Reading and Germantown, Pennsylvania, where little evidence exists of interchurch conflict; Wolf, *Urban Village,* 221–22, and Laura

Becker, "Diversity and Its Significance in an Eighteenth-Century Pennsylvania Town," in Zuckerman, ed., *Friends and Neighbors*, 206–14. Overall, interchurch relations seem to have improved temporarily in the 1730s and more permanently after 1750.

22. Balmer, "The Dutch Church in an English World," 144–66, describes how a number of these same issues strained Anglican–Dutch Reformed relations.

23. Robert Bolton, *History of the Protestant Episcopal Church in the County of Westchester* (New York: Stanford & Swords, 1855), 242–69; Thomas Poyer to the Secretary, June 14, 1731, SPG Records, Letterbooks Series A, 23: 328–29 (microfilm). All future citations from the SPG records are from the microfilm copy at the Billy Graham Center Archives, Wheaton, Ill. See also Rev. Mr. Colgan to the Secretary, June 14, 1734, *ERNY*, 4: 2645–46; Kreider, *Lutheranism in New York*, 78–80.

24. Benjamin Ferris, MS Journal of Benjamin Ferris of Oblong, N.Y., 1732, Ferris Papers, Friends Historical Library, Swarthmore College, Swarthmore, Pa.; Revs. Boel, Mutzelius and Mancius, to the Classis of Amsterdam, Apr. 14, 1743, *ERNY*, 4: 2798–2800.

25. *Lutheran Church: Records in Hamburg*, 57.

26. Monica Taller, "The Assimilation of Jews in Colonial New York City, 1740–1776," 1, Jews in New York City file, Trinity Parish Archives, New York City; Hyman B. Grinstein, *The Rise of the Jewish Community of New York, 1654–1860* (Philadelphia: Porcupine Press, 1976), 165–66.

27. Hartwick to Pieters (see n.72, chap. one).

28. Bonomi, "'Watchful against the Sects,'" 2–13. Similar arguments have been advanced regarding East Jersey Scottish Presbyterians and Quakers in Chester County, Pennsylvania. See Ned Landsman, "The Scottish Proprietors and the Planning of East New Jersey," in Zuckerman, ed., *Friends and Neighbors*, 65–89, and Susan Forbes, "Quaker Tribalism," in ibid., 145–73.

29. Butler, *Huguenots in America*, 190–91.

30. Howard, "Education and Ethnicity in Colonial New York," 280–81, 314–22.

31. Robert Tenney to the Secretary, July 30, 1735, SPG Records, Letterbooks Series A, 26: 64–67.

32. This conflict began in 1703 and lasted until the early 1730s. It may be traced in *ERNY*, 3: 1690, 1892–96, 2021, 2043–44, 2114–15, 2128–38, 2392, 4: 2623–24.

33. Taller, "Assimilation of Jews," 4–5, 10; Marcus, *Early American Jewry*, 1: 47, 84–94. Not all Jews responded to diversity in this way; Grinstein, *Jewish Community of New York*, 333–35, points out a growing laxity among certain members in the 1740s and '50s.

34. Cf. Bonomi and Eisenstadt, "Church Adherence in American Colonies," 247–48.

35. James Wetmore to the Secretary, Dec. 5, 1735, SPG Records, Letterbooks Series A, 26: 88–90.

36. Ibid., 1743, SPG Records, Letterbooks Series B, 11: 151.

37. Mr. Stouppe to the Secretary, Aug. 10, 1733, SPG Records, Letterbooks Series A, 24: 465–67; Flint Dwight to the Secretary, Nov. 12, 1735, SPG Records, Letterbooks Series A, 26: 75–76; Thomas Colgan to the Secretary, 1735, SPG Records, Letterbooks Series A, 26: 96–98; Rev. Mr. Colgan to the Secretary, Mar. 28, 1749, *ERNY*, 4: 3056.

38. Arthur J. Worrall, *Quakers in the Colonial Northeast* (Hanover, N.H.: University Press of New England, 1980), 78–80.

39. Muhlenberg, *Journals*, 1: 339.

40. Crèvecoeur, *Letters from an American Farmer*, 48–51.

41. Field Horne, ed., *The Diary of Mary Cooper: Life on a Long Island Farm 1768–1773* (Oyster Bay, N.Y.: Oyster Bay Historical Society, 1981). Quotation is from entry for June 27, 1772.

42. See Anne Grant, *Memoirs of An American Lady* (New York: D. Appleton, 1846), 30, and Carl Bridenbaugh, ed., *Gentleman's Progress: The Itinerarium of Dr. Alexander Hamilton* (Chapel Hill: University of North Carolina Press, 1948), 74, for accounts by two contemporary observers of this development. Barry Levy, "The Birth of the 'Modern Family' in Early America: Quaker and Anglican Families in the Delaware Valley, Pennsylvania, 1681–1750," in Zuckerman, ed., *Friends and Neighbors*, 54–56, finds that competition from Quakers in southeastern Pennsylvania brought a decline in the involvement and interest of many local Anglicans in their church. Frantz, "Awakening among the German Settlers," 267–70, argues that some German colonists became irreligious as a result of the spiritual confusion aroused by religious competition.

43. Muhlenberg, *Journals*, 1: 236.

44. Theodore J. Frelinghuysen, *Sermons by Theodore J. Frelinghuysen*, trans. W. Demarest (New York, 1856), 168–69.

45. William Livingston et al., *The Independent Reflector*, ed. Milton M. Klein (Cambridge, Mass.: Harvard University Press, 1963), 276.

46. Samuel Seabury to the Society, Sept. 30, 1745, SPG Records, Letterbooks Series B, 13: 241.

47. Rev. Gualterus Du Bois to the Rev. Classis of Amsterdam, May 14, 1741, *ERNY*, 4: 2756.

48. Dutch Reformed Collegiate Church call for a Minister to preach in English, Jan. 18, 1763, *ERNY*, 6: 3853–56; Maynard, *Huguenot Church of New York*, 139; *Protocol of Lutheran Church in New York City*, 421–22, 463–67.

49. Dietmar Rothermund, *The Layman's Progress: Religious and Political Experience in Colonial Pennsylvania, 1740–1770* (Philadelphia, 1961), argues in chaps. 2 and 3 that the Great Awakening brought about a heightened denominational consciousness set in a framework of "competitive coexistence." In New York, it was a short-term trend, soon replaced by signs of interchurch cooperation.

50. Extract from a letter of George Michael Weiss, Apr. 25, 1742, *ERNY*, 4: 2774; the Church of Minnisink to the Classis of Amsterdam, July 18, 1747, *ERNY*, 4: 2964.

51. All the SPG missionaries in lower New York commented on the activity of New Light preachers in their 1743 correspondence with the society. See SPG Records, Letterbooks Series B, 11: 134–52.

52. On Reformed Orthodoxy in New York, see Balmer, "The Dutch Church in an English World," 180–204. On Lutheran Orthodoxy in New York, see Kreider, *Lutheranism in New York*, 81–104.

53. Trinterud, *Forming of an American Tradition*, 50–76, discusses Presbyterian subscription to the Westminster Confession and Catechism. Congregationalists generally relied on the Cambridge Platform of 1648 and the Saybrook Platform of 1708.

54. Mills, *Bishops by Ballot*, 5–6, 60, 79, 137; John F. Woolverton, *Colonial Anglicanism in North America* (Detroit: Wayne State University Press, 1984), 123–26, 192.

55. No one has yet come up with an adequate label for these religionists. I prefer *Orthodox Protestants* because it conveys the loyalty of these people to the doctrinal and liturgical traditions of the 1600s and is the term employed by eighteenth-century Lutheran and Reformed colonists. *Confessionalists* applies well to the Lutherans and Reformed, but less well or not at all to Anglicans, Presbyterians, and Congregationalists. *Conservative* may be misleading to modern readers who are used

to thinking of evangelicals, and not their opponents, as conservatives. *Traditionalists* works well for most of these folk but I have already used the term in chap. one for a different purpose. Of course, *Orthodox Protestants* and *European Orthodoxy* may also be misunderstood. I am at no point referring to anything connected with what is today called the Orthodox Church, or the Greek Orthodox Church, or Eastern Orthodoxy. My terms are also distinct from the notion of Christian orthodoxy, which refers to conformity to the long-held, established doctrines of the Christian church.

56. Alan Heimert, *Religion and the American Mind: From the Great Awakening to the Revolution* (Cambridge, Mass.: Harvard University Press, 1966), 318.

57. Gerrit Lydekker, Preface, *Theological Theses, containing the Chief Heads of the Christian Doctrine,* by Isaac Sigfrid and Daniel Wyttenbach (New York: Samuel Brown, 1766), i. For a defense of Orthodoxy from a New York minister earlier in the century, see Gualterus Du Bois, *Kort-Begryp der waare Christelyke Leere, uit den Heidelgergischen Catechismus uitgetrokken, door ordre der Christelyke Synod te Dordrecht, Anno 1618 & 1619* (New York, 1706).

58. For examples of their pastoral approach, see Lambertus De Ronde, *The True Spiritual Religion* (New York: John Holt, 1767), and the Anglican-sponsored 1767 reprint of John Rotheram, *An Essay on Faith and Its Connection with Good Works* (New York: J. Parker, 1767).

59. De Jong, *Dutch Reformed Church in Colonies,* 172–76.

60. James Tanis, "Reformed Pietism in the Colonial America," in Stoeffler, ed., *Continental Pietism and Early American Christianity,* 45–47; James Tanis, *Dutch Calvinistic Pietism in the Middle Colonies: A Study in the Life and Theology of Theodorus Jacobus Frelinghuysen* (The Hague: Martinus Nijhoff, 1957), 42–88.

61. O'Callaghan, ed., *Documentary History of New York,* 3: 316–20.

62. Ibid., 3: 193–94; *ERNY,* 5: 3354.

63. Jon Butler, "Enthusiasm Described and Decried: The Great Awakening as Interpretative Fiction," *Journal of American History* 69 (1982): 322. Kammen, *Colonial New York,* 230–31, agrees with this assessment of the awakening's impact. Several recent works that attribute more significance to evangelical religion in New York are Frantz, "Awakening among the German Settlers," 274–88; Howard, "Education and Ethnicity in Colonial New York," 418, 444–78; Balmer, "The Dutch Church in an English World," chap. 7.

64. John Rodgers was minister of the Wall St. and Brick Presbyterian churches in New York City; John Gano pastored the First Baptist Church of New York City; Thomas Rankin was one of the first Methodist missionaries sent by Wesley to America. This list should probably be expanded to include more radical enthusiasts, such as New Light Baptists or Presbyterian pastor James Davenport.

65. Frantz, "Awakening among the German Settlers," 282–83, explains the unity of all German Pietists on these points despite their other differences.

66. Samuel Buell, *The Excellence and Importance of the Saving Knowledge of the Lord Jesus Christ in the Gospel Preacher* (New York: James Parker, 1761), 3, 14, 17–19.

67. Nelson, "Critical Study of Muhlenberg's Lutheranism," 54–58, 136, 354–55. Nelson suggests that Muhlenberg approved of Whitefield's instantaneous conversions but thought gradual awareness was appropriate, too.

68. For a recent discussion of how the new birth was central to the evangelical revivals in both America and Great Britain, see Timothy L. Smith, "George Whitefield and Wesleyan Perfectionism," *Wesleyan Theological Journal* 19 (1984): 63–85.

69. Nelson, "Critical Study of Muhlenberg's Lutheranism," 344–45. On Tennent, see Milton J. Coalter, Jr., "The Life of Gilbert Tennent: A Case Study of Continental Pietism's Influence on the First Great Awakening in the Middle Colonies" (Ph.D. diss., Princeton University, 1982). Evangelicals also did not always agree

within single congregations. For example, both New York City's Presbyterian and Baptist churches split over changes in hymnody.

70. Adrian C. Leiby, *The United Churches of Hackensack and Schraalenburgh, New Jersey 1686–1822* (River Edge, N.J.: Bergen County Historical Society, 1976), 89.

71. Samuel Auchmuty to Samuel Johnson, Dec. 21, 1764, Schneider and Schneider, eds., *Samuel Johnson*, 1: 348–49; Morgan Dix et al., *A History of the Parish of Trinity Church in the City of New York,* 6 vols. (New York: G. P. Putnam's Sons, 1898–1962), 1: 356, 2: 39.

72. Baker, "Early American Methodism," 9.

73. Joseph B. Wakeley, *Lost Chapters recovered from the Early History of American Methodism* (New York: By the Author, 1858), 208–10.

74. George Whitefield, *The Works of George Whitefield,* 6 vols. (London: Edward & Charles Dilly, 1771), 3: 301–6, 312–14, 424–25, records his many successful efforts in New York in 1763–64 and 1770. While in 1764 his impact was particularly strong among congregations on Long Island, in 1770 he preached most effectively at the Hudson Valley towns of Albany, Schenectady, Poughkeepsie, Fishkill, New Rumbout, New Windsor, and Peekskill.

75. Samuel Buell, *A Faithful Narrative of the Revival at East-Hampton in 1764* (New York: Samuel Brown, 1766). Cf. a copy of a letter written by Buell describing this revival to an unknown party, dated July 10, 1764, in the Isaac Backus Papers, American Baptist Historical Society, Rochester, N.Y. Buell, a 1741 Yale graduate, ministered in Easthampton from 1746 till his death in 1798. This congregation had experienced a revival in 1741–42 under the previous pastor, and in 1749 a large number of young people were converted, though no general awakening took place. Samuel Buell, *The Import of the Saint's Confession* (New London, Conn.: T. Green & Son, [1792]), 43–45.

76. MS Records of the Baptist Church of Christ in Paulings Precinct, 28, New York Church Records, American Baptist Historical Society.

77. On Smith, see Nichols, *Presbyterianism in New York State,* 49; on Deacon's successful ministries, see Gillette, ed., *Minutes of the Philadelphia Baptist Association,* 107–58, for 1769–80; on the pastoral work of Bostwick and Rodgers at the Wall St. and Brick Presbyterian churches in New York City, see Shepherd Knapp, *A History of the Brick Presbyterian Church in the City of New York* (New York: The Brick Presbyterian Church, 1909), and Samuel Miller, *Memoirs of the Rev. John Rodgers, D.D.* (New York: Whiting & Watson, 1813).

78. Mrs. Grant's Account of the circumstances under which Rev. Theodore Frelinghuysen left Albany, 1759, *ERNY,* 5: 3739–44; Kenney, *Gansevoorts of Albany,* 45.

79. Asbury, *Journal and Letters,* 1: 81, 126.

80. Samples or discussions of these pastors' sermons may be found in Sermons of Rev. Archibald Laidlie, pastor of the Middle Dutch Church [1763–1778], New York Historical Society; Earl William Kennedy, "From Providence to Civil Religion: Some 'Dutch' Reformed Interpretations of America in the Revolutionary Era," *Reformed Review* 30 (1976): 111–23; Alexander Gunn, *Memoirs of the Rev. John Henry Livingston, D.D.* (New York: Reformed Protestant Dutch Church, 1856); 19 Discourses of Rev. John Rodgers 1755–1807, New York Historical Society; Joseph Treat, *A Thanksgiving Sermon, occasioned by the glorious news of the reduction of the Havannah* (New York: Hugh Gaine, 1762); and Nichols, *Presbyterianism in New York State,* 47–57.

81. The Moravians began with fewer than 100 attenders and had close to 300 by the mid-1750s; Stocker, *Moravian Church in New York City,* 75, 110. The Baptists went from 27 members to 139 by the Revolution; Gillette, ed., *Minutes . . . Phila-*

delphia Baptist Association, 89, 158. The handful of Methodists who organized a society in 1766 increased to over 220 closely disciplined members by 1774; *Minutes of the Methodist Conferences, annually held in America: 1773–1813* (New York: David Hitt & Thomas Ware, 1813), 8. On Methodist growth in New York, see Doris Andrews, "Popular Religion and the Revolution in the Middle Atlantic Ports: The Rise of the Methodists, 1770–1800" (Ph.D. diss., University of Pennsylvania, 1986).

82. Kreider, *Lutheranism in New York,* 112–20, 142.

83. Samuel Auchmuty to Samuel Johnson, Dec. 21, 1764, Schneider and Schneider, eds., *Samuel Johnson,* 1: 348–49.

84. Most of the attacks I have located came from either Anglican or Dutch Reformed ministers. For two samples, see Thomas Chandler to Samuel Johnson, Aug. 20, 1764, ibid., 342–45, and Conferentie to Classis of Amsterdam, June 21, 1764, *ERNY* 6: 3927–30.

85. For one example, see Buell, *Saving Knowledge of the Lord Jesus Christ,* 18–19.

86. See the correspondence of Thomas Chandler to Samuel Johnson in Schneider and Schneider, eds., *Samuel Johnson,* 1: 415–17, 432–34, 442–45.

87. Klein, *Politics of Diversity,* 68–69. Livingston expressed many of his religious ideas in *The Independent Reflector.* In particular see essay 31, 276.

88. Charles W. Akers, "Religion and the American Revolution: Samuel Cooper and the Brattle Street Church," *William and Mary Quarterly* 3d. Ser., 35 (1978): 477–98; Edmund S. Morgan, *The Gentle Puritan: A Life of Ezra Stiles, 1727–1795* (New Haven, Conn.: Yale University Press, 1962).

89. Woolverton, *Colonial Anglicanism in North America,* 192, 216.

90. Abel C. Thomas, *A Century of Universalism in Philadelphia and New-York* (Philadelphia, 1872), 256–61; Ernest Cassara, ed., *Universalism in America: A Documentary History* (Boston: Beacon Press, 1971), 10–14, 55–77; Russell E. Miller, *The Larger Hope: The First Century of the Universalist Church in America, 1770–1870* (Boston: Unitarian Universalist Association, 1979), 10–14, 681; and Stephen A. Marini, *Radical Sects of Revolutionary New England* (Cambridge, Mass.: Harvard University Press, 1982), 68–69.

91. Leo Hershkowitz and Isidore S. Meyer, eds., *Letters of the Franks Family, 1733–1748* (Waltham, Mass.: American Jewish Historical Society, 1968), xxii, 7–8, 12.

92. Quoted in Winthrop Hudson, *Religion in America,* 3d ed. (New York: Charles Scribner's Sons, 1980), 80–81.

93. Ibid., 81–82.

94. Nelson, "Critical Study of Muhlenberg's Lutheranism," 341–49.

95. Tappert, "Influence of Pietism in Colonial Lutheranism," 29; Muhlenberg records this proposal in his *Journals,* 1: 448.

96. For examples, see Muhlenberg, *Journals,* 2: 181, and Asbury, *Journal and Letters,* 1: 133.

97. In New York, evangelical Dutch Reformed and Presbyterian ministers exchanged their pulpits frequently. See Rev. Anthonius Curtenius to the Classis of Amsterdam, Nov. 5, 1754, *ERNY,* 5: 3518–19.

98. Extract from a Letter of Rev. John Ritzema to Rev. W. Budde, Apr. 1, 1763, *ERNY,* 6: 3865.

99. Asbury, *Journal and Letters,* 1: 81–82, 131–33.

100. Dutchess Presbytery MS Minutes 1762–1795, 8–19, Dutchess Presbytery MSS, Presbyterian Historical Society.

101. Bolton, *Episcopal Church in Westchester,* 500–502.

102. Brenda Hough, "The Archives of the Society for the Propagation of the Gospel," *Historical Magazine of the Protestant Episcopal Church* 46 (1977): 315–16.

103. Samson Occom, *A Choice Collection of Hymns and Spiritual Song; Intended for the Edification of Sincere Christians, of all Denominations* (New London, Conn.: Timothy Green, 1774), 4.

104. The most noteworthy interdenominational services were those conducted by Whitefield and Asbury. See Whitefield, *Works*, 3: 299, 301, 424; and Asbury, *Journal and Letters*, 1: 137. Ann Moore and Benjamin Ferris, Quaker Itinerants, both recorded conducting similar religious meetings in the Hudson Valley in the 1750s. Ann Moore, MS Journal of journey from Maryland to Pennsylvania, New York, and New England, visiting Friends Meetings, 1756–58, 24–25, Friends Historical Library; Ferris, MS Journal of Benjamin Ferris of Oblong, N.Y., July 1754, Ferris Papers.

105. Heimert, *Religion and the American Mind*, 140.

106. Mead, "Fact of Pluralism and Persistence of Sectarianism," 255–62.

Three. "An Equal Footing for All"

1. Smith, *Religion and Trade in New Netherland*, 11–14, 236–46; Pratt, *Religion, Politics, and Diversity*, 3–67. Smith's work is particularly valuable for its examination of the European roots of New York's religious order during Dutch rule.

2. Kammen, *Colonial New York*, 85–86, and Howard, "Education and Ethnicity in Colonial New York," 147–55, discuss how this system of multiple establishments worked in practice.

3. Cody, "Church and State in the Middle Colonies," 50–90; Cynthia A. Kierner, "A Concept Rejected: New York's Anglican 'Establishment,' 1693–1715," *Essays in History* 26 (1982): 71–100.

4. *ERNY*, 3: 1690, 1892–96, 2021, 2043–44, 2114–15, 2128–38, 2392, 4: 2623–24, 6: 4180, 4231–34.

5. Nichols, *Presbyterianism in New York State*, 25; Charles W. Baird, *History of Bedford Church* (New York: Dodd, Mead, and Co., 1882), 24–44.

6. A number of these early grievances were listed in a pamphlet published by dissenters, *Reasons for the Present Glorious Combination of the Dissenters in the City* (New York, 1769).

7. Worrall, *Quakers in the Colonial Northeast*, 126–27.

8. Hershkowitz and Meyer, eds., *Letters of the Franks Family*, 4.

9. Howard, "Education and Ethnicity in Colonial New York," 420–25, 436–38.

10. Archbishop Secker to Samuel Johnson, Sept. 27, 1758, Schneider and Schneider eds., *Samuel Johnson*, 3: 256–60.

11. The best general treatment of this college's history in the eighteenth century is David Humphrey, *From King's College to Columbia, 1746–1800* (New York: Columbia University Press, 1976).

12. Joseph Ellis, *The New England Mind in Transition: Samuel Johnson of Connecticut, 1696–1772* (New Haven, Conn.: Yale University Press, 1973), 181; Schneider and Schneider, eds., *Samuel Johnson*, 5: 191–207.

13. Throughout this chapter, the terms *Anglican hierarchy* and *Anglican leadership* refer collectively to the colony's Anglican clergy, most royal officials in the province, and the majority of Anglican members of New York's political and economic elite. Certainly a minority group of elite Anglicans existed who disagreed with the politics of their church.

14. Livingston et al., *The Independent Reflector*, 178. Cf. Dorothy Dillon, *The New York Triumvirate: A Study of the Legal and Political Careers of William Livingston, John Morin Scott, and William Smith, Jr.* (New York: Columbia University Press, 1949). Some historians, including Beverly McAnear, "American Imprints concerning King's College," *Papers of the Bibliographical Society of America* 44 (1950): 301–39, have

argued that the aims of the Livingston faction in the college controversy were primarily to establish a platform upon which to challenge the DeLanceys' strong-hold in the provincial government. While political ambition may have been part of Livingston's motivation, this explanation overlooks his strong interest in the colony's religious and educational life. A more recent analysis, Donald F.M. Geradi, "The King's College Controversy 1753–1756 and the Ideological Roots of Toryism in New York," *Perspectives in American History* 11 (1977–1978): 145–96, argues that the debate over the college marked the start of a division in the colony between Tory ideology and Whig.

15. McAnear, "American Imprints concerning King's College," 311.

16. Ellis, *New England Mind*, 181. Intellectually, no one had a profounder impact on Johnson than George Berkeley. The experience of living in pluralistic Rhode Island had persuaded Berkeley that diversity encouraged an indifference to religion and that, therefore, one had to move beyond charity and tolerance to advocacy. For both him and Johnson, that meant advancing the claims and cause of Anglicanism. Cf. Edwin S. Gaustad, *George Berkeley in America* (New Haven, Conn.: Yale University Press, 1979), 116–19.

17. Samuel Johnson to Thomas Clap, Feb. 5, 1754, and Johnson to Clap, Feb. 19, 1754, Schneider and Schneider eds., *Samuel Johnson* 1: 175–82.

18. Ellis, *New England Mind*, 176.

19. S. Johnson to Bishop Thomas Secker, Oct. 25, 1754, *ERNY*, 5: 3503–4.

20. Samuel Johnson to the Archbishop of Canterbury, June 29, 1753, *ERNY*, 5: 3388–89.

21. Ellis, *New England Mind*, 198.

22. New York *Gazette: or the Weekly Post Boy*, June 3, 1754. This advertisement was reprinted in New York Historical Society, *Collections, 1870* (New York: By the Society, 1871), 166–69.

23. Milton M. Klein, "Church, State, and Education: Testing the Issue in Colo-nial New York," *New York History* 45 (1964): 291–303. Klein also points out that Livingston's educational plan formed the basis of the New York State Board of Regents, founded in 1787.

24. Livingston et al., *The Independent Reflector*, 178–83.

25. Ibid., 391.

26. Klein, "Church, State, and Education," 295.

27. William Livingston's protest against the King's College Board of Trustees Petition to the New York Assembly, Schneider and Schneider, eds., *Samuel Johnson*, 4: 185–90.

28. Livingston et al., *The Independent Reflector*, 207–14.

29. For Anglican concern over maintaining good relations with the Dutch Reformed, see Rev. Henry Barclay to William Smith, Feb. 12, 1755, William Smith MSS, Hawks Papers, Archives of the Protestant Episcopal Church, Austin, Tex., and Samuel Johnson to the Archbishop of Canterbury, July 10, 1754, *ERNY*, 5: 3484–85. For a Presbyterian attempt to influence the Dutch Reformed, see *ERNY*, 5: 3459–60.

30. "Report on the Personal Petition of Dominie Ritzema for an Additional Charter to King's College, for a Dutch Professor of Divinity therein. May 13, 1755," *ERNY*, 5: 3544.

31. Rev. John Ritzema censured by the Consistory of the Collegiate Church. Aug. 11, 1755, *ERNY*, 5: 3574–77.

32. A Dutch Reformed, a Lutheran, and a French Protestant minister accepted the offer, and as a result pastors Ritzema, Weygand, and Carle, and at least portions of their congregations, became much more closely tied to the Anglican establish-ment. For their participation on the board, see minutes for 1755–1763, *Columbia*

University: Early Minutes of the Trustees, 1755–1770 (New York: By the University, 1932).

33. *ERNY*, 5: 3459–60.

34. Ellis, *New England Mind*, 204.

35. For evidence of Frelinghuysen's authorship, see McAnear, "American Imprints concerning King's College," 327–38.

36. Theodore Frelinghuysen [David Marin Ben Jesse], *A Remonstrance* (New York, 1755), 2.

37. Theodore Frelinghuysen [David Marin Ben Jesse], *A Remark on the Disputes and Contentions in the Province* (New York: Hugh Gaine, 1755), 106.

38. Anglican minister Henry Barclay commented favorably on the board's makeup in a letter written to Samuel Johnson in November 1754. *ERNY*, 5: 3517–18.

39. McAnear, "American Imprints concerning King's College," 323, 334.

40. Dillon, *New York Triumvirate*, 40–42. She explains that until 1761 "the library's facilities were at the disposal of all residents of the province, though naturally non-subscribers had fewer privileges. In that year, however, because of great damage and loss of volumes, borrowing privileges were withdrawn from non-subscribers. The initial subscription amounted to five pounds New York currency and ten shillings every year thereafter," 41. Cf. Austin Baxter Keep, *History of the New York Society Library* (New York: DeVinne Press, 1908), 123–78.

41. Abraham Keteltas, *The Religious Soldier: or, the military character of King David* (New York: Hugh Gaine, 1759), portrayed the British and American effort in this way.

42. Chauncey Graham, *God will trouble the Troublers of his People* (New York: Hugh Gaine, 1759); Klett, ed., *Minutes of the Presbyterian Church*, 312, 333; *A Serious Call from the City to the Country* (Woodridge, N.J., 1757).

43. "A Letter of July 13, 1753, Appended by William Smith to the London Edition of Johnson's *Elements Philosophica*," Schneider and Schneider, eds., *Samuel Johnson*, 3: 248–53.

44. Isaac Brown and Thomas B. Chandler to His Grace of Canterbury, Jan. 29, 1755, Samuel Johnson MSS, Hawks Papers.

45. Episcopal Clergy of New York to the Secretary of the Society, Nov. 3, 1755, Schneider and Schneider, eds., *Samuel Johnson*, 4: 39–41.

46. For example, see Samuel Johnson to Thomas Secker, Archbishop of Canterbury, Mar. 1, 1759, and Johnson's "Questions Relating to the Union and Government of the Plantations," appended to a letter from him to the archbishop, July 13, 1760, Schneider and Schneider, eds., *Samuel Johnson*, 1: 282–87, 3: 297–301. Mills, *Bishops by Ballot*, 53, notes that there is little or no evidence that the Anglican laity of the northeastern region supported their clergy's proposal for bishops in America.

47. Schneider and Schneider, eds., *Samuel Johnson*, 1: 282–87, 3: 297–301.

48. Gerald Goodwin, "The Anglican Reaction to the Great Awakening," *Historical Magazine of the Protestant Episcopal Church* 35 (1966): 349–53; William M. Hogue, "The Religious Conspiracy Theory of the American Revolution: Anglican Motive," *Church History* 45 (1976): 280–81.

49. Hogue, "Religious Conspiracy Theory," 288. On the episcopate issue in general, see Carl Bridenbaugh, *Mitre and Sceptre: Transatlantic Faiths, Ideas, Personalities, and Politics, 1689–1775* (New York: Oxford University Press, 1962); Arthur L. Cross, *The Anglican Episcopate and the American Colonies* (Cambridge, Mass.: Harvard University Press, 1902); Evarts B. Greene, "The Anglican Outlook on the American Colonies in the Early Eighteenth Century," *American Historical Review* 20 (1914): 64–84; and Mills, *Bishops by Ballot*.

50. Archbishop Secker to Samuel Johnson, Sept. 27, 1758, Schneider and Schneider, eds., *Samuel Johnson*, 3: 267–70.

51. Address of the Episcopal Clergy of the Province of New York to the Bishop of London, Dr. Osbaldistone, Sept. 12, 1762, Schneider and Schneider, eds., *Samuel Johnson*, 1: 322–34.

52. Ellis, *New England Mind*, 184.

53. *ERNY*, 6: 4083–99.

54. Ibid., 3805–6, 4026, 4074–75, 4083–84.

55. Samuel Auchmuty to Samuel Johnson, Feb. 1[O?], 1767, Johnson MSS, Hawks Papers.

56. O'Callaghan, ed., *Documentary History of New York*, 3: 489–95.

57. E. B. O'Callaghan and Berthold Fernow, eds., *Documents relating to the Colonial History of the State of New York*, 15 vols. (Albany N.Y.: Weed, Parsons, & Co., 1853–1887), 7: 585–86. *ERNY*, 6: 4041, 4098–99.

58. [John Rodgers], *The Case of the Scotch Presbyterians, of the City of New York* (New York, 1773), 8. For Presbyterian attempts to gain a charter, see Bridenbaugh, *Mitre and Sceptre*, 127–28, 158, 181, 218, 252, 260–62, 330–31; and *ERNY*, 3–6: 1672–73, 2173–76, 3427–29, 4046–48, 4081, 4083, 4095. Despite the declaration of the King's Order in Council in 1767, dissenting congregations continued to submit petitions to obtain charters until the Revolution. Among them were the Dutch Reformed Churches in Schenectady (1774) and Flatbush (1775), the Presbyterian Church in Jamaica (1775), and the First Baptist Church in New York City (1775), as recorded in E. B. O'Callaghan, ed., *Calendar of Historical Manuscripts in the Office of the Secretary of State*, 2 vols. (Albany, N.Y.: Weed, Parsons, & Co., 1866), 2: 824–29, 833–34. That the English government was willing to grant such charters if provincial officials approved is indicated in a letter from the Earl of Dartmouth to Governor Tryon, dated May 4, 1775, in O'Callaghan and Fernow, eds., *Documents*, 8: 472–74.

59. [Rodgers], *Case of Scotch Presbyterians*, 8.

60. Jordan, "Anglican Establishment," 428. For an example of the English hierarchy's response to colonial appeals, see the correspondence from Archbishop Secker to Samuel Johnson in Schneider and Schneider, eds., *Samuel Johnson*, 3: 256–63, 269–71, 286–88.

61. Samuel Johnson to Archbishop Secker, Dec. 20, 1763, Schneider and Schneider, eds., *Samuel Johnson*, 3: 279–81.

62. Samuel Johnson to the Archbishop of Canterbury, Nov. 10, 1766, Schneider and Schneider, eds., *Samuel Johnson*, 1: 278–81.

63. Mills, *Bishops by Ballot*, 41–53.

64. Walter E. Stowe, ed., "The Seabury Minutes of the New York Clergy Conventions of 1766 and 1767," *Historical Magazine of the Protestant Episcopal Church* 10 (1941): 124–62. Samuel Seabury and Ezra Stiles exchanged heated letters over the respective purposes of these two meetings. See Stiles to Seabury, Mar. 8, 1768, and Seabury to Stiles, June 4, 1768, Samuel Seabury Papers, microfilm copy, Colgate-Rochester Divinity School, Rochester, N.Y.

65. John W. Lydekker, *The Life and Letters of Charles Inglis* (London: Society for Promoting Christian Knowledge, 1936), 53–54. Also see [Charles Inglis], *A Vindication of the Bishop of Landaff's Sermon* (New York: John Holt, 1768).

66. Ellis, *New England Mind*, 250.

67. New York *Gazette: or the Weekley Post Boy*, Mar. 14, 1768.

68. Hogue, "Religious Conspiracy Theory," 290–91.

69. William Smith, Jr., *Historical Memoirs of William Smith*, ed. William H. W. Sabine, 2 vols. (New York: Colburn & Tegg, 1956–1958), 1: 42–43; William

Livingston, *A Letter to the Right Reverend Father . . . lord bishop of Landaff* (Boston: Kneeland & Adams, 1768).

70. *Minutes of the General Convention of Delegates appointed by the Synod of New York and Philadelphia and the General Association of Connecticut 1766 to 1775* (Philadelphia: Presbyterian Board of Publication, 1904), 17–41. For the Society of Dissenters, see Herbert Osgood, ed., "The Society of Dissenters founded at New York in 1769," *American Historical Review* 6 (1901): 498–507. The society's members came from three evangelical congregations: John Rodgers's Brick Presbyterian, John Mason's Scottish Presbyterian Church, and John Gano's First Baptist Church.

71. *Reasons for the Combination of Dissenters.*

72. Ibid.

73. Osgood, "Society of Dissenters," 504–5.

74. Heimert, *Religion and the American Mind*, 367.

75. James S. Olsen, "The New York Assembly, the Politics of Religion, and the Origins of the American Revolution, 1768–1771," *Historical Magazine of the Protestant Episcopal Church* 43 (1974): 23, 26. The most provocative recent analysis of New York politics in this period is Edward Countryman, *A People in Revolution: The American Revolution and Political Society in New York, 1760–1790* (Baltimore: Johns Hopkins University Press, 1981), 72–98.

76. *To the Dissenting Electors of All Denominations* (New York, 1770).

77. *To the Freeholders of the City and County of New York: The Querist, No. 1 and No. 2* (New York, 1769); *Observations on the Reasons Lately Published for the Malicious Combination* (New York, 1769). Bonomi, *A Factious People*, 248–54, discusses the ways in which the religious issue was used as a political tool in the election of 1769. For three differing views on this election, see Roger Champagne, "Family Politics versus Constitutional Principles: The New York Assembly Elections of 1768 and 1769," *William and Mary Quarterly* 3d Ser., 20 (1963): 57–79; Bernard Friedman, "The New York Assembly Elections of 1768 and 1769: The Disruption of Family Politics," *New York History* 46 (1965): 3–24; and Lawrence H. Leder, "The New York Elections of 1769: An Assault on Privilege," *Mississippi Valley Historical Review* 49 (1963): 675–82.

78. *ERNY*, 6: 4149–50, 4176–81. Also see the prodissenter tract *To the Public, Few are Ignorant . . .* (New York, 1770).

79. Olsen, "New York Assembly," 26–27.

80. Jordan, "Anglican Establishment," 350, comments perceptively on this development: "If the same two groups are divided from each other on ethnic, religious, political and economic lines, they are likely to come to consider themselves two nations, and act accordingly. New York was still far from so completely polarized a situation, but religious and political divisions had come largely to coincide and that was an ominous sign to anyone who wished to preserve the social fabric."

81. [John Rodgers], "A Brief View of the State of religious Liberty in the Colony of New York," *Massachusetts Historical Society Collections* 11 (1804): 140–55.

82. Gillette, ed., *Minutes of the Philadelphia Baptist Association*, 107, 114, 141.

83. Kenney, *Struggle for Liberty*, 143–45.

84. Beardslee, "Reformed Church and the American Revolution," 28.

85. New York Yearly Meeting MS Minutes, 1759. On this committee's work prior to the Revolution, see New York Meeting for Sufferings MS Minutes, 1758–1796, 3–35, Friends Historical Library.

86. Dix, *History of Trinity Parish*, 2: 31–37. Provoost may have gained both his political and his theological liberalism studying in England under Dr. John Jebb, the Anglican liberal. See John N. Norton, *Life of Bishop Provoost of New York* (New York: General Protestant Episcopal Sunday School Union, and Church Book Society, 1859).

87. Dix, *History of Trinity Parish*, 1: 325.

88. Ibid., 356.

89. Livingston et al., *The Independent Reflector*, 312.

90. *ERNY*, 6: 4013–14. Kammen, *Colonial New York*, 150, explains how this was a long-standing notion among some of New York's Dutch Reformed.

91. *To the Freeholders and Freemen of the City and County of New-York, in Communion with the Reformed Dutch Church* (New York, 1769).

92. *ERNY*, 5: 3605–7, 6: 3851–53.

93. Worrall, *Quakers in the Colonial Northeast*, 126–27; Jordan, "Anglican Establishment," 214, 220.

94. Archibald Kennedy, *A Speech . . . by a Member Dissenting from the Church* (New York, 1755).

95. Steiner, *Samuel Seabury*, 177.

96. Lydekker, *Life and Letters of Inglis*, 95. One such privilege urged by Cadwallader Colden was a new charter for King's College. O'Callaghan and Fernow, eds., *Documents*, 8: 486.

97. On the Yonkers matter, see *A Letter from a Gentleman in New-York to his Friend in the Country* (New York, 1772). For the legal battle in Jamaica, see *ERNY*, 6: 4180, 4231–34; and Dillon, *New York Triumvirate*, 50–52.

98. Jordan, "Anglican Establishment," 441. For an example of this type of appeal, see the address of the Anglican clergy of New York and New Jersey to Lord Hillsborough in 1771, in Cross, *Anglican Episcopate*, 254–55.

99. Ellis, *New England Mind*, 267.

100. Steiner, *Samuel Seabury*, 127.

101. For this problem as it affected the religious institutions of Catholic, Lutheran, and Jewish immigrants in the next century, see Eric McKitrick and Stanley Elkins, "Institutions in Motion," *American Quarterly* 12 (1960): 188–97.

Four. "A Shocken Time"

1. Bernard Mason, *The Road to Independence: The Revolutionary Movement in New York, 1773–1777* (Lexington: University of Kentucky Press, 1967). For the military history of the war in New York, see Alexander C. Flick, ed., *The American Revolution in New York* (Albany: University of the State of New York, 1926) and Milton M. Klein, *New York in the American Revolution: A Bibliography* (Albany, N.Y., 1974).

2. "Minutes of the Presbytery of New York, 1775–1782," *New York History* 50 (1969 supplement): 30; *Acts and Proceedings of the General Synod*, 57. Cf. Charles Royster, *A Revolutionary People at War* (Chapel Hill: University of North Carolina Press, 1979), 13–15, 153–62, and Gordon S. Wood, *The Creation of the American Republic, 1776–1787* (Chapel Hill: University of North Carolina Press, 1969), 114–18, on the use of the theme of America's need for repentance and reformation during the war by the clergy.

3. Dutchess Presbytery MS Minutes, 90.

4. *Acts and Proceedings of the General Synod*, 57.

5. Quoted in Maynard, *Huguenot Church of New York*, 203. The original statement, in French, is found in the Memoranda of Jacques Buvelot, Elder of the French Church du St. Esprit, N.Y.C. 1771–1775, N.Y. City Churches MSS, New York Historical Society. On that same fast day, Stephen Van Voorhees told his Reformed congregation in Poughkeepsie that unless Americans repented of their sins, "God will brake up our Armies and give us up to be scourged by our wicked Enemies"; Stephen Van Voorhees, Sermon of July 20, 1775, Sermons of Stephen Van Voorhees [1773–1795], New York Public Library.

6. Gillette, ed., *Minutes of the Philadelphia Baptist Association*, 149; Dutchess Presbytery MS Minutes, 97.

7. Knapp, *History of the Brick Presbyterian Church,* 44. See Roger Champagne, *Alexander McDougall and the American Revolution in New York* (Schenectady, N.Y.: New York State American Revolution Bicentennial Commission in conjunction with Union College Press, 1975), for information on McDougall and these other Presbyterian patriots.

8. Barbara Wingo, "Politics, Society, and Religion: The Presbyterian Clergy of Pennsylvania, New Jersey, and New York, and the Formation of the Nation, 1775–1808" (Ph.D. diss., Tulane University, 1976), 17–18.

9. Discourses of Rev. John Rodgers 1755–1807, New York Historical Society; Sermons of Rev. Archibald Laidlie, pastor of the Middle Dutch Church [1763–1778], New York Historical Society.

10. Klett, ed., *Minutes of the Presbyterian Church,* 544.

11. Ibid., 543. From this point on, Rodgers openly endorsed the colonial cause. According to loyalist historian Thomas Jones, Rodgers repeatedly prayed during worship services for the success of General Montgomery's campaign in Quebec in November 1775. Jones described him as "a person of rigid republican principles, a rebellious, seditious, preacher, a man who had given more encouragement to rebellion, by his treasonable harangues from the pulpit, than any other republican preacher, perhaps, upon the continent"; Thomas Jones, *History of New York during the Revolutionary War,* ed. Edward F. DeLancey, 2 vols. (New York: New York Historical Society, 1879), 1: 3–4.

12. Laidlie, Sermon of May 21, 1775. See Kennedy, "From Providence to Civil Religion," 11–23, for an analysis of Laidlie's political views.

13. Thomas B. Chandler, Memorandums 1775–1786, 1–4, MS Diary, typescript copy, General Theological Seminary, New York City.

14. *Journals of the Provincial Congress, Provincial Convention, Committee of Safety and Council of Safety of the State of New York 1775–1777,* 2 vols. (Albany, N.Y.: Thurlow Weed, 1842), 1: 9–11. In his journal, Presbyterian William Smith, Jr., commented on the Episcopal clergy's presence at these sessions: "The Power of the Congress appears in this for Nothing but Fear would bring the Episcopal clergy to this Se[r]vice"; Smith, *Historical Memoirs,* 1: 225.

15. New York Meeting for Sufferings MS Minutes, 14–15.

16. Ibid., 24, 26, 28.

17. John Wesley to James Dempster, May 19, 1775, and Wesley to Thomas Rankin, May 19, 1775, in Wesley, *Letters of John Wesley,* 6: 149–51.

18. MS Records of the Baptist Church in Paulings Precinct, 28; Gillette, ed., *Minutes of the Philadelphia Baptist Association,* 155; Royden W. Vosburgh, ed., *Records of the Reformed Dutch Church of Kinderhook,* 3 vols. (New York: New York Genealogical and Biographical Society, 1921), vol. 2. The Kinderhook congregation experienced consistent growth between 1771 and 1775, as eighty-three members were added, sixty-seven by confession of faith.

19. "Occupation of New York City by the British: Extracts from the Diary of the Moravian Congregation," *Pennsylvania Magazine of History and Biography* 1 (1877): 134.

20. New York Yearly Meeting MS Minutes, 1775.

21. These requests were made by the Provincial Congress in the summer of 1775. *Journals of the Provincial Congress. . . ,* 1: 67, 99.

22. Asbury, *Journal and Letters,* 1: 188.

23. *Journals of the . . . Provincial Convention. . . ,* 1: 515–21.

24. Jordan, "Anglican Establishment," 559, 573. Prior to the war, ministers of most denominations felt a responsibility to pray for the king, whether it was required by their liturgy or not. Even patriot John Rodgers had continued praying for the king through 1775; Rivington's *New-York Gazetteer,* June 12, 1775.

25. Joseph S. Tiedemann, "Patriots by Default: Queens County, New York, and the Brtish Army, 1776–1783," *William and Mary Quarterly* 3d Ser., 43 (1986): 36–37, suggests that 60 percent of this county's adult males were neutral immediately before the war.

26. Michael Kammen, "The American Revolution as a *Crise de Conscience:* The Case of New York," in Richard Jellison, ed., *Society, Freedom, and Conscience* (New York: Norton, 1976), 140; Thomas J. Wertenbaker, *Father Knickerbocker Rebels: New York City during the Revolution* (New York: Charles Scribner's Sons, 1948), 49–52.

27. The strongest case for explaining the Revolution as a product of religious differences, and for understanding the conflict in New York as a religious war, was made by Carl Bridenbaugh, *Mitre and Sceptre.* Recent works treating the question of Revolutionary decisions in New York include Robert A. East and Jacob Judd, eds., *The Loyalist Americans: A Focus on Greater New York* (Tarrytown, N.Y.: Sleepy Hollow Restorations, 1975); Bruce Wilkenfeld, "Revolutionary New York," in Milton M. Klein, ed., *New York: The Centennial Years 1676–1976* (Port Washington, N.Y.: Kennikat Press, 1976), 43–74; and Rick J. Ashton, "The Loyalist Experience: New York, 1763–1789" (Ph.D. diss., Northwestern University, 1973).

28. Jordan, "Anglican Establishment," 586, 618.

29. The historiography on this point is quite extensive. See Heimert, *Religion and the American Mind*; Edmund S. Morgan, "The Puritan Ethic and the American Revolution," in Morgan, ed., *The Challenge of the American Revolution* (New York: Norton, 1976), 88–138; Nathan Hatch, *The Sacred Cause of Liberty: Republican Thought and the Millennium* (New Haven, Conn.: Yale University Press, 1977); William G. McLoughlin, "The Role of Religion in the Revolution," in Stephen G. Kurtz and James H. Hutson, eds., *Essays on the American Revolution* (Chapel Hill: University of North Carolina Press, 1973), 197–255; and Royster, *A Revolutionary People at War*, 5–23, 152–61.

30. Gary B. Nash, *The Urban Crucible: Social Change, Political Consciousness, and the Origins of the American Revolution* (Cambridge, Mass.: Harvard University Press, 1979), 342–45.

31. Ibid., 372.

32. Among works on the Middle Colonies, see Adrian Leiby, *The Revolutionary War in the Hackensack Valley: The Jersey Dutch and the Neutral Ground, 1775–1783* (New Brunswick, N.J.: Rutgers University Press, 1962); Alice B. Kenney, "The Albany Dutch, Loyalists and Patriots," *New York History* 42 (1961): 331–50; Beardslee, "Reformed Church and the American Revolution," 17–33; and Leiby, *United Churches*, 150–51.

33. Beardslee, "Reformed Church and the American Revolution," 19–20.

34. For the evidence in New Jersey, see the books by Leiby, and for the Hudson Valley, see the articles by Kenney and Beardslee.

35. Jordan, "Anglican Establishment," 577; *History of the First Reformed Protestant Dutch Church of Breuckelen Now Known as the First Reformed Church of Brooklyn, 1654 to 1896* (Brooklyn, N.Y.: By the Consistory, 1896), 21–27; Joseph S. Tiedemann, "Response to Revolution: Queens County, New York, during the Era of the American Revolution" (Ph.D. diss., City University of New York, 1976), 35, 41, 45. Tiedemann found that in 1775 in Queens county, the Dutch Reformed percentages were 12.5 Whig, 33 Tory, and 53.7 uncommitted.

36. Lydekker, *Life and Letters of Inglis*, 195–96. Gerald De Jong, *The Dutch in America, 1609–1974* (Boston: Twayne, 1975), 109–16, gives a summary of Dutch Reformed attitudes in the American Revolution.

37. Dix, *History of Trinity Parish*, 1: 356, 2: 34; Mills, *Bishops by Ballot*, 7, 37; Jordan, "Anglican Establishment," 417; Woolverton, *Colonial Anglicanism in North America*, 232.

38. Gano, *Biographical Memoirs,* 92–95. William G. McLoughlin asserts that on the whole there was much less sympathy for the Revolution among Baptists in the Middle Colonies than among those in the Southern Colonies and New England; McLoughlin, ed., *The Diary of Isaac Backus,* 3 vols. (Providence, R.I.: Brown University Press, 1979), 2: 917.

39. Tiedemann, "Response to Revolution," 45–52; Charles S. Wightman, "History of the Baptist Church of Oyster Bay," in *Minutes of the Seventh Session of the Long Island Baptist Association* (New York: E. H. Jones, 1873), 40–41.

40. Kreider, *Lutheranism in New York,* 192; Karl Kretzmann, *The Oldest Lutheran Church in America* (New York: The Evangelical Lutheran Church of Saint Matthew, 1914), 28. Henry Muhlenberg encouraged all Lutheran ministers to remain neutral during the war and wrote that it was impossible for respectable preachers to engage in political activity. Ironically, a decade earlier, Muhlenberg himself had been active in the effort to oppose the introduction of royal government in Pennsylvania. Muhlenberg, *Journals,* 3: 101–2; Nash, *Urban Crucible,* 288. See Charles Mampoteng, "The Lutheran Governors of King's College," *Columbia University Quarterly* 27 (1935): 443–52, for Houseal's ties to the Anglican college.

41. Jordan, "Anglican Establishment," 206–9; Wertenbaker, *Father Knickerbocker Rebels,* 50–51. Cf. Leopold S. Launitz-Schurer, *Loyal Whigs and Revolutionaries: The Making of the Revolution in New York* (New York: New York University Press, 1980), on the loyalism of the DeLancey family.

42. Charles H. Stitt, *History of the Huguenot Church and Settlement at New Paltz* (Kingston, N.Y.: William H. Romeyn, 1863), 19–23.

43. Stocker, *Moravian Church in New York City,* 120.

44. Marcus, *Early American Jewry,* 1: 94; David De Sola Pool and Tamar De Sola Pool, *An Old Faith in the New World: Portrait of Shearith Israel, 1654–1954* (New York: Columbia University Press, 1955), 168.

45. Wingo, "Politics, Society, and Religion," 242–45; Harman C. Westervelt, "The Presbyterian Church, and Other Denominations in New York," 1–2, in Essays on Various Features of New York City File, New York Public Library Manuscript Room.

46. Tiedemann, "Response to Revolution," 35.

47. Worrall, *Quakers in the Colonial Northeast,* 140–41.

48. Cf. Kammen, "American Revolution as a *Crise de Conscience,*" 188–89, for a similar statement on this point.

49. Kelley, *The Cultural Pattern in American Politics,* 63–70.

50. *Journals of the . . . Provincial Convention. . . ,* 1:554.

51. The discussion of New York's constitutional process that follows is based principally on chap. 4 of John Pratt's *Religion, Politics, and Diversity,* 82–89.

52. Quoted in Leonard W. Levy, *Constitutional Opinions: Aspects of the Bill of Rights* (New York and Oxford: Oxford University Press, 1986), 157; *Journals of the . . . Provincial Convention. . . ,* 1: 846.

53. Thomas E. Buckley, *Church and State in Revolutionary Virginia, 1776–1787* (Charlottesville: University of Virginia Press, 1977), 6–7, 23–28, 192–96.

54. William H. Bennett, *Catholic Footsteps in Old New York: A Chronicle of Catholicity in the City of New York from 1524 to 1808* (1909; reprint ed., New York: United States Catholic Historical Society, 1973), 337.

55. *Journals of the . . . Provincial Convention. . . ,* 1: 844–45. Richard B. Morris, ed., Introduction, *John Jay: The Making of a Revolutionary—Unpublished Papers, 1745–1780* (New York: Harper & Row, 1975), 15, attributes Jay's anti-Catholic prejudice to Jay's Huguenot refugee background.

56. Pratt, *Religion, Politics, and Diversity,* 95–96; William C. Webster, "Comparative Study of the State Constitutions of the American Revolution," *Annals of the*

American Academy of Political and Social Sciences 9 (1897): 89. Cf. *The Constitution of the State of New-York* (Fish-Kill, N.Y.: Samuel Loudon, 1777).

57. Morton Borden, "Federalists, Antifederalists, and Religious Freedom," *Journal of Church and State* 21 (1979): 472–75. Among the restrictions included in other state constitutions were limiting the holding of public office to Protestants or "Christians"; requiring officeholders to acknowledge the inspiration of Scripture; and making allowance for public taxation to support the Protestant clergy; Webster, "Comparative Study of State Constitutions," 88–89.

58. Lewis Perry, *Intellectual Life in America: A History* (New York: Franklin Watts, 1984), 147–56.

59. My discussion of the Presbyterian role in state constitution-making is based on Wingo, "Politics, Society, and Religion," 163, 260–66, 277–80.

60. David O. Thomas, *The Honest Mind: The Thought and Work of Richard Price* (Oxford, England: Clarendon Press, 1977), 186.

61. Morgan, *Ezra Stiles,* 178–79.

62. Gordon Wood, "The Democratization of Mind in the American Revolution," in Robert H. Horwitz, ed., *The Moral Foundations of the American Republic* (Charlottesville: University of Virginia Press, 1977), 123–26.

63. Bennett, *Catholic Footsteps,* 249, notes that despite persecution and animosity from Protestants earlier in the century, a few Catholics had openly identified themselves with the Roman church.

64. Pratt, *Religion, Politics, and Diversity,* 113. This again contrasts with the situation in Virginia, where a group of Episcopalian rationalists led by James Madison favored the total withdrawal of government from religion. See Buckley, *Church and State in Revolutionary Virginia,* 99–109, 130–36, 179–81, 196–98.

65. John H. Livingston to Robert R. Livingston, Feb. 28, 1777, Robert R. Livingston Papers, New York Historical Society.

66. John H. Livingston to Robert R. Livingston, Mar. 17, 1777, Robert R. Livingston Papers. In the final letter, dated Apr. 8, 1777, John expressed his conviction that for political reasons the constitution should bar Catholics from holding public office.

67. [Jacob Green], *Observations on the Reconciliation of Great-Britain and the Colonies* (New York: John Holt, 1776), 12–13.

68. Smith, *Historical Memoirs,* 2: 421.

69. Pratt, *Religion, Politics, and Diversity,* 66.

70. Mills, *Bishops by Ballot,* 120.

71. "Presbyterians and the American Revolution: A Documentary Account," *Journal of Presbyterian History* 52 (1974): 446–48.

72. *Acts and Proceedings of the General Synod,* 83–86.

73. Buckley, *Church and State in Revolutionary Virginia,* 180–82.

74. Larry Gerlach, ed., *New Jersey in the American Revolution 1763–1783: A Documentary History* (Trenton, 1975), 452.

75. Flick, *American Revolution in New York,* 243; W. C. Abbot, *New York in the American Revolution* (New York, 1929), 113–17, 157, 208; Oscar T. Barck, *New York City during the War for Independence* (New York: Columbia University Press, 1931), 155–65; Wertenbaker, *Father Knickerbocker Rebels,* 80, 105–08.

76. Wesley, *Letters of John Wesley,* 6: 150–51.

77. Francis Asbury to [John Wesley], Sept. 20, 1783, in Asbury, *Journal and Letters,* 3: 29–32.

78. Barck, *New York City during the War,* 161–63; William L. Brower and Henry P. Miller eds., *Collegiate Reformed Protestant Dutch Church of the City of New York: Her Organization and Development* (New York: By the Consistory, 1928), 19.

79. Trinterud, *Forming of an American Tradition,* 255; "Presbyterians and the

American Revolution," 412; Samuel I. Prime, "Early Ministers of Long Island," *Journal of the Presbyterian Historical Society* 23 (1945): 181.

80. *ERNY*, 6: 4303–4. See Marius Schoonmaker, *The History of Kingston, New York* (New York: Burr Printing House, 1888), 221, for an example of a Dutch Reformed church (Kingston) that was destroyed during the war. Charles E. Corwin, "Incidents of Reformed Church Life in New York City during the Revolutionary War," *Journal of the Presbyterian Historical Society* 9 (1918): 364–66, details what happened to the Dutch Reformed church buildings in New York City.

81. Hough, "Archives of the SPG," 315.

82. Tiedemann, "Patriots by Default," 48.

83. O'Callaghan, ed., *Documentary History of New York*, 3: 1055–58.

84. Steiner, *Samuel Seabury*, 166–67.

85. Kammen, "American Revolution as a *Crise de Conscience*," 162–63.

86. Arthur J. McKeel, ed., "New York Quakers in the American Revolution," *Bulletin of Friends Historical Association* 29 (1940): 55; Peter Brock, *Pacifism in the United States, from the Colonial Era to the First World War* (Princeton, N.J.: Princeton University Press, 1968), 274–75.

87. First Baptist Church of New York to Philadelphia Baptist Association, Oct. 5, 1784, Philadelphia Baptist Association Letters, McKesson Papers.

88. Bolton, *Episcopal Church in Westchester*, 325; Charles W. Baird, *Chronicle of a Border Town: History of Rye* (New York: Anson D. F. Randolph & Co., 1871), 335–37. See Otto Hufeland, *Westchester County during the American Revolution 1775–1783* (White Plains, N.Y.: Westchester County Historical Society, 1926), for a detailed account of the war's devastation in this part of New York.

89. Baird, *History of Bedford Church*, 65.

90. Vandenberge, *Historical Directory*, 70.

91. George E. DeMille, *A History of the Diocese of Albany, 1704–1923* (Philadelphia: Church Historical Society, 1946), 22–25.

92. John W. Lydekker, "The Rev. John Stuart," *Historical Magazine of the Protestant Episcopal Church* 11 (1942): 36.

93. Bolton, *Episcopal Church in Westchester*, 510–11.

94. Dutchess Presbytery MS Minutes, 106.

95. Ibid., 120.

96. Royster, *A Revolutionary People at War*, 160–69, 273–78.

97. "Occupation of New York City: Moravian Congregation," 251.

98. Cf. William A. Polf, *Garrison Town: The British Occupation of New York City, 1776–1783* (Albany, N.Y.: New York State American Revolution Bicentennial Commission, 1976).

99. Corporation of Trinity Church, Minutes of the Vestry, 1: 409, 413, Trinity Parish Archives; Dix, *History of Trinity Parish*, 1: 427; Corwin, "Incidents of Reformed Church Life," 364–67.

100. Thomas B. Chandler Diary, Memorandums 1775–1786, 41, 46–47.

101. Jordan, "Anglican Establishment," 560.

102. Wakeley, *Lost Chapters of Methodism*, 281–87. The city's Anglican congregations also benefited from the presence of new hearers, many of whom were loyalist refugees from other colonies. By July 1782, their services were so crowded that the governor allowed them to worship in the large courtroom of City Hall, and even this room had to have additional seats placed in it. Barck, *New York City during the War*, 159–60.

103. Mark A. Noll et al., eds., *Eerdmans' Handbook to Christianity in America* (Grand Rapids, Mich.: Wm. B. Eerdmans, 1983), 147, make this same point with respect to the patriot side.

104. "Presbyterians and the American Revolution," 406–7; Gano, *Biographical Memoirs*, 92–116.

105. Vandenberge, *Historical Directory,* 63, 65, 106, 145; Corwin, "Incidents of Reformed Church Life," 360–63.

106. The records of the following churches were examined: the Reformed congregations in Kinderhook, Livingston, Hillsdale, Gallatin, Germantown, Schoharie, Coxsackie, Claverack, New Paltz, Red Hook, Ghent, Rochester, and Kingston; and the Lutheran congregations in West Camp, Athens, Schoharie, Claverack, Red Hook, Rhinebeck, and Germantown. A transcript of the Rochester Reformed Church records and the published records of the Kingston congregation, *Baptismal and Marriage Registers of the Old Dutch Church of Kingston,* ed. R. R. Hoes (New York: DeVinne Press, 1891), may be found at the Archives Room of the Senate House Museum, Kingston, N.Y. The records of the New Paltz church were published in *Collections of the Holland Society of New York* (New York: Holland Society, 1896), vol. 3, and those of Kinderhook in Vosburgh, ed., *Records of the Reformed Dutch Church of Kinderhook.* Transcribed and indexed copies of all the other records have been made by Arthur C. M. Kelley and can be found at the Columbia County Historical Society, Kinderhook, N.Y.

107. John Close served the New Windsor church in Orange County and the Newburgh church in Ulster County, while Ichabod Lewis was at Philip's Patent in Dutchess County.

108. Trinterud, *Forming of an Americna Tradition,* 254, incorrectly states that the Dutchess Presbytery, like the Suffolk Presbytery, did not function during the war. While it did not meet in 1779 or 1782, the Dutchess Presbytery did meet in the other years from 1775 through 1783. See Dutchess Presbytery MS Minutes, 103–18.

109. *Acts and Proceedings of the General Synod,* 65. These particular assemblies, along with one in New Brunswick, N.J., had been formed in 1771 to serve as regional representative bodies to which member congregations sent ministerial and lay delegates for annual meetings. Each particular assembly, in turn, sent delegates to the annual meeting of the General Body.

110. John Asplund, *The Universal Register of the Baptist Denomination in North America for the years 1790, 1791, 1792, 1793, and part of 1794* (Boston: John W. Folsom, 1795), 18–20. While all were Baptist, these congregations held differing views on other doctrines. The church in Canaan, for instance, held the Arminian view of the nature of Christ's atonement, while the other congregations were strict Calvinists. McLoughlin, ed., *Diary of Isaac Backus,* 2: 1093–95.

111. Worrall, *Quakers in the Colonial Northeast,* 174–75, 226.

112. My discussion of this congregation's history is based on A. P. Van Gieson, *Anniversary Discourse and History of the First Reformed Church of Poughkeepsie, New York* (Poughkeepsie, N.Y., 1893), 22, 65–68, and Edwin C. Coon, *Old First: A History of the Reformed Church of Poughkeepsie, New York* (New York: The William-Frederick Press, 1967), 32–38.

113. My discussion of Christ Church is based on Helen Wilkinson Reynolds, ed., *The Records of Christ Church, Poughkeepsie, New York* (Poughkeepsie, N.Y.: Frank B. Howard, 1911), 47–68, 83.

114. Minutes of Baptist, Presbyterian, Dutch Reformed, and Quaker bodies were examined. They were the only denominations that had active assemblies representing New York congregations during the war.

115. Gillette, ed., *Minutes of the Philadelphia Baptist Association,* 167–69.

116. Klett, ed., *Minutes of the Presbyterian Church,* 556, 560, 562, 568.

117. John Rodgers, *Holiness the Nature and Design of the Gospel of Christ* (Hartford, Conn.: Hudson & Goodwin, 1779), iii.

118. *Acts and Proceedings of the General Synod,* 68–69, 93. See Gillette, ed., *Minutes of the Philadelphia Baptist Association,* 159, for a similar home missions project started by Baptists in 1778. They established a voluntary fund the interest of which would

be used to send preachers to the back settlements.

119. New York Yearly Meeting MS Minutes, 1775, 1779, 1780.

120. *Acts and Proceedings of the General Synod,* 71; Klett, ed., *Minutes of the Presbyterian Church,* 568.

121. Gillette, ed., *Minutes of the Philadelphia Baptist Association,* 179. Another illustration of poor communication is the fact that New York's Methodist Society, though very active during the war, had no correspondence with the annual Methodist Conferences between 1778 and 1784. *Minutes of the Methodist Conferences,* 14–45.

122. One classic example of this type of omission comes in the minutes of the Suffolk Presbytery, which nowhere mention the 1764 revival in Easthampton, when hundreds were converted. See Suffolk Presbytery MS Minutes, 100–13.

123. New York Meeting for Sufferings MS Minutes, 179–80.

124. Captain Franklin Ellis, *History of Columbia County, New York* (Philadelphia: Everts & Ensign, 1878), 307; Marini, *Radical Sects,* 52–53, 75–80.

125. Principles and Rules of a Praying Society formed in the City of New York during the war of the American Revolution by the Scotch Presbyterian Patriots, New York City Misc. MSS, New York Historical Society.

126. Arthur C. M. Kelley, *Settlers and Residents: Town of Livingston 1719–1899,* 3 vols. (Rhinebeck, N.Y.: By the Compiler, 1978), 3: pt. 1. A few of these new members were transfers from other Reformed congregations, but most were admitted upon a confession of faith.

127. Wakeley, *Lost Chapters of Methodism,* 285–87. The strongest indication that the society's classes were well attended is the increasing size of collections (offerings) received from these classes.

128. Moore, MS Journal of journey . . . to Pennsylvania and New York, 1778, 75–76; New York Meeting for Sufferings MS Minutes, 94.

129. New York Meeting for Sufferings MS Minutes, 103, 106.

130. Samuel Waldo to Philadelphia Baptist Association, [1782], Philadelphia Baptist Association Letters, McKesson Papers; also see Epherim Pain [church clerk of Amenia Precinct] to Philadelphia Baptist Association, Oct. 9, 1782, Philadelphia Baptist Association Letters, McKesson Papers.

131. McLoughlin, ed., *Diary of Isaac Backus,* 2: 1092.

132. James Benedict to Philadelphia Baptist Association, Oct. 6, 1779, Philadelphia Baptist Association Letters, McKesson Papers.

133. Charles Inglis, *A Farewell-Sermon, preached at St. George's and St. Paul's Chapels in the City of New-York, October 26, 1783* (London: C. Buckton, 1784), 23–24.

134. Wakeley, *Lost Chapters of Methodism,* 299; Stocker, *Moravian Church in New York City,* 120, 145.

135. Pratt, *Religion, Politics, and Diversity,* 114.

136. Azel Roe, God blesseth the Provision of Grace to his Church, Roe MSS, Presbyterian Historical Society. Roe preached this sermon four times in New York during the Revolution, the last time at Hartford South, N.Y., on Nov. 23, 1983.

Five. "An Uncommon Train of Providences"

1. Israel Evans, *A Discourse Delivered in New York* (New York: John Holt, 1784), 8–13.

2. John Rodgers, *The Divine Goodness Displayed in the American Revolution: A Sermon* (New York: Samuel Loudon, 1784), 29–36.

3. Marcus, *Early American Jewry,* 1: 100–101.

4. Abraham Beach, *A Thanksgiving Discourse delivered in Trinity Church* (New York, 1784), 38.

5. *Journal of the Senate of the State of New-York . . . Seventh Session* (New York: E. Holt, 1784), 31–32, 45–49. See *Acts and Proceedings of the General Synod*, 129, 141–42, 156–67, and *ERNY*, 6: 4346, for the Dutch Reformed effort in the 1780s to get a special amendment passed to the incorporation act allowing for the incorporation of Dutch Reformed congregations according to their own church order.

6. *Laws of the State of New-York . . . Seventh Session* (New York: E. Holt, 1784), 21–25.

7. Ibid., 42–45.

8. Ibid., 69–71.

9. Bennett, *Catholic Footsteps*, 367.

10. Countryman, *A People in Revolution*, 238–42, discusses these acts in light of New York's political context in 1784.

11. Rodgers, *Divine Goodness Displayed*, 26–27.

12. Stocker, *Moravian Church in New York City*, 145.

13. First Baptist Church of New York to Philadelphia Baptist Association, Oct. 5, 1784, Philadelphia Baptist Association Letters, McKesson Papers; Second Baptist Church of New York to Philadelphia Baptist Association, Oct. 2, 1787, Philadelphia Baptist Association Letters, McKesson Papers.

14. Wakeley, *Lost Chapters of Methodism*, 282, 299.

15. Reynolds, ed., *Records of Christ Church, Poughkeepsie*, 65, 399.

16. Dutchess Presbytery MS Minutes, 151–52.

17. *Acts and Proceedings of the General Synod*, 112–14.

18. Klett, ed., *Minutes of the Presbyterian Church*, 596.

19. New York, Presbytery MS Minutes 1775–1797, 153–59, New York Presbytery MSS, Presbyterian Historical Society; Suffolk Presbytery MS Minutes, 175–85; Dutchess Presbytery MS Minutes, 128–29.

20. Frederick V. Mills, Sr., "The Protestant Episcopal Churches in the United States 1783–1789: Suspended Animation or Remarkable Recovery?" *Historical Magazine of the Protestant Episcopal Church* 46 (1977): 153–54.

21. Kreider, *Lutheranism in New York*, 140–47.

22. *Acts and Proceedings of the General Synod*, 115.

23. Klett, ed., *Minutes of the Presbyterian Church*, 587.

24. *Acts and Proceedings of the General Synod*, 135–36; Dutchess Presbytery MS Minutes, 124.

25. *Acts and Proceedings of the General Synod*, 109–10.

26. Johannes C. Rubel, *An Answer to Several Church Meetings* (New York: J. McLean, 1784), 14–15.

27. *ERNY*, 6: 4332–36.

28. Dix, *History of Trinity Parish*, 2: 1–30.

29. Trustees of the Corporation of Trinity Parish to Rev. Samuel Provoost, Jan. 8, 1784, Benjamin Moore file, Trinity Parish Archives.

30. Among the numerous studies adhering to this view are Robert Baird, *Religion in the United States of America* (1844; reprinted., New York: Arno Press, 1969); Leonard Woolsey Bacon, *A History of American Christianity* (New York: The Christian Literature Co., 1897); William Warren Sweet, *The Story of Religion in America* (New York: Harper & Bros., 1930); Hudson, *Religion in America;* Ahlstrom, *Religious History of the American People;* and Nathan Hatch et al., *The Search for Christian America* (Westchester, Ill.: Crossway, 1983), 113.

31. Sweet, *Story of Religion in America*, 322.

32. See Douglas H. Sweet, "Church Vitality and the American Revolution: Historiographical Consensus and Thoughts towards a New Perspective," *Church History* 45 (1976): 341–59, for a discussion of the development and limitations of this historiography. Among the few works that present a positive view of American

religion in this period are Thomas Hanley O'Brien, *The American Revolution and Religion: Maryland 1770–1800* (Washington, D.C.: The Catholic University of America Press, Consortium Press, 1971); Frederick A. Norwood, *The Story of American Methodism: A History of the United Methodists and Their Relations* (Nashville, Tenn.: The Abingdon Press, 1974); Mills, "Protestant Episcopal Churches 1783–1789"; De-Mille, *Diocese of Albany,* 26–41.

33. William S. Perry, ed., *Journals of General Conventions of the Protestant Episcopal Church, in the United States, 1785–1821,* 3 vols. (Claremont, N.H.: Claremont Manufacturing Co., 1874), 1: 18–25. See A. Dean Calcote, "The Proposed Prayer Book of 1784," *Historical Magazine of the Protstant Episcopal Church* 46 (1977): 275–95, for the controversy surrounding the proposed liturgical changes.

34. *Journals of the Conventions of the Protestant Episcopal Church in the Diocese of New York* (New York: Henry M. Onderdonk, 1844), 18.

35. Ibid., 24–30. Mills, *Bishops by Ballot,* 288, discusses how Provoost and the other postwar bishops were the type of bishops that Samuel Johnson and Thomas Chandler had argued for earlier: strictly spiritual, with no ties to the state.

36. *Minutes of the Methodist Conferences,* 49–51.

37. Freeborn Garrettson, *The Experience and Travels of Mr. Freeborn Garrettson* (Philadelphia: Joseph Crukshank, 1794), 225.

38. Jones, *Quakers in the American Colonies,* 261; David Benedict, *A General History of the Baptist Denomination in America* (New York: Lewis Colby & Co., 1848), 486, 543, 546.

39. Suffolk Presbytery MS Minutes, 189, 193, 196.

40. Nichols, *Presbyterianism in New York State,* 68; Trinterud, *Forming of an American Tradition,* 279–306.

41. Klett, ed., *Minutes of the Presbyterian Church,* 636–37.

42. *Acts and Proceedings of the General Synod,* 104, 115.

43. Ibid., 128; *ERNY,* 6: 4323–25.

44. Kreider, *Lutheranism in New York,* 127–29.

45. *Translation of the German Minutes of the Evangelical Lutheran Ministerium of the State of New York and adjacent states and counties,* trans. Theodore E. Palleske (Staten Island, N.Y., 1937), 1.

46. Ibid., 2.

47. Trinterud, *Forming of an American Tradition,* 306.

48. Nathan Bangs, *The Life of the Rev. Freeborn Garrettson* (New York: Emory & Waugh, 1830), 219.

49. New York Meeting for Sufferings MS Minutes, 185.

50. Asplund, *Universal Register of Baptist Denomination,* 18–20, 90.

51. Mills, "Protestant Episcopal Churches 1783–1789," 163; *Journals of the Conventions of the Episcopal Diocese of New York,* 46–47.

52. Howard, "Education and Ethnicity in Colonial New York," 211–15, 314–22, 450.

53. Unlike the other communions, New York's Baptists had few restrictions on who could preach, and laymen often became preachers with little or no formal training.

54. New York Presbytery MS Minutes, 159, 288. See S.D. Alexander, *The Presbytery of New York, 1738–1888* (New York: Anson D.F. Randolph & Co., 1888), for more information on how this presbytery responded to the problems of the postwar period.

55. Dutchess Presbytery MS Minutes, 151–52.

56. Suffolk Presbytery MS Minutes, 181–89; Trinterud, *Forming of an American Tradition,* 306. The seven ministers were Noah Wetmore, Asa Hillyer, Aaron Woolworth, Nathan Woodhull, Joshua Williams, Thomas Russel, and Wait Cornwell.

57. Klett, ed., *Minutes of the Presbyterian Church*, 597–98.
58. Humphrey, *From King's College to Columbia*, 269–82.
59. *Journals of the Conventions of the Episcopal Diocese of New York*, 46–47. Cf. Mills, "Protestant Episcopal Churches 1783–1789," 153–56, on the national trend among Episcopalians toward an American born and trained clergy.
60. Kreider, *Lutheranism in New York*, 122; Muhlenberg, *Journals*, 3: 656–57.
61. Humphrey, *From King's College to Columbia*, 285, points out that the student body in the 1780s included fifteen men who became pastors in the Episcopal, Dutch Reformed, Presbyterian, Baptist, German Reformed, and Associate Reformed churches.
62. Rev. Dr. John H. Livingston to Rev. Dr. Eilardus Westerlo, Oct. 22, 1783, *ERNY*, 6: 4312–13.
63. *Acts and Proceedings of the General Synod*, 123–25.
64. Vandenberge, *Historical Directory*, 7, 17, 23, 89, 163.
65. *ERNY*, 6: 4338–39. The Dutch Reformed also eased their ministerial shortage by beginning to accept pastors trained and ordained in other communions. Presbyterian William Linn became the first such minister when he joined John Livingston at the Collegiate Church in 1787. Ten others entered from other denominations between 1792 and 1800. Corwin, *Manual of Dutch Reformed Church*, 75, 157. In addition, Dirck Romeyn, Dutch Reformed pastor at Schenectady, established an academy there in the mid-1780s, that later became Union College.
66. New York Yearly Meeting MS Minutes, 1780.
67. Worrall, *Quakers in the Colonial Northeast*, 181–83.
68. Methodists did take steps in the next decade to provide for education when the General Conference outlined a plan for seminaries of learning in 1796. *Journals of the General Conference of the Methodist Episcopal Church, 1796–1836*, 3 vols. (New York: Carlton & Phillips, 1855), 1: 17–20.
69. Asbury, *Journal and Letters*, 1: 539–43, 599–601; Garrettson, *Experience and Travels*, 225–47.
70. Asbury, *Journal and Letters*, 1: 726, 729.
71. First Baptist Church of New York to Philadelphia Baptist Association, Sept. 25, 1787, Philadelphia Baptist Association Letters, McKesson Papers; Gillette, ed., *Minutes of the Philadelphia Baptist Association*, 229.
72. McLoughlin, ed., *Diary of Isaac Backus*, 2: 1095, 3: 1385.
73. *Acts and Proceedings of the General Assembly of the Presbyterian Church in the United States of America, A.D. 1789* (Philadelphia: Francis Bailey, 1789), 8.
74. Synod of New York and New Jersey MS Minutes 1788–1822, 11, Synod of New York and New Jersey MSS, Presbyterian Historical Society; New York Presbytery MS Minutes, 288; Dutchess Presbytery MS Minutes, 150–52.
75. *Journals of the Conventions of the Episcopal Diocese of New York*, 38–39.
76. *Acts and Proceedings of the General Synod*, 114–15.
77. Ibid., 180–81.
78. Vandenberge, *Historical Directory*, 370.
79. De Jong, *Dutch Reformed Church in Colonies*, 224, 229.
80. *Acts and Proceedings of the General Synod*, 184–85. New York's Lutherans, led by Johann Kunze, also took steps toward Americanization with the reintroduction of English services in the 1780s, the printing in English of the New York Ministerium's constitution in the 1790s, and the establishment of an American Lutheran theological seminary in the early 1800s. Kreider, *Lutheranism in New York*, 123, 129, 134. Cf. Armin G. Weng, "The Language Problem in the Lutheran Church in Pennslyvania, 1742–1820," *Church History* 5 (1936): 359–75.
81. Synod of New York and New Jersey MS Minutes, 11.
82. Royster, *A Revolutionary People at War*, 160–74, discusses the role played by

chaplains during the war. For examples of typical war-time sermons preached by chaplains on the patriot side, see John Rodgers, *Holiness the Nature and Design of the Gospel of Christ;* William Linn, *A Military Discourse* (Philadelphia, 1776); Israel Evans, *A Discourse Delivered Near York in Virginia* (Philadelphia: Francis Bailey, 1782); and Israel Evans, *A Discourse, Delivered on the 18th Day of December, 1777* (Lancaster, Pa.: Francis Bailey, 1778). Gano, *Biographical Memoirs,* 93–116, provides a glimpse of the life and ministry of one chaplain during the Revolution.

83. Rodgers, *Divine Goodness Displayed,* 30, 35–36.

84. Trinterud, *Forming of an American Tradition,* 277–78.

85. "Letters of Uzal Ogden," *The Methodist Magazine* 6 (1823): 112–13.

86. Uzal Ogden, *A Sermon . . . May 16, 1786, Before a Convention of Clerical and Lay Deputies of the Protestant Episcopal Church in the State of New Jersey* (New York: Samuel & John Loudon, 1786), 17.

87. Uzal Ogden, *An Address to those Persons at Elizabeth-Town . . . Who have lately been seriously impressed with a Desire to obtain Salvation* (New York: J. McLean, 1785), 21–22.

88. Thomas Moore, *A Sermon . . . before the Convention of the Protestant Episcopal Church* (New York: Hugh Gaine, 1789), 14–15.

89. Jeremiah Leaming, *Dissertations upon Various Subjects* (New Haven, Conn.: Thomas & Samuel Green, 1788), 32–33.

90. Winthrop S. Hudson, "Denominationalism as a Basis of Ecumenicity: A Seventeenth Century Conception," *Church History* 24 (1955): 32–50, gives the classic definition of the denominational theory of the church.

91. Jedediah Chapman, "A Synodical Discourse," in David Austin, ed., *The American Preacher, or a Collection of Sermons,* 4 vols. (Elizabethtown, N.J.: Kollock, 1791, 1793), 2: 177–80.

92. Ibid., 181–87.

93. Robert C. Monk, "Unity and Diversity among Eighteenth-Century Colonial Anglicans and Methodists," *Historical Magazine of the Protestant Episcopal Church* 38 (1969): 54, 69; Asbury, *Journal and Letters,* 1: 442, 467; 2: 54, 130, 355; "Letters of Uzal Ogden," *Methodist Magazine* 5 (1822): 422–24, 460–62.

94. Humphrey, *From King's College to Columbia,* 292.

95. David Schuyler Bogart, *A Discourse delivered before a Religious Society, upon the Admission of a Member* (New York: J. & A. M'Lean, [1788]), 4–5, 11.

96. John Barent Johnson, MS Diary 1787–1803, Aug. 25, 1787, and May 11, 1788, Columbiana Collection, Columbia University Library, New York City. Johnson developed a particularly close friendship with John Mitchell Mason and the rest of his family (Mason's father was an Associate Reformed pastor in the city), and recorded attending the worship services of at least five denominations in 1787–1788.

97. Corporation of Trinity Church, Minutes of the Vestry, 1: 482, 485.

98. Gillette, ed., *Minutes of the Philadelphia Baptist Association,* 247–48; *Journals of the Conventions of the Episcopal Church,* 1: 85; Synod of New York and New Jersey MS Minutes, 12.

99. Klett, ed., *Minutes of the Presbyterian Church,* 592–93, 603–7, 610–11, 629, 637–38; *Acts and Proceedings of the General Synod,* 121, 132, 190–91, 199. The Presbyterian New York and New Jersey Synod also reestablished in 1788 a friendly correspondence with the Congregational General Association in Connecticut. Synod of New York and New Jersey MS Minutes, 12.

100. Washington wrote this in a letter of thanks to the Episcopal General Convention for their congratulatory address sent to him after his election to the presidency. *Journals of the Conventions of the Episcopal Church,* 1: 131–34.

101. Asbury, *Journal and Letters*, 1: 599–600, 692, 764; Garrettson, *Experience and Travels*, 225–27, 242; Bangs, *Life of Freeborn Garrettson*, 194.

102. Asbury, *Journal and Letters*, 1: 601.

103. Ibid., 1: 542, 726; Garrettson, *Experience and Travels*, 235.

104. Donald G. Mathews, "The Second Great Awakening as an Organizing Process, 1780–1830: An Hypothesis," *American Quarterly* 21 (1969): 36.

105. De Sola Pool and De Sola Pool, *An Old Faith in the New World*, 448–49, 457.

106. Corporation of Trinity Church, Minutes of the Vestry, 1: 477. Cf. Mary Christine Taylor, *A History of the Foundations of Catholicism in Northern New York* (New York: United States Catholic Historical Society, 1976), and Martin J. Becker, *A History of Catholic Life in the Diocese of Albany, 1609–1864* (New York: United States Catholic Historical Society, 1975) for information on Catholics in upper New York after the Revolution.

107. For the Lutherans and Dutch Reformed, I sampled the records listed in n. 106, chap. four. For the Presbyterians I examined "Records of the First and Second Presbyterian Churches of the City of New York," *The New York Genealogical and Biographical Records* 11 (1880): 83, 120–24; 14 (1883): 118–23.

108. Thomas, *A Century of Universalism*, 261–62.

109. Marini, *Radical Sects*, 88–94, 127–32.

110. Bennett, *Catholic Footsteps*, 368–83; Leo R. Ryan, *Old St. Peter's: The Mother Church of Catholic New York (1785–1935)* (New York: United States Catholic Historical Society, 1935), 36–70. Ryan says there were about two hundred Catholics in New York City in the mid-1780s.

111. De Sola Pool and De Sola Pool, *An Old Faith in the New World*, 47, 213–14, 260–63, 298, 352–53.

112. Gillette, ed., *Minutes of the Philadelphia Baptist Association*, 216, 225, 234, 252; Buell, *Import of the Saint's Confession*, 44–45; *Minutes of the Methodist Conferences*, 66, 75, 83.

113. Baird, *Religion in the United States*, 221–24; Sweet, *Story of Religion in America*, 322.

Six. "A Glorious Enterprize"

1. *Minutes of the New-York Baptist Association . . . 1803* (n.p., n.d.), 7.

2. Alexander MacWhorter, *The Blessedness of the Liberal* (New York: T. & J. Swords, 1796), 26.

3. On the unifying character of the awakening, see Perry Miller, "From the Covenant to the Revival," in James Ward Smith and A. Leland Jamison, eds., *The Shaping of American Religion* (Princeton, N.J.: Princeton University Press, 1961), 332–68; on its organizing character, see William Warren Sweet, *Religion in the Development of American Culture 1765–1840* (New York: Charles Scribner's Sons, 1952); T. Scott Miyakawa, *Protestants and Pioneers: Individualism and Conformity on the American Frontier* (Chicago: University of Chicago Press, 1964); and Mathews, "Second Great Awakening," 27–43.

4. Hudson, *Religion in America*, 134–36; Franklin H. Littell, *From State Church to Pluralism: Protestant Interpretation of Religion in American History* (Garden City, N.Y.: Anchor Books, 1962), 30; and William McLoughlin, *Revivals, Awakenings, and Reform: An Essay on Religion and Social Change in America, 1607–1977* (Chicago: University of Chicago Press, 1978), 106–22. Recent studies that have challenged this view include Richard D. Shiels, "The Second Great Awakening in Connecticut: Critique of the Traditional Interpretation," *Church History* 49 (1980): 401–15; Marini, *Radical Sects*, 40–59, 82–101; Douglas H. Sweet, "Church and Community: Town Life and Ministerial Ideals in Revolutionary New Hampshire" (Ph.D. diss., Columbia Uni-

versity, 1978); Randolph A. Roth, "Whence This Strange Fire? Religious and Reform Movements in the Connecticut River Valley of Vermont, 1791–1843" (Ph.D. diss., Yale University, 1981); and Martha T. Blauvelt, "Society, Religion, and Revivalism: The Second Great Awakening in New Jersey, 1780–1830," (Ph.D. diss., Princeton University, 1975).

5. Hudson, *Religion in America* 131–35; H. Shelton Smith, Robert T. Handy, and Lefferts A. Loetscher, *American Christianity: An Historical Interpretation with Representative Documents,* 2 vols. (New York: Charles Scribner's Sons, 1960), 1: 519.

6. *Acts and Proceedings of the General Assembly of the Presbyterian Church . . . 1795 and 1796* (Philadelphia: Samuel Smith, 1796), 12; *Acts and Proceedings of the General Assembly of the Presbyterian Church . . . 1798* (Philadelphia: Samuel Smith, 1798), 11–14.

7. Gillette, ed., *Minutes of the Philadelphia Baptist Association,* 318–20.

8. *Minutes of the New-York Baptist Association . . . 1796* (n.p., n.d.), 4; *Journals of the General Conference of the Methodist Episcopal Church,* 1: 25.

9. Associated Westchester Presbytery MS Constitution and Records 1792–1830, 30, Associated Westchester Presbytery MSS, Presbyterian Historical Society; Hudson Presbytery MS Records 1795–1806, 45, Hudson Presbytery MSS, Presbyterian Historical Society.

10. John Mitchell Mason, *A Sermon, preached September 20th, 1793* (New York: Samuel Loudon & Son, 1793), 8–14, 17. Blauvelt, "Society, Religion, and Revivalism," 76–77, suggests that the strong sense of declension among the clergy was partly the result of the new national vision adopted by various emerging denominations in the late eighteenth century. As the clergy's vision grew, so did their fear that they would be unable to fulfill it.

11. "Address of the New York Missionary Society," *Edinburgh Missionary Magazine* 2 (1797): 67.

12. *United States Christian Magazine* 1 (1796): 64.

13. Gillette, ed., *Minutes of the Philadelphia Baptist Association,* 321.

14. Cf. Martin E. Marty, *The Infidel: Free Thought and American Religion* (Cleveland and New York: World Publishing Co., 1961), 19–20.

15. Lois W. Banner, "Religious Benevolence as Social Control: A Critique of an Interpretation," *Journal of American History* 60 (1973): 33–34; Mark Noll, *Christians in the American Revolution* (Washington, D.C.: Christian University Press, 1977), 158–60.

16. May, *Enlightenment in America,* 233–34.

17. Thomas, *A Century of Universalism,* 262–68; Miller, *The Larger Hope,* 681–82. The 1790s also saw the publication in New York City of another defense of universal salvation, Joseph Young's *Calvinism and Universalism Contrasted.*

18. For example, the minutes and circular letters of the Philadelphia Baptist Association for 1775, 1778, and 1796 all lament a declining zeal among believers and the triumph of iniquity. Gillette, ed., *Minutes of the Philadelphia Baptist Association,* 149, 167–68, 318–21.

19. This is essentially the nature of the argument in Mathews, "Second Great Awakening," 23–43.

20. First Baptist Church of New York to Philadelphia Baptist Association, Sept. 25, 1787.

21. Stephen Van Voorhees, Sermons of Nov. 17, 1775, and June 1795, Sermons of Stephen Van Voorhees [1773–1795]. Since Van Voorhees preached his sermons many times, the dates on them are only helpful for identification purposes; Stitt, *Huguenot Church at New Paltz,* 24.

22. "Letters to Dr. Rippon from New York," *Transactions of the Baptist Historical Society* 1 (1909): 69–79.

23. I do not mean to imply that ministers did not play an important role in the religious developments of this era. Instead, the point is simply that this particular aspect of their efforts did not by itself create an awakening.

24. Matthews, "Second Great Awakening," 25.

25. "An Account of the Revival of Religion at Bridgehampton," *New York Missionary Magazine* 1 (1800): 375–81.

26. "An Account of a remarkable Revival of Religion in Bern, Albany County," *New York Missionary Magazine* 1 (1800): 286–91.

27. *Acts and Proceedings of the General Assembly of the Presbyterian Church . . . 1799* (Philadelphia: William Woodward, 1799), 14; *Minutes of the New-York Baptist Association . . . 1796*, 4.

28. Buell, *Import of the Saint's Confession*, 45.

29. John Street Methodist Church Records, bk. 1A, vol. 233, Methodist Episcopal Church Records, New York Public Library Manuscript Room; Asbury, *Journal and Letters*, 1: 624, 652.

30. Wakeley, *Lost Chapters of Methodism*, 368, 396.

31. Asbury, *Journal and Letters*, 2: 118–19, 122; *Minutes of the Methodist Conferences*, 190.

32. "History of the Stillwater Baptist Church," in *Seventy-Third Anniversary of the Saratoga Baptist Association* (Amsterdam, N.Y.: The "Democrat" Steam Printing House, 1877), 12–13.

33. *Minutes of the Shaftsbury Association . . . 1794* (Canaan, N.Y.: Elihu Phinny, 1794), 3; Asplund, *Universal Register of Baptist Denomination*, 20.

34. *Minutes of the Shaftsbury Association . . . 1800* (Troy, N.Y.: R. Moffitt & Co., 1800), 6, 15.

35. Report to Synod of Presbytery of New York, Oct. 10, 1797, Associate Reformed Synod Papers 1782–1803, New York Historical Society.

36. *Minutes of the Shaftsbury Association . . . M, DCC, XCI* (Bennington, Vt.: Anthony Haswell, 1791), 3; *Minutes of the Shaftsbury Association . . . 1794*, 6; Asplund, *Universal Register of Baptist Denomination*, 19.

37. Vosburgh, ed., *Records of the Reformed Church of Kinderhook*, vol. 2; Ellis, *History of Columbia County*, 231.

38. *Minutes of the Methodist Conferences*, 94–242.

39. *Acts and Proceedings of the General Assembly of the Presbyterian Church . . . 1790 and 1791* (Philadelphia: R. Aitken & Son, 1791), 16–17.

40. Philander Chase, *Bishop Philander Chase's Reminiscences: An Autobiography*, 2d ed., 2 vols. (Boston: James B. Dow, 1848), 1: 30, 36–41.

41. DeMille, *Diocese of Albany*, 41–42; Ammi Rogers, *Memoirs of the Rev. Ammi Rogers*, 6th ed. (Troy, N.Y.: By the Author, 1834), 28, 34.

42. *Acts and Proceedings of the General Synod*, 307.

43. Ellis, *History of Columbia County*, 385.

44. Asher Wickham to Elder Comer Bullock, July 9, 1797, Envelope 3, MS Records of the Stanford Baptist Church, New York Baptist Church Records, American Baptist Historical Society.

45. Asher Wickham to Elder Bullock, June 9, 1799, Envelope 3, MS Records of the Stanford Baptist Church.

46. For contemporary accounts of other revivals in New York, see Rippon, *Baptist Annual Register, 1790–1793*, 100; McLoughlin, ed., *Diary of Isaac Backus*, 3: 1287, 1299, 1310; *New York Missionary Magazine* 1 (1800): 119, 158–59, 2 (1801): 469–71; *Edinburgh Missionary Magazine* 3 (1798): 90, 5 (1800): 220; John Rippon, *The Baptist Annual Register, 1801–1802* (London, 1802), 610–11; MS Records of the Baptist Church in Paulings Precinct, 33. Such religious fervor continued an eighteenth-century tradition of spiritual interest on the American frontier. See Smith,

"Congregation, State, and Denomination," 155–76, and Bonomi and Eisenstadt, "Church Adherence," 248, 262–68, 275.

47. May, *Enlightenment in America,* 223–25.

48. William Linn, *The Blessings of America* (New York: Thomas Greenleaf, 1791), 33–34. On Linn, see Philip J. Anderson, "William Linn, 1752–1808: American Revolutionary & Anti-Jeffersonian," *Journal of Presbyterian History* 55 (1977): 381–94.

49. Hatch, *Sacred Cause of Liberty,* 96–175.

50. *Minutes of the New-York Baptist Association . . . 1802* (n.p., n.d.), 8; Gillette, ed., *Minutes of the Philadelphia Baptist Association,* 363.

51. New York Baptist Association to Philadelphia Baptist Association, May 23, 1794, Philadelphia Baptist Association Letters, McKesson Papers.

52. *Minutes of the New-York Baptist Association . . . 1793* (n.p., n.d.), 8.

53. Minister John Stanford, a recent immigrant from England, gave this report to the Warwick Baptist Association and probably to the New York Association. Stanford had apparently heard it from a correspondent in England—perhaps John Rippon, for Isaac Backus received the same report. See *Minutes of the Warwick Baptist Association . . . 1794* (n.p., n.d.), 3; *Minutes of the New-York Baptist Association . . . 1794* (n.p., n.d.), 7–8; and McLoughlin, ed., *Diary of Isaac Backus,* 3: 1371.

54. New York Baptist Associaton to Philadelphia Baptist Association, May 23, 1794.

55. Kennedy, "From Providence to Civil Religion," 119–20.

56. "Address of the New York Missionary Society," 65 (n. 11 above); Mac-Whorter, *Blessedness of the Liberal,* 26, 28.

57. Northern Missionary Society in the State of New York, *The Constitution of the Northern Missionary Society in the State of New York* (Schenectady, N.Y.: C. P. Wyckoff, 1797), 2, 13–15.

58. Preface, *The Theological Magazine* 3 (1798): 3–4.

59. "Thoughts on the Plan for Social Prayer, Proposed by the Directors of the New York Missionary Society," *Edinburgh Missionary Magazine* 3 (1798): 490–94.

60. Shiels, "Second Great Awakening in Connecticut," 413.

61. While evangelicals were displeased by 1798 by the turn of events in France, they still believed progress was being made toward the millennium. See William Linn, *A Discourse on National Sins* (New York: T. & J. Swords, 1798), iv–v, 24, 30–31, 35–36.

62. For one example, see John H. Livingston, *The Triumph of the Gospel: A Sermon delivered before the New York Missionary Society* (New York: T. & J. Swords, 1804). Cf. Oliver W. Elsbree, *The Rise of the Missionary Spirit in America, 1790–1815* (Williamsport, Pa.: Williamsport Printing & Binding Co., 1928), for the connection of the missionary spirit with postmillennialism. See Lois W. Banner, "Presbyterians and Voluntarism in the Early Republic," *Journal of Presbyterian History* 50 (1972): 188–90, and Lefferts A. Loetscher, "The Problem of Christian Unity in Early Nineteenth-Century America," *Church History* 32 (1963): 3–6, for the role of postmillennialism in stimulating Christian unity.

63. Samuel Austin, *Disinterested Love, the Ornament of the Christian, and the Duty of Man* (New York: William Durell, 1791).

64. Other noteworthy attempts were made by Samuel Miller, *A Discourse Delivered in the New Presbyterian Church, New-York* (New York: F. Childs, 1795), and Francis Asbury, *The Causes, Evils, and Cures, of the Heart and Church Divisions* (Philadelphia: Perry Hall, 1792).

65. William Linn, *Discourses on the Signs of the Times* (New York: Thomas Greenleaf, 1794), 20, 136.

66. Linn's notion of what the basis of Christian union should be was apparently typical of evangelicals at this time. Loetscher, "Problem of Christian Unity," 11, suggests that the core of "essential" truths on which the host of evangelical voluntary societies was founded were "those truths which were considered necessary for conversion and for the devout life."

67. Linn, *Signs of the Times*, 94–97, 102–07.

68. Ibid., 181.

69. Asbury, *Journal and Letters*, 2: 96. Asbury expressed this judgment at a meeting of the leaders of the classes of the New York City Methodist Society in August 1796. When revival broke out there six months later, Asbury believed his message had been partly responsible (2: 119).

70. Linn, *Signs of the Times*, 92–93, 95.

71. Ibid., 197–99. Linn himself was a member of this society and considered its informal doctrinal statement highly acceptable: "Here is a good confession, and proves what I asserted, that the generality of Christians are agreed in all the essential articles of faith; and that were they to continue themselves to these, and not unwarrantably extend them, a foundation for union would appear."

72. *The Constitution of the New-York Society for promoting Christian Knowledge and Piety* (New York: Loudon & Brewer, 1794), 3, 7, 9–12.

73. Stocker, *Moravian Church in New York City*, 176–77.

74. David Austin, Preface, *American Preacher*, 1: iii, vi.

75. John H. Livingston, "Growth in Grace, Part 2," in Austin, ed., *American Preacher*, 1: 148.

76. *Experienced Christian's Magazine* 1 (1796): 3, 121.

77. *Methodist Magazine* 1 (1797): 3, 5, 13.

78. Minute Book, 13, 55–56, MS Records of the Stanford Baptist Church.

79. Robert Scott et al. to Elder Bullock and the Brethren of the Baptist Church in Stanford, Aug. 15, 1798, Envelope 3, MS Records of the Stanford Baptist Church.

80. Minute Book, 62–63, MS Records of the Stanford Baptist Church.

81. Northern Missionary Society, *Constitution of the Northern Missionary Society*, 3, 11–12; *United States Christian Magazine* 1 (1796): 230–36. Besides being the basis for membership, these confessions were to serve as the doctrinal core of the preaching and teaching conducted by the missionaries sent out by these societies. See "Instructions from the Directors of the New-York Missionary Society to their Missionaries among the Indians," in John H. Livingston, *Two Sermons Delivered before the New-York Missionary Society* (New York: Isaac Collins, 1799), 86–92.

82. Shiels, "Second Great Awakening in Connecticut," 413–14.

83. New York Presbytery (Associate Reformed Church of North America) MS Minutes 1782–1805, Jan. 15, 1797, Presbyterian Historical Society. Apparently, some Dutch Reformed New Yorkers prepared a similar petition respecting vice and immorality for the State Legislature's consideration in late 1797. See Johnson, MS Diary 1787–1803, Dec. 18, 1797, and Dec. 28, 1797, Columbiana Collection.

84. Synod of New York and New Jersey MS Minutes, 114. The idea for these congregational committees originated in the General Assembly meeting in 1798.

85. Wingo, "Politics, Society, and Religion," 184–86.

86. Long Island Presbytery (formerly Suffolk Presbytery) MS Minutes 1790–1800, 118, Long Island Presbytery MSS, Presbyterian Historical Society; Hudson Presbytery MS Minutes, 93–94; New York Presbytery MS Minutes, 175.

87. Developments in New York fit into the three patterns of Christian unity identified by Lefferts Loetscher: federative action by ecclesiastical bodies, organic union between denominations, and cooperation by individual Christians in volun-

tary societies. Loetscher, "Problem of Christian Unity," 6–7.

88. *Acts and Proceedings of the General Synod,* 258, 268–69, 282–89.

89. Ibid., 258.

90. *Translation of the German Minutes of the New York Ministerium,* 18; *Journals of the Conventions of the Episcopal Diocese of New York,* 86–87; Monk, "Unity and Diversity among Colonial Anglicans and Methodists," 65–67; "Thomas Coke to Bishop White Apr. 24, 1791," in Asbury, *Journal and Letters,* 3: 95–98.

91. William Linn, *Sermons Historical and Characteristical* (New York: Childs & Swaine, 1791), was sponsored by ministers from the Dutch Reformed, Presbyterian, Associate Reformed, Episcopal, Quaker, Baptist, and Congregationalist denominations, as well as by Vice-President John Adams, sixty-four congressmen, and forty-eight state legislators. John M'Donald, Presbyterian pastor in Albany, and John Bassett, Dutch Reformed pastor in Albany, co-edited John Brown, *An Introduction to the Right Understanding of the Oracles of God* (Albany, N.Y.: Barber & Southwick, 1793).

92. Both pastors wrote two pamphlets. Linn initiated the debate in *The Character of Simon the Sorcerer: A Sermon designed to prove that Baptism is not Regeneration* (New York: Thomas Greenleaf, 1793), after reading a book by Benjamin Moore on the doctrine of regeneration. Moore responded to Linn's pamphlet with *An Address . . . occasioned by the Appendix to Dr. Linn's Sermon* (New York: Hugh Gaine, 1793). Then Linn wrote *Remarks on Dr. Moore's Address* (New York: Thomas Greenleaf, 1793), and finally Moore retaliated in *The Doctrine of Baptismal Regeneration vindicated against the objections of Dr. Linn, and others* (New York: Hugh Gaine, 1793).

93. Johnson, MS Diary 1787–1803, September 1798, and Feb. 26, 1799, Columbiana Collection; Miller, *Memoirs of John Rodgers;* Charles G. Sommers, *Memoir of John Stanford, D.D.* (New York: Stanford & Swords, 1844); Alexander Gunn, *Memoirs of John Henry Livingston.*

BIBLIOGRAPHY

Primary Sources

Manuscripts

American Baptist Historical Society, Rochester, New York
    Isaac Backus Papers
    New York Baptist Church Records
    Philadelphia Baptist Association Letters, McKesson Papers
    Robert Scott Papers
    John Sutcliffe Papers
Archives of the Protestant Episcopal Church, Austin, Texas
    Samuel Johnson MSS, Hawks Papers
    William Smith MSS, Hawks Papers
Billy Graham Center Archives, Wheaton College, Wheaton, Illinois
    Society for the Propagation of the Gospel Records
Colgate–Rochester–Bexley Hall–Crozer Divinity School, Rochester, New York
    Samuel Seabury Papers
Columbia County Historical Society, Kinderhook, New York
    Collection of Arthur C. M. Kelley's transcripts of Hudson Valley
        Dutch Reformed and Lutheran Church Records
Columbiana Collection, Columbia University Library, New York City
    John Barent Johnson Diary
Friends Historical Library, Swarthmore College, Swarthmore, Pennsylvania
    Benjamin Ferris Journal, Ferris Papers
    Ann Moore Journal
    New York Meeting for Sufferings Minutes
General Theological Seminary, New York City
    Thomas B. Chandler Diary
Haviland Records Room of the New York Yearly Meeting—Religious Society of
    Friends, New York City
    New York Yearly Meeting Minutes
New York Historical Society, New York City
    Associate Reformed Synod Papers
    Memoranda of Jacques Buvelot
    Thomas Ellison MSS
    John Christopher Hartwick MSS
    Sermons of Archibald Laidlie
    Robert R. Livingston Papers
    Sermons of Abel Morgan
    New York City Miscellaneous MSS
    John Rodgers Discourses and Papers
New York Public Library, New York City
    Mary Cooper Diary
    Emmett Collection
    Jared Lane Papers
    Gilbert Livingston Papers

Methodist Episcopal Church Records
Sermons of Stephen Van Voorhees
Presbyterian Historical Society, Philadelphia, Pennsylvania
Associated Westchester Presbytery MSS
Dutchess Presbytery MSS
Hudson Presbytery MSS
Long Island Presbytery MSS
New York Presbytery MSS
New York Presbytery MSS (Associate Reformed Church of North America)
John Rodgers MSS
Azel Roe MSS
Suffolk Presbytery MSS
Synod of New York and New Jersey MSS
Senate House Museum, Kingston, New York
Rochester Dutch Reformed Church Records
Trinity Parish Archives, New York City
Minutes of the Vestry
Benjamin Moore File
Jews in New York City File
University of Rochester, Rochester, New York
Tallcott-Howland Family Papers

Newspapers and Periodicals

Arminian Magazine, 1790–1800
Connecticut Evangelical Magazine, 1800–1801
Edinburgh Missionary Magazine, 1793–1800
Evangelical Magazine, 1793–1800
Experienced Christian's Magazine, 1796–1800
Independent Reflector, 1752–1753
James Rivington's New York *Gazetteer,* 1773–1775
Massachusetts Baptist Missionary Magazine, 1807
Methodist Magazine, 1797–1800
New-York *Gazette: or the Weekly Post Boy,* 1750–1773
New York *Mercury,* 1752–1768
New York Missionary Magazine, 1800–1803
Theological Magazine, 1796–1798
United States Christian Magazine, 1796

Published Sources

Acts and Proceedings of the General Assembly of the Presbyterian Church in the United States of America, A.D., 1789. Philadelphia: Francis Bailey, 1789.
Acts and Proceedings of the General Assembly of the Presbyterian Church . . . 1790 and 1791. Philadelphia: R. Aitken & Son, 1791.
Acts and Proceedings of the General Assembly of the Presbyterian Church . . . 1795 and 1796. Philadelphia: Samuel Smith, 1796.
Acts and Proceedings of the General Assembly of the Presbyterian Church . . . 1798. Philadelphia: Samuel Smith, 1798.
Acts and Proceedings of the General Assembly of the Presbyterian Church . . . 1799. Philadelphia: William Woodward, 1799.
The Acts and Proceedings of the General Synod of the Reformed Protestant Dutch Church in North America, 1771–1812. New York: Board of Publication of the Reformed Protestant Dutch Church, 1859.
"Advertisement: To such Parents as have now . . . Children prepared to be educated

in the College of NEW YORK." In New York Historical Society, *Collections, 1870.* New York: By the Society, 1871.

Asbury, Francis. *The Causes, Evils and Cures, of the Heart and Church Divisions.* Philadelphia: Perry Hall, 1792.

———. *The Journal and Letters of Francis Asbury.* 3 vols. Edited by Elmer T. Clark. London: Epworth Press, 1958.

Asplund, John. *The Universal Register of the Baptist Denomination in North America for the years 1790, 1791, 1792, 1793, and part of 1794.* Boston: John W. Folsom, 1795.

Austin, David, ed. *The American Preacher, or a Collection of Sermons.* 4 vols. Elizabethtown, N.J.: Kollock, 1791, 1793.

Austin, Samuel. *Disinterested Love, the Ornament of the Christian, and the Duty of Man.* New York: William Durell, 1791.

Baker, Frank. "Early American Methodism: A Key Document." *Methodist History* 3 (1965): 3–15.

Beach, Abraham. *A Thanksgiving Discourse delivered in Trinity Church.* New York, 1784.

Bealey, Joseph. *Observations Upon the Rev. Mr. Owen's Sermon.* Warrington, England: W. Eyres, 1790.

Berkenmeyer, William. *Geheime unt offentlicke Anspracke, samt einer Schluss-rede, an Herren Johann Christopher Hartwick, mit Etlicken zur Erlauterung, und zur Entdeckung des Cripto-Herrnhuthianismi, dieneden Anmerkungen nack der Vorschrift unsrer Nieu-Yorksen K[erken] O[rdinantie], P.II, Cap.2, art.6* [Private and Public Address, with an Epilogue, to Johann Christopher Hartwick, with some relevant observations to set forth and expose the secret cherishing of Moravian teachings, as prescribed by our New York Church Constitution, Part II, Chapter 2, article 6]. New York: John Zenger, 1749.

Bogart, David Schuyler. *A Discourse delivered before a Religious Society, upon the Admission of a Member.* New York: J. & A. M'Lean, [1788].

Bridenbaugh, Carl, ed. *Gentleman's Progress: The Itinerarium of Dr. Alexander Hamilton.* Chapel Hill: University of North Carolina Press, 1948.

Brown, John. *An Introduction to the Right Understanding of the Oracles of God.* Edited by John M'Donald and John Bassett. Albany, N.Y.: Barber & Southwick, 1793.

Buell, Samuel. *A Faithful Narrative of the Revival at East-Hampton in 1764.* New York: Samuel Brown, 1766.

———. *The Excellence and Importance of the Saving Knowledge of the Lord Jesus Christ in the Gospel Preacher.* New York: James Parker, 1761.

———. *The Import of the Saint's Confession.* New London, Conn.: T. Green & Son, [1792].

Burnaby, Andrew. *Travels Through the Middle Settlements in North America in the Years 1759 and 1760.* 2d ed. London: T. Payne, 1775.

Chase, Philander. *Bishop Philander Chase's Reminiscences: An Autobiography.* 2d ed. 2 vols. Boston: James B. Dow, 1848.

Columbia University: Early Minutes of the Trustees, 1755–1770. New York: By the University, 1932.

The Constitution of the New-York Society for promoting Christian Knowledge and Piety. New York: London & Brewer, 1794.

The Constitution of the State of New-York. Fish-Kill, N.Y.: Samuel Loudon, 1777.

Crèvecoeur, de, J. Hector St. John. *Letters from an American Farmer.* London: J. M. Dent & Sons, 1926.

De Ronde, Lambertus. *A System: . . . . Suitable to the Heidelberg Catechism.* New York: H. Gaine, 1763.

———. *The True Spiritual Religion.* New York: John Holt, 1767.

Dern, John P., ed. *The Albany Protocol: Wilhelm Christoph Berkenmeyer's Chronicle of Lutheran Affairs in New York Colony, 1731–1750.* Translated by Simon Hart and Sibrandina Geertruid Hart-Runeman. Ann Arbor, Mich.: By the Editors, 1971.

Du Bois, Gualterus. *Kort-Begryp der waare Christelyke Leere, uit den Heidelgergishen Catechismus uitgetrokken, door ordre der Christelyke Synod te Dordrecht, Anno 1618 & 1619.* New York, 1706.

Dwight, Timothy. *The Nature and Danger of Infidel Philosophy.* 3d ed. Cambridge, England: B. Flower, 1804.

Evans, Israel. *A Discourse Delivered in New York.* New York: John Holt, 1784.

———. *A Discourse Delivered Near York in Virginia.* Philadelphia: Francis Bailey, 1782.

———. *A Discourse, Delivered on the 18th Day of December, 1777.* Lancaster, Pa.: Francis Bailey, 1778.

Frelinghuysen, Theodore [David Marin Ben Jesse]. *A Remark on the Disputes and Contentions in the Province.* New York: Hugh Gaine, 1755.

———. [David Marin Ben Jesse]. *A Remonstrance.* New York, 1755.

Frelinghuysen, Theodore J., *Sermons by Theodore J. Frelinghuysen.* Translated by W. Demarest. New York, 1856.

Gano, John. *Biographical Memoirs of the late Rev. John Gano.* New York: Southwick & Hardcastle, 1806.

Garrettson, Freeborn. *The Experience and Travels of Mr. Freeborn Garrettson.* Philadelphia: Joseph Crukshank, 1794.

Gerlach, Larry, ed. *New Jersey in the American Revolution 1763–1783: A Documentary History.* Trenton, 1975.

Gillette, A. D., ed. *Minutes of the Philadelphia Baptist Association from 1707 to 1807.* Philadelphia: American Baptist Publication Society, 1851.

Graham, Chauncey. *Enthusiasm Detected: A Letter to Those who have Separated from The Presbyterian Church in Rumbout.* New York: James Parker, 1751.

———. *God will trouble the Troublers of his People.* New York: Hugh Gaine, 1759.

Grant, Anne. *Memoirs of An American Lady, with sketches of manners and scenery in America, as they existed previous to the Revolution.* New York: D. Appleton, 1846.

[Green, Jacob.] *Observations on the Reconciliation of Great-Britain and the Colonies.* New York: John Holt, 1776.

Griffith, John. *A Journal of the Life, Travels, and Labours in the Work of the Ministry of John Griffith.* London: Joseph Crukshank, 1780.

Hastings, Hugh, and Corwin, E. T., eds. *Ecclesiastical Records of the State of New York.* 7 vols. Albany, N.Y.: J. E. Lyon Co., 1901–6.

Hershkowitz, Leo, and Meyer, Isidore S., eds. *Letters of the Franks Family, 1733–1748.* Waltham, Mass.: American Jewish Historical Society, 1968.

Hoes, R. R., ed. *Baptismal and Marriage Registers of the Old Dutch Church of Kingston.* New York: DeVinne Press, 1891.

Horne, Field, ed. *The Diary of Mary Cooper: Life on a Long Island Farm 1768–1773.* Oyster Bay, N.Y.: Oyster Bay Historical Society, 1981.

Horne, Melville. *Letter on Missions.* Schenectady, N.Y.: C.P. Wyckoff, 1797.

Inglis, Charles. *A Farewell-Sermon, preached at St. George's and St. Paul's Chapels in the City of New-York, October 26, 1783.* London: C. Buckton, 1784.

[Inglis, Charles.] *A Vindication of the Bishop of Landaff's Sermon.* New York: John Holt, 1768.

"Instructions from the Directors of the New-York Missionary Society to their Missionaries among the Indians." In John H. Livingston, *Two Sermons Delivered before the New-York Missionary Society,* 86–92. New York: Isaac Collins, 1799.

Jones, Thomas. *History of New York during the Revolutionary War.* 2 vols. Edited by Edward F. DeLancey. New York: New York Historical Society, 1879.

Journal of the Senate of the State of New-York . . . Seventh Session. New York: E. Holt, 1784.

Journals of the Conventions of the Protestant Episcopal Church in the Diocese of New York. New York: Henry M. Onderdonk, 1844.

Journals of the General Conference of the Methodist Episcopal Church, 1796–1836. 3 vols. New York: Carlton & Phillips, 1855.

Journals of the Provincial Congress, Provincial Convention, Committee of Safety and Council of Safety of the State of New York 1775–1777. 2 vols. Albany, N.Y.: Thurlow Weed, 1842.

Kelley, Arthur C. M. *Settlers and Residents: Town of Livingston 1710–1899.* 3 vols. Rhinebeck, N.Y.: By the Compiler, 1978.

Kennedy, Archibald. *A Speech . . . by a Member Dissenting from the Church.* New York, 1755.

Keteltas, Abraham. *The Religious Soldier: or, the military character of King David.* New York: Hugh Gaine, 1759.

Klett, Guy S., ed. *Minutes of the Presbyterian Church in America 1706–1788.* Philadelphia: Presbyterian Historical Society, 1976.

Knox, Hugh. *The Moral and Religious Miscellany.* New York: Hodge & Schober, 1775.

Laws of the State of New-York . . . Seventh Session. New York: E. Holt, 1784.

Leaming, Jeremiah. *Dissertations upon Various Subjects.* New Haven, Conn.: Thomas & Samuel Green, 1788.

A Letter from a Gentleman in New-York to his Friend in the Country. New York, 1772.

"Letters of Uzal Ogden." *The Methodist Magazine* 5 (1822): 347–49, 384–87, 422–24, 457–62; 6 (1823): 26–29, 59–62, 111–13, 145–47.

"Letters to Dr. Rippon from New York." *Transactions of the Baptist Historical Society* 1 (1909): 69–79.

Linn, William. *The Blessings of America.* New York: Thomas Greenleaf, 1791.

———. *The Character of Simon the Sorcerer: A Sermon designed to prove that Baptism is not Regeneration.* New York: Thomas Greenleaf, 1793.

———. *A Discourse on National Sins.* New York: T. & J. Swords, 1798.

———. *Discourses on the Signs of the Times.* New York: Thomas Greenleaf, 1794.

———. *A Military Discourse.* Philadelphia, 1776.

———. *Remarks on Dr. Moore's Address.* New York: Thomas Greenleaf, 1793.

———. *Sermons Historical and Characteristical.* New York: Childs & Swaine, 1791.

Livingston, John H. *The Triumph of the Gospel: A Sermon delivered before the New York Missionary Society.* New York: T. & J. Swords, 1804.

Livingston, William. *A Letter to the Right Reverend Father . . . lord bishop of Landaff.* Boston: Kneeland & Adams, 1768.

Livingston, William; Scott, John Morin; and Smith, Jr., William. *The Independent Reflector.* Edited by Milton M. Klein. Cambridge, Mass.: Harvard University Press, 1963.

Lutheran Church in New York and New Jersey 1722–1760: Lutheran Records in the Ministerial Archives of the Staatsarchiv, Hamburg, Germany. Translated by Simon Hart and Harry J. Kreider. New York: United Lutheran Synod of New York and New England, 1962.

Lydekker, Gerrit. Preface, *Theological Theses, containing the Chief Heads of the Christian Doctrine,* by Isaac Sigfrid and Daniel Wyttenbach. New York: Samuel Brown, 1766.

Lydekker, John W. *The Life and Letters of Charles Inglis.* London: Society for Promoting Christian Knowledge, 1936.

McLoughlin, William G., ed. *The Diary of Isaac Backus.* 3 vols. Providence, R.I.: Brown University Press, 1979.

MacWhorter, Alexander, *The Blessedness of the Liberal.* New York: T. & J. Swords, 1796.
Mason, John Mitchell. *A Sermon, preached September 20th, 1793.* New York: Samuel Loudon & Son, 1793.
Miller, John. *A description of the province and city of New York.* Edited by John Gilmary Shea. New York: W. Gowans, 1862.
Miller, Samuel. *A Discourse Delivered in the New Presbyterian Church, New-York.* New York: F. Childs, 1795.
Minutes of the General Convention of Delegates appointed by the Synod of New York and Philadelphia and the General Association of Connecticut 1766 to 1775. Philadelphia: Presbyterian Board of Publication, 1904.
Minutes of the Methodist Conferences, annually held in America: 1773–1813. New York: David Hitt & Thomas Ware, 1813.
Minutes of the New-York Baptist Association . . . 1793. n.p., n.d.
Minutes of the New-York Baptist Association . . . 1794. n.p., n.d.
Minutes of the New-York Baptist Association . . . 1796. n.p., n.d.
Minutes of the New-York Baptist Association . . . 1802. n.p., n.d.
Minutes of the New-York Baptist Association . . . 1803. n.p., n.d.
"Minutes of the Presbytery of New York, 1775–1782." *New York History* 50 (1969 Supplement): 22–43.
Minutes of the Shaftsbury Association . . . M, DCC, XCI. Bennington, Vt.: Anthony Haswell, 1791.
Minutes of the Shaftsbury Association . . . 1794. Canaan, N.Y.: Elihu Phinny, 1794.
Minutes of the Shaftsbury Association . . . 1800. Troy, N.Y.: R. Moffitt & Co., 1800.
Minutes of the Warwick Baptist Association . . . 1794. n.p. n.d.
Moore, Benjamin. *An Address . . . occasioned by the Appendix to Dr. Linn's Sermon.* New York: Hugh Gaine, 1793.
———. *The Doctrine of Baptismal Regeneration vindicated against the objections of Dr. Linn, and others.* New York: Hugh Gaine, 1793.
Moore, Thomas. *A Sermon . . before the Convention of the Protestant Episcopal Church.* New York: Hugh Gaine, 1789.
Morris, Richard B., ed. *John Jay: The Making of a Revolutionary—Unpublished Papers, 1745–1780.* New York: Harper & Row, 1975.
Muhlenberg, Henry M. *The Journals of Henry Melchior Muhlenberg.* 3 vols. Translated by Theodore G. Tappert and John W. Doberstein. Philadelphia: Evangelical Lutheran Ministerium of Pennsylvania and Muhlenberg Press, 1942–58.
Northern Missionary Society in the State of New York. *The Constitution of the Northern Mssionary Society in the State of New York.* Schenectady, N.Y.: C. P. Wyckoff, 1797.
Observations on the Reasons Lately Published for the Malicious Combination. New York, 1769.
O'Callaghan, E. B., ed. *The Documentary History of the State of New York.* 4 vols. Albany, N.Y.: Weed, Parsons & Co., 1850.
O'Callaghan, E. B., and Fernow, Berthold, eds. *Documents relating to the Colonial History of the State of New York.* 15 vols. Albany, N.Y.: Weed, Parsons, & Co., 1853–87.
Occom, Samson. *A Choice Collection of Hymns and Spiritual Song; Intended for the Edification of Sincere Christians, of all Denominations.* New London, Conn.: Timothy Green, 1774.
"Occupation of New York City by the British: Extracts from the Diary of the Moravian Congregation." *Pennsylvania Magazine of History and Biography* 1 (1877): 133–48, 250–62, 467–68; 10 (1886): 418–45.

Ogden, Uzal. *An Address to those Persons at Elizabeth-Town . . . Who have lately been seriously impressed with a Desire to obtain Salvation.* New York: J. McLean, 1785.

———. *A Sermon . . . May 16, 1786, Before a Convention of Clerical and Lay Deputies of the Protestant Episcopal Church in the State of New Jersey.* New York: Samuel & John Loudon, 1786.

Osgood, Herbert, ed. "The Society of Dissenters founded at New York in 1769." *American Historical Review* 6 (1901): 498–507.

Perry, William S., ed. *Journals of General Conventions of the Protestant Episcopal Church, in the United States, 1785–1821.* 3 vols. Claremont, N.H.: Claremont Manufacturing Co., 1874.

Presbyterian Church in the U.S.A. Synod of New York and Philadelphia. *An Account of the Annual Contribution . . . As Returned . . . 20 May 1769.* Philadelphia, 1769.

Price, Richard. *Additional Observations on the Nature and Value of Civil Liberty, and the War with America.* Philadelphia: Hall & Sellars, 1778.

———. *Observations on the Importance of the American Revolution.* Boston: Powers & Willis, 1784.

———. *Observations on the Nature of Civil Liberty.* London: T. Cadell, 1776.

Prime, Ebenezer. *Two Ordination Sermons.* New York: Hugh Gaine, 1758.

Protocol of the Lutheran Church in New York City, 1702–1750. Translated by Simon Hart and Harry J. Kreider. New York: United Lutheran Synod of New York and New England, 1958.

Reasons for the Present Glorious Combination of the Dissenters in the City. New York, 1769.

The Records in the Lutheran Church at Amsterdam, Holland, relating to Lutheranism in Colonial New York. Translated by Arnold J. F. Van Laer. New York: The United Lutheran Synod of New York, 1942.

"Records of the First and Second Presbyterian Churches of the City of New York." *The New York Genealogical and Biographical Records* 11 (1880): 83, 120–24; 14 (1883): 188–23.

"Records of the Reformed Dutch Church of New Paltz, New York." In *Collections of the Holland Society of New York.* New York: Holland Society, 1896.

Reynolds, Helen Wilkinson, ed. *The Records of Christ Church, Poughkeepsie, New York.* Poughkeepsie, N.Y.: Frank B. Howard, 1911.

Rippon, John. *The Baptist Annual Register, 1790–1793.* London, 1793.

———. *The Baptist Annual Register, 1801–1802.* London, 1802.

[Rodgers, John.] "A Brief View of the State of religious Liberty in the Colony of New York." *Massachusetts Historical Society Collections* 11 (1804): 140–55.

[Rodgers, John.] *The Case of the Scotch Presybterians, of the City of New York.* New York, 1773.

Rodgers, John. *The Divine Goodness Displayed in the American Revolution: A Sermon.* New York: Samuel Loudon, 1784.

———. *Holiness the Nature and Design of the Gospel of Christ.* Hartford, Conn.: Hudson & Goodwin, 1779.

Rogers, Ammi. *Memoirs of the Rev. Ammi Rogers.* 6th ed. Troy, N.Y.: By the Author, 1834.

Rotheram, John. *An Essay on Faith and Its Connection with Good Works.* New York: James Parker, 1767.

Rubel, Johannes C. *An Answer to Several Church Meetings.* New York: J. McLean, 1784.

Schneider, Herbert, and Schneider, Carol, eds. *Samuel Johnson, President of King's College, His Career and Writings.* 4 vols. New York: Columbia University Press, 1929.

A Serious Call from the City to the Country. Woodbridge, N.J., 1757.

Smith, William, Jr. *Historical Memoirs of William Smith.* 2 vols. Edited by William H. W. Sabine. New York: Colburn & Tegg, 1956–58.

To the Dissenting Electors of All Denominations. New York, 1770.

To the Freeholders and Freemen of the City and County of New-York, in Communion with the Reformed Dutch Church. New York, 1769.

To the Freeholders of the City and County of New York: The Querist, No. 1 and No. 2. New York, 1769.

To the Public, Few are Ignorant. . . . New York, 1770.

Translation of the German Minutes of the Evangelical Lutheran Ministerium of the State of New York and adjacent states and counties. Translated by Theodore E. Palleske. Staten Island, N.Y., 1937.

Treat, Joseph. *A Thanksgiving Sermon, occasioned by the glorious news of the reduction of the Havannah.* New York: Hugh Gaine, 1762.

Two Treatises, Containing Reasons Why the People Called Quakers do not pay Tithes. Philadelphia: Joseph Crukshank, 1771.

Vosburgh, Royden W., ed. *Records of the Reformed Dutch Church of Kinderhook.* 3 vols. New York: New York Genealogical and Biographical Society, 1921.

Wesley, John. *The Letters of the Rev. John Wesley, A.M..* 8 vols. Edited by John Telford. London: Epworth Press, 1931.

———. *The Works of John Wesley.* 14 vols. Grand Rapids, Mich.: Zondervan, 1958.

Weygand, John A. *The Whole System of the Augsbourgh Confession compared with the Translations of the Moravians.* New York: Parker & Weyman, 1766.

Whitefield, George. *The Works of George Whitefield.* 6 vols. London: Edward & Charles Dilly, 1771.

Wooley, Charles. *A Two Years Journal in New York.* In *Historic Chronicles of New Amsterdam, Colonial New York and Early Long Island.* Edited by Cornell Jaray. 1st series. 1860; reprint edition, Port Washington, N.Y.: Ira J. Friedman, Inc., 1968.

Woolman, John. *The Journal and Major Essays of John Woolman.* Edited by Phillips P. Moulton. New York: Oxford University Press, 1971.

Secondary Sources

Books

Abbot, W. C. *New York in the American Revolution.* New York, 1929.

Ahlstrom, Sydney E. *A Religious History of the American People.* 2 vols. Garden City, N.Y.: Doubleday and Co., Inc., Image Books, 1975.

Alexander, S. D. *The Presbytery of New York, 1738–1888.* New York: Anson D. F. Randolph & Co., 1888.

Archdeacon, Thomas. *New York City, 1664–1710: Conquest and Change.* Ithaca, N.Y.: Cornell University Press, 1976.

Bacon, Leonard Woolsey. *A History of American Christianity.* New York: The Christian Literature Co., 1897.

Baird, Charles W. *Chronicle of a Border Town: History of Rye.* New York: Anson D. F. Randolph & Co., 1871.

———. *History of Bedford Church.* New York: Dodd, Mead, and Co., 1882.

Baird, Robert. *Religion in the United States of America.* 1844; reprint edition, New York: Arno Press, 1969.

Bangs, Nathan. *The Life of the Rev. Freeborn Garrettson.* New York: Emory & Waugh, 1830.

Barck, Oscar T. *New York City during the War for Independence.* New York: Columbia University Press, 1931.

Becker, Martin J. *A History of Catholic Life in the Diocese of Albany, 1609–1864.* New York: United States Catholic Historical Society, 1975.

Benedict, David. *A General History of the Baptist Denomination in America.* New York: Lewis Colby & Co., 1848.

Bennett, William H. *Catholic Footsteps in Old New York: A Chronicle of Catholicity in the City of New York from 1524 to 1808.* 1909; reprint edition, New York: United States Catholic Historical Society, 1973.

Bolton, Robert. *History of the Protestant Episcopal Church in the County of Westchester.* New York: Stanford & Swords, 1855.

Bonomi, Patricia U. *A Factious People: Politics and Society in Colonial New York.* New York: Columbia University Press, 1971.

———. *Under the Cope of Heaven: Religion, Society, and Politics in Colonial America.* New York: Oxford University Press, 1986.

Bonwick, Colin. *English Radicals and the American Revolution.* Chapel Hill: University of North Carolina Press, 1977.

Bridenbaugh, Carl. *Mitre and Sceptre: Transatlantic Faiths, Ideas, Personalities, and Politics, 1689–1775.* New York: Oxford University Press, 1962.

Bridenbaugh, Carl, and Bridenbaugh, Jessica. *Rebels and Gentlemen: Philadelphia in the Age of Franklin.* New York: Oxford University Press, 1965.

Brock, Peter. *Pacifism in the United States, from the Colonial Era to the First World War.* Princeton, N.J.: Princeton University Press, 1968.

Brower, William L., and Miller, Henry P., eds. *Collegiate Reformed Protestant Dutch Church of the City of New York: Her Organization and Development.* New York: By the Consistory, 1928.

Buckley, Thomas E. *Church and State in Revolutionary Virginia, 1776–1787.* Charlottesville: University of Virginia Press, 1977.

Bushman, Richard L. *From Puritan to Yankee: Character and Social Order in Connecticut, 1690–1765.* Cambridge, Mass.: Harvard University Press, 1967.

Butler, Jon. *Huguenots in America: A Refugee People in New World Society.* Cambridge, Mass.: Harvard University Press, 1983.

———. *Power, Authorty, and the Origins of American Denominational Order: The English Churches in the Delaware Valley 1680–1730.* Philadelphia: American Philosophical Society, 1978.

Cappon, Lester J., et al., eds., *The Atlas of Early American History: The Revolutionary Era, 1760–1790.* Princeton, N.J.: Princeton University Press, 1976.

Cassara, Ernest, ed. *Universalism in America: A Documentary History.* Boston: Beacon Press, 1971.

Champagne, Roger. *Alexander McDougall and the American Revolution in New York.* Schenectady, N.Y.: New York State American Revolution Bicentennial Commission in conjunction with Union College Press, 1975.

Coon, Edwin C. *Old First: A History of the Reformed Church of Poughkeepsie, New York.* New York: The William-Frederick Press, 1967.

Corwin, Edwin T. *A Manual of the Reformed Protestant Dutch Church in North America.* 3d & 4th eds. New York: Reformed Protestant Dutch Church, 1879, 1902.

Countryman, Edward. *A People in Revolution: The American Revolution and Political Society in New York, 1760–1790.* Baltimore: Johns Hopkins University Press, 1981.

Cross, Arthur L. *The Anglican Episcopate and the American Colonies.* Cambridge, Mass.: Harvard University Press, 1902.

De Jong, Gerald F. *The Dutch in America, 1609–1974.* Boston: Twayne, 1975.

———. *The Dutch Reformed Church in the American Colonies.* Grand Rapids, Mich.: Wm. B. Eerdmans, 1978.

DeMille, George E. *A History of the Diocese of Albany 1704–1923.* Philadelphia: Church Historical Society, 1946.

De Sola Pool, David, and De Sola Pool, Tamar. *An Old Faith in the New World: Portrait of Shearith Israel, 1654–1954.* New York: Columbia University Press, 1955.

Dexter, Franklin B. *Biographical Sketches of the Graduates of Yale College.* 6 vols. New York: Henry Holt & Co., 1896.

Dillon, Dorothy. *The New York Triumvirate: A Study of the Legal and Political Careers of William Livingston, John Morin Scott, and William Smith, Jr..* New York: Columbia University Press, 1949.

Dix, Morgan, et al. *A History of the Parish of Trinity Church in the City of New York.* 6 vols. New York: G. P. Putnam's Sons, 1898–1962.

East, Robert A., and Judd, Jacob, eds. *The Loyalist Americans: A Focus on Greater New York.* Tarrytown, N.Y.: Sleepy Hollow Restorations, 1975.

Ellis, Captain Franklin. *History of Columbia County, New York.* Philadelphia: Everts & Ensign, 1878.

Ellis, David M.; Frost, James A.; Syrett, Harold C.; and Carman, Harry J. *A Short History of New York State.* Ithaca, N.Y.: Cornell University Press, 1957.

Ellis, Joseph. *The New England Mind in Transition: Samuel Johnson of Connecticut, 1696–1772.* New Haven, Conn.: Yale University Press, 1973.

Ellsbree, Oliver W. *The Rise of the Missionary Spirit in America, 1790–1815.* Williamsport, Pa.: Williamsport Printing & Binding Co., 1928.

Flick, Alexander C., ed. *The American Revolution in New York.* Albany, N.Y.: University of the State of New York, 1926.

Gaustad, Edwin S. *George Berkeley in America.* New Haven, Conn.: Yale University Press, 1979.

———. *Historical Atlas of Religion in America.* Revised ed. New York: Harper & Row, 1976.

Greenberg, Douglas. *Crime and Law Enforcement in the Colony of New York, 1691–1776.* Ithaca, N.Y.: Cornell University Press, 1976.

Greene, Evarts B., and Harrington, Virginia D. *American Population before the Federal Census of 1790.* New York: Columbia University Press, 1932.

Grinstein, Hyman B. *The Rise of the Jewish Community of New York, 1654–1860.* Philadelphia: Porcupine Press, 1976.

Gunn, Alexander. *Memoirs of the Rev. John Henry Livingston, D.D.* New York: Reformed Protestant Dutch Church, 1856.

Hatch, Nathan. *The Sacred Cause of Liberty: Republican Thought and the Millennium.* New Haven, Conn.: Yale University Press, 1977.

Hatch, Nathan et al. *The Search for Christian America.* Westchester, Ill.: Crossway Books, 1983.

Heimert, Alan. *Religion and the American Mind: From the Great Awakening to the Revolution.* Cambridge, Mass.: Harvard University Press, 1966.

Higginbotham, Don. *The War of American Independence.* New York: Macmillan Co., 1971.

History of the First Reformed Protestant Dutch Church of Breuckelen Now Known as the First Reformed Church of Brooklyn, 1654 to 1896. Brooklyn, N.Y.: By the Consistory, 1896.

Hudson, Winthrop. *American Protestantism.* Chicago: University of Chicago Press, 1961.

———. *Religion in America.* 3d ed. New York: Charles Scribner's Sons, 1980.

Hufeland, Otto. *Westchester County during the American Revolution 1775–1783.* White Plains, N.Y.: Westchester County Historical Society, 1926.

Humphrey, David. *From King's College to Columbia, 1746–1800.* New York: Columbia University Press, 1976.

Jones, Rufus M. *The Quakers in the American Colonies*. London: Macmillan and Co., Ltd., 1923.

Kammen, Michael. *Colonial New York: A History*. New York: Charles Scribner's Sons, 1975.

Keep, Austin Baxter. *History of the New York Society Library*. New York: DeVinne Press, 1908.

Kelley, Robert. *The Cultural Pattern in American Politics*. New York: Alfred A. Knopf, 1979.

Kenney, Alice P. *The Gansevoorts of Albany: Dutch Patricians in the Upper Hudson Valley*. Syracuse, N.Y.: Syracuse University Press, 1969.

———. *Stubborn for Liberty: The Dutch in New York*. Syracuse, N.Y.: Syracuse University Press, 1975.

Klein, Milton M. *New York in the American Revolution: A Bibliography*. Albany, N.Y., 1974.

———. *Politics of Diversity: Essays in the History of Colonial New York*. Port Washington, N.Y.: Kennikat Press, 1974.

Knapp, Shepherd. *A History of the Brick Presbyterian Church in the City of New York*. New York: The Brick Presbyterian Church, 1909.

Kreider, Harry J. *Lutheranism in Colonial New York*. New York: Edwards Bros., Inc., 1942.

Kretzmann, Karl. *The Oldest Lutheran Church in America*. New York: The Evangelical Lutheran Church of Saint Matthew, 1914.

Kross, Jessica. *The Evolution of an American Town: Newtown, New York, 1642–1775*. Philadelphia: Temple University Press, 1983.

Lamb, Martha J. *History of the City of New York*. 2 vols. New York: A.S. Barnes, 1877.

Launitz-Schurer, Leopold S. *Loyal Whigs and Revolutionaries: The Making of the Revolution in New York*. New York: New York University Press, 1980.

Leiby, Adrian C. *The Revolutionary War in the Hackensack Valley: The Jersey Dutch and the Neutral Ground, 1775–1783*. New Brunswick, N.J.: Rutgers University Press, 1962.

———. *The United Churches of Hackensack and Schraalenburgh, New Jersey 1686–1822*. River Edge, N.J.: Bergen County Historical Society, 1976.

Levy, Leonard W. *Constitutional Opinions: Aspects of the Bill of Rights*. New York and Oxford: Oxford University Press, 1986.

Littell, Franklin H. *From State Church to Pluralism: Protestant Interpretation of Religion in American History*. Garden City, N.Y.: Anchor Books, 1962.

Lovejoy, David S. *The Glorious Revolution in America*. New York: Harper & Row, 1972.

McLoughlin, William. *Revivals, Awakenings, and Reform: An Essay on Religion and Social Change in America, 1607–1977*. Chicago: University of Chicago Press, 1978.

Marcus, Jacob R. *Early American Jewry: The Jews of New York, New England, and Canada 1649–1794*. 2 vols. Philadelphia: The Jewish Publication Society of America, 1951–53.

Marini, Stephen A. *Radical Sects of Revolutionary New England*. Cambridge, Mass.: Harvard University Press, 1982.

Marty, Martin E. *The Infidel: Free Thought and American Religion*. Cleveland and New York: World Publishing Co., 1961.

Mason, Bernard. *The Road to Independence: The Revolutionary Movement in New York, 1773–1777*. Lexington: University of Kentucky Press, 1967.

Maxson, Charles H. *The Great Awakening in the Middle Colonies*. Chicago: University of Chicago Press, 1920.

May, Henry F. *The Enlightenment in America*. New York: Oxford University Press, 1976.

Maynard, John A. F. *The Huguenot Church of New York: A History of the Church of Saint-Esprit.* New York: By the Church, 1938.

Mead, Sidney. *The Lively Experiment.* New York: Harper & Row, 1963.

Miller, Russell E. *The Larger Hope: The First Century of the Universalist Church in America, 1770–1870.* Boston: Unitarian Universalist Association, 1979.

Miller, Samuel. *Memoirs of the Rev. John Rodgers, D.D.* New York: Whiting & Watson, 1813.

Mills, Frederick V., Sr. *Bishops by Ballot: An Eighteenth-Century Ecclesiastical Revolution.* New York: Oxford University Press, 1978.

Miyakawa, T. Scott. *Protestants and Pioneers: Individualism and Conformity on the American Frontier.* Chicago: University of Chicago Press, 1964.

Morgan, Edmund S. *The Gentle Puritan: A Life of Ezra Stiles, 1727–1795.* New Haven, Conn.: Yale University Press, 1962.

Nash, Gary B. *The Urban Crucible: Social Change, Political Consciousness, and the Origins of the American Revolution.* Cambridge, Mass.: Harvard University Press, 1979.

Nichols, Robert H. *Presbyterianism in New York State.* Philadelphia: Westminster Press, 1963.

Noll, Mark. *Christians in the American Revolution.* Washington, D.C.: Christian University Press, 1977.

Norton, John N. *Life of Bishop Provoost of New York.* New York: General Protestant Episcopal Sunday School Union, and Church Book Society, 1859.

Norwood, Frederick A. *The Story of American Methodism: A History of the United Methodists and Their Relations.* Nashville, Tenn.: The Abingdon Press, 1974.

O'Brien, Thomas Hanley. *The American Revolution and Religion: Maryland 1770–1800.* Washington, D.C.: The Catholic University of America Press, Consortium Press, 1971.

O'Callaghan, E.B., ed. *Calendar of Historical Manuscripts in the Office of the Secretary of State.* 2 vols. Albany, N.Y.: Weed, Parsons & Co., 1866.

Parkinson, William. *Jubilee: A Sermon, containing a history of the origin of the First Baptist Church in the City of New-York.* New York: By the Church, 1813.

Perry, Lewis. *Intellectual Life in America: A History.* New York: Franklin Watts, 1984.

Polf, William A. *Garrison Town: The British Occupation of New York City, 1776–1783.* Albany, N.Y.: New York State American Revolution Bicentennial Commission, 1976.

Pratt, John W. *Religion, Politics, and Diversity: The Church-State Theme in New York History.* Ithaca, N.Y.: Cornell University Press, 1967.

Rothermund, Dietmar. *The Layman's Progress: Religious and Political Experience in Colonial Pennsylvania, 1740–1770.* Philadelphia, 1961.

Royster, Charles. *A Revolutionary People at War.* Chapel Hill: University of North Carolina Press, 1979.

Ryan, Leo R. *Old St. Peter's: The Mother Church of Catholic New York (1785–1935).* New York: United States Catholic Historical Society, 1935.

Schoonmaker, Marius. *The History of Kingston, New York.* New York: Burr Printing House, 1888.

Smith, George L. *Religion and Trade in New Netherland.* Ithaca, N.Y.: Cornell University Press, 1973.

Smith, H. Shelton; Handy, Robert T.; and Loetscher, Lefferts A. *American Christianity: An Historical Interpretation with Representative Documents.* 2 vols. New York: Charles Scribner's Sons, 1960.

Sommers, Charles G. *Memoir of the Rev. John Stanford, D.D.* New York: Stanford & Swords, 1844.

Sprague, William. *Annals of the American Pulpit.* 9 vols. New York: Robert Carter & Bros., 1869.

Steiner, Bruce E. *Samuel Seabury 1729–1796: A Study in High Church Tradition.* Oberlin: Ohio University Press, 1971.

Stitt, Charles H. *History of the Huguenot Church and Settlement at New Paltz.* Kingston, N.Y.: William H. Romeyn, 1863.

Stocker, Harry E. *A History of the Moravian Church in New York City.* New York: By the Author, 1922.

Sweet, William Warren. *Religion in the Development of American Culture 1765–1840.* New York: Charles Scribner's Sons, 1952.

———. *The Story of Religion in America.* New York: Harper & Bros., 1930.

Tanis, James. *Dutch Calvinistic Pietism in the Middle Colonies: A Study in the Life and Theology of Theodorus Jacobus Frelinghuysen.* The Hague: Martinus Nijhoff, 1967.

Taylor, Mary Christine. *A History of the Foundations of Catholicism in Northern New York.* New York: United States Catholic Historical Society, 1976.

Thomas, Abel C. *A Century of Universalism in Philadelphia and New-York.* Philadelphia, 1872.

Thomas, David O. *The Honest Mind: The Thought and Work of Richard Price.* Oxford, England: Clarendon Press, 1977.

Trinterud, Leonard. *The Forming of an American Tradition: A Reexamination of Colonial Presbyterianism.* Philadelphia: Westminster Press, 1948.

Vandenberge, Peter N. *Historical Directory of the Reformed Church in America 1628–1978.* Grand Rapids, Mich.: Wm. B. Eerdmans, 1978.

Van Gieson, A.P. *Anniversary Discourse and History of the First Reformed Church of Poughkeepsie, New York.* Poughkeepsie, N.Y., 1893.

Wakeley, Joseph B. *Lost Chapters recovered from the Early History of American Methodism.* New York: By the Author, 1858.

Watson, William W. *The Huguenots of Westchester and the Parish of Fordham.* New York: W.H. Kelley & Bros., 1864.

Weis, Frederick L. *The Colonial Clergy of the Middle Colonies.* Worcester, Mass.: American Antiquarian Society, 1957.

Wenner, George. *The Lutherans of New York: Their Story and Their Problems.* New York: The Petersfield Press, 1918.

Wertenbaker, Thomas J. *Father Knickerbocker Rebels: New York City during the Revolution.* New York: Charles Scribner's Sons, 1948.

———. *The Founding of American Civilization: The Middle Colonies.* New York: Charles Scribner's Sons, 1938.

Wolf, Stephanie G. *Urban Village: Population, Community, and Family Structure in Germantown, Pennsylvania, 1683–1800.* Princeton, N.J.: Princeton University Press, 1976.

Wood, Gordon S. *The Creation of the American Republic, 1776–1787.* Chapel Hill: University of North Carolina Press, 1969.

Woolverton, John F. *Colonial Anglicanism in North America.* Detroit: Wayne State University Press, 1984.

Worrall, Arthur J. *Quakers in the Colonial Northeast.* Hanover, N.H.: University Press of New England, 1980.

Zuckerman, Michael, ed. *Friends and Neighbors: Group Life in America's First Plural Society.* Philadelphia: Temple University Press, 1982.

Zwierlein, Frederick J. *Religion in New Netherland, 1623–1664.* Rochester, N.Y.: John P. Smith, 1910.

Articles

Akers, Charles W. "Religion and the American Revolution: Samuel Cooper and the Brattle Street Church." *William and Mary Quarterly* 3d. Ser., 35 (1978): 477–98.

Anderson, Philip J. "William Linn, 1752–1808: American Revolutionary & Anti-Jeffersonian." *Journal of Presbyterian History* 55 (1977): 381–94.

Babcock, Mary. "Difficulties and Dangers of Pre-Revolutionary Ordinations." *Historical Magazine of the Protestant Episcopal Church* 12 (1943): 225–41.

Banner, Lois W. "Presbyterians and Voluntarism in the Early Republic." *Journal of Presbyterian History* 50 (1972): 187–205.

———. "Religious Benevolence as Social Control: A Critique of an Interpretation." *Journal of American History* 60 (1973): 23–41.

Beardslee, John, III. "The Reformed Church and the American Revolution." In *Piety and Patriotism: Bicentennial Studies of the Reformed Church in America, 1776–1976*, 17–33. Edited by James W. Van Hoeven. Grand Rapids, Mich.: Wm. B. Eerdmans, 1976.

Bielinski, Stefan. "The Refounding and Anglicization of Albany, New York, under English Rule." Paper presented to the Social Science History Association, November 1980.

Bonomi, Patricia U. "'Watchful against the Sects': Religious Renewal in Pennsylvania's German Congregations, 1720–1750." Paper presented to the Organization of American Historians, April 1983.

Bonomi, Patricia U., and Eisenstadt, Peter R. "Church Adherence in the Eighteenth-Century British American Colonies." *William and Mary Quarterly* 3d. Ser., 39 (1982): 245–86.

Borden, Martin. "Federalists, Antifederalists, and Religious Freedom." *Journal of Church and State* 21 (1979): 469–82.

Burr, Nelson R. "The Episcopal Church and the Dutch in Colonial New York and New Jersey—1664–1787." *Historical Magazine of the Protestant Episcopal Church* 19 (1950): 90–111.

Butler, Jon. "Enthusiasm Described and Decried: The Great Awakening as Interpretative Fiction." *Journal of American History* 69 (1982): 305–25.

———. "Magic, Astrology, and the Early American Religious Heritage, 1600–1760." *American Historical Review* 84 (1979): 317–46.

———. "A Spiritual Tower of Babel: Shifting Structures of Religious Diversity in Colonial Pennsylvania, 1680–1760." Paper presented to the Newberry Library Early American history seminar, January 1983.

Calcote, A. Dean. "The Proposed Prayer Book of 1785." *Historical Magazine of the Protestant Episcopal Church* 46 (1977): 275–95.

Champagne, Roger. "Family Politics versus Constitutional Principles: The New York Assembly Elections of 1768 and 1769." *William and Mary Quarterly* 3d. Ser., 20 (1963): 57–79.

Coalter, Milton J. "The Radical Pietism of Count Nicholas Zinzendorf as a Conservative Influence on the Awakener Gilbert Tennent." *Church History* 49 (1980): 35–46.

Corwin, Charles E. "Incidents of Reformed Church Life in New York City during the Revolutionary War." *Journal of the Presbyterian Historical Society* 9 (1918): 355–67.

Frantz, John B. "The Awakening of Religion among the German Settlers in the Middle Colonies." *William and Mary Quarterly* 3d. Ser., 33 (1976): 266–88.

Friedman, Bernard. "The New York Assembly Elections of 1768 and 1769: The Disruption of Family Politics." *New York History* 46 (1965): 3–24.

Gerardi, Donald F. M. "The King's College Controversy 1753–1756 and the Ideological Roots of Toryism in New York." *Perspectives in American History* 11 (1977–78): 145–96.

Goodwin, Gerald. "The Anglican Reaction to the Great Awakening." *Historical Magazine of the Protestant Episcopal Church* 35 (1966): 342–71.

Greenberg, Douglas. "The Middle Colonies in Recent American Historiography." *William and Mary Quarterly* 3d. Ser., 36 (1979): 396–427.

Greene, Evarts B. "The Anglican Outlook on the American Colonies in the Early Eighteenth Century." *American Historical Review* 20 (1914): 64–84.

Greene, Jack P. "Political Mimesis: A Consideration of the Historical and Cultural Roots of Legislative Behavior in the British Colonies in the Eighteenth Century." *American Historical Review* 75 (1969): 337–60.

———. "Search for Identity: An Interpretation of the Meaning of Selected Patterns of Social Response in Eighteenth-Century America." *Journal of Social History* 3 (1970): 189–220.

Handy, Robert T. "John Rodgers, 1727–1811: 'A Life of Usefulness on Earth'." *Journal of Presbyterian History* 34 (1956): 69–82.

"History of the Stillwater Baptist Church." In *Seventy-Third Anniversary of the Saratoga Baptist Association,* 12–14. Amsterdam, N.Y.: The "Democrat" Steam Printing House, 1877.

Hogue, William M. "The Religious Conspiracy Theory of the American Revolution: Anglican Motive." *Church History* 45 (1976): 279–92.

Hough, Brenda. "The Archives of the Society for the Propagation of the Gospel." *Historical Magazine of the Protestant Episcopal Church* 46 (1977): 309–22.

Hudson, Winthrop S. "Denominationalism as a Basis of Ecumenicity: A Seventeenth Century Conception." *Church History* 24 (1955): 32–50.

Kammen, Michael. "The American Revolution as a *Crise de Conscience:* The Case of New York." In *Society, Freedom, and Conscience,* 125–89. Edited by Richard Jellison. New York: Norton, 1976.

Kennedy, Earl William. "From Providence to Civil Religion: Some 'Dutch' Reformed Interpretations of America in the Revolutionary Era." *Reformed Review* 30 (1976): 111–23.

Kenney, Alice B. "The Albany Dutch, Loyalists and Patriots." *New York History* 42 (1961): 331–50.

———. "Private Worlds in the Middle Colonies: An Introduction to Human Tradition in American History." *New York History* 51 (1970): 5–31.

Kierner, Cynthia A. "A Concept Rejected: New York's Anglican 'Establishment,' 1693–1715." *Essays in History* 26 (1982): 71–100.

Kim, Sung Bok. "A New Look at the Great Landlords of Eighteenth-Century New York." *William and Mary Quarterly* 3d. Ser., 27 (1970): 581–614.

Kimnach, Wilson H. "Jonathan Edwards' Early Sermons: New York, 1722–1723." *Journal of Presbyterian History* 55 (1977): 255–66.

Kingdon, Robert M. "Why Did the Huguenot Refugees in the American Colonies Become Episcopalian?" *Historical Magazine of the Protestant Episcopal Church* 48 (1980): 317–35.

Klein, Milton M. "Church, State, and Education: Testing the Issue in Colonial New York." *New York History* 45 (1964): 291–303.

———. "New York in the American Colonies: A New Look." *New York History* 53 (1972): 132–56.

———. "Shaping the American Tradition: The Microcosm of Colonial New York." *New York History* 59 (1978): 173–97.

Launitz-Schurer, Leopold S. "Whig-Loyalists: The DeLanceys of New York." *New-York Historical Society Quarterly* 56 (1977): 179–98.

Lawrence, Thea. "Unity without Uniformity: An Exploration into the History of the Churches of Rhinebeck, N.Y." *The Hudson Valley Regional Review* 1 (1984): 97–114.

Leder, Lawrence H. "The New York Election of 1769: An Assault on Privilege." *Mississippi Valley Historical Review* 49 (1963): 675–82.

Lodge, Martin E. "The Crisis of the Churches in the Middle Colonies, 1720–1750." *Pennsylvania Magazine of History and Biography* 95 (1971): 195–220.

Loetscher, Lefferts A. "The Problem of Christian Unity in Early Nineteenth-Century America." *Church History* 32 (1963): 3–16.

Lydekker, John W. "The Rev. John Stuart." *Historical Magazine of the Protestant Episcopal Church* 11 (1942): 18–64.

McAnear, Beverly. "American Imprints concerning King's College." *Papers of the Bibliographical Society of America* 44 (1950): 301–39.

McCloy, Frank D. "John Mitchell Mason: Pioneer in American Theological Education." *Journal of Presbyterian History* 44 (1966): 141–55.

McKeel, Arthur J., ed. "New York Quakers in the American Revolution." *Bulletin of Friends Historical Association* 29 (1940): 47–55.

McKitrick, Eric and Elkins, Stanley. "Institutions in Motion." *American Quarterly* 12 (1960): 188–97.

McLoughlin, William G. "The Role of Religion in the Revolution." In *Essays on the American Revolution,* 197–255. Edited by Stephen G. Kurtz and James H. Hutson. Chapel Hill: University of North Carolina Press, 1973.

Mampoteng, Charles. "The Lutheran Governors of King's College." *Columbia University Quarterly* 27 (1935): 443–52.

Mathews, Donald G. "The Second Great Awakening as an Organizing Process, 1780–1830: An Hypothesis." *American Quarterly* 21 (1969): 23–43.

Mead, Sidney. "Christendom, Enlightenment, and the Revolution." In *Religion and the American Revolution,* 29–54. Edited by Jerald C. Brauer. Philadelphia: Fortress Press, 1976.

———. "The Fact of Pluralism and the Persistence of Sectarianism." In *The Religion of the Republic,* 247–66. Edited by Elwyn Smith. Philadelphia: Fortress Press, 1971.

Miller, Perry. "From the Covenant to the Revival." In *The Shaping of American Religion,* 332–68. Edited by James Ward Smith and A. Leland Jamison. Princeton, N.J.: Princeton University Press, 1961.

Mills, Frederick V., Sr. "The Protestant Episcopal Churches in the United States 1783–1789: Suspended Animation or Remarkable Recovery?" *Historical Magazine of the Protestant Episcopal Church* 46 (1977): 151–76.

Monk, Robert C. "Unity and Diversity among Eighteenth-Century Colonial Anglicans and Methodists." *Historical Magazine of the Protestant Episcopal Church* 38 (1969): 51–69.

Morgan, Edmund S. "The Puritan Ethic and the American Revolution." In *The Challenge of the American Revolution,* 88–138. Edited by Edmund S. Morgan. New York: Norton, 1976.

Murrin, John M. "Pluralism and Predatory Power: Early New York as a Social Failure." *Reviews in American History* 6 (1978): 473–79.

Nichols, Robert H. "The First Synod of New York, 1745–1758, and Its Permanent Effects." *Church History* 14 (1945): 239–55.

Nybakken, Elizabeth. "New Light on the Old Side: Irish Influences on Colonial Presbyterianism." *Journal of American History* 68 (1982): 813–32.

O'Connor, T. F. "Religious Toleration in New York, 1664–1700." *New York History* 17 (1936): 391–410.

Olsen, James S. "The New York Assembly, the Politics of Religion, and the Origins of the American Revolution, 1768–1771." *Historical Magazine of the Protestant Episcopal Church* 43 (1974): 21–28.

Potter, J. "The Growth of Population in America, 1700–1860." In *Population in History: Essays in Historical Demography,* 631–88. Edited by D. V. Glass and D. E. C. Eversley. Chicago: Aldine Publishing Co., 1965.

"Presbyterians and the American Revolution: A Documentary Account." *Journal of Presbyterian History* 52 (1974): 303–487.

Prime, Samuel I. "Early Ministers of Long Island." *Journal of the Presbyterian Historical Society* 23 (1945): 180–94.

"St. Peter's Roman Catholic Church on Barclay Street." St. Peter's Roman Catholic Church File, Trinity Parish Archives.

Shiels, Richard D. "The Scope of the Second Great Awakening: Andover, Massachusetts, As A Case Study." *Journal of the Early Republic* 5 (1985): 223–46.

———. "The Second Great Awakening in Connecticut: Critique of the Traditional Intrepretation." *Church History* 49 (1980): 401–15.

Smith, Timothy L. "Congregation, State, and Denomination: The Forming of the American Religious Structure." *William and Mary Quarterly* 3d. Ser., 25 (1968): 155–76.

———. "George Whitefield and Wesleyan Perfectionism." *Wesleyan Theological Journal* 19 (1984): 63–85.

Stowe, Walter E., ed. "The Seabury Minutes of the New York Clergy Conventions of 1766 and 1767." *Historical Magazine of the Protestant Episcopal Church* 10 (1941): 124–62.

Sweet, Douglas H. "Church Vitality and the American Revolution: Historiographical Consensus and Thought towards a New Perspective." *Church History* 45 (1976): 341–59.

Taller, Monica. "The Assimilation of Jews in Colonial New York City, 1740–1776." Jews in New York City File, Trinity Parish Archives.

Tanis, James. "Reformed Pietism in Colonial America." In *Continental Pietism and Early American Christianity*, 34–73. Edited by F. Ernest Stoeffler. Grand Rapids, Mich.: Wm. B. Eerdmans, 1976.

Tappert, Theodore G. "The Influence of Pietism in Colonial American Lutheranism." In *Continental Pietism and Early American Christianity*, 13–33. Edited by F. Ernest Stoeffler. Grand Rapids, Mich.: Wm. B. Eerdmans, 1976.

Tiedemann, Joseph S. "Patriots by Default: Queens County, New York, and the British Army, 1776–1783." *William and Mary Quarterly* 3d. Ser., 43 (1986): 35–63.

Wall, Alexander. "The Controversy in the Dutch Church in New York concerning Preaching in English, 1754–1758." *New-York Historical Society Quarterly Bulletin* 12 (1928): 39–58.

Webster, William C. "Comparative Study of the State Constitutions of the American Revolution." *Annals of the American Academy of Political and Social Sciences* 9 (1897): 64–104.

Weng, Armin. "The Language Problem in the Lutheran Church in Pennsylvania, 1742–1820." *Church History* 5 (1936): 359–75.

Westervelt, Harman C. "The Presbyterian Church, and Other Denominations in New York." Essays on Various Features of New York City File, New York Public Library Manuscript Room.

Wightman, Charles S. "History of the Baptist Church of Oyster Bay." In *Minutes of the Seventh Session of the Long Island Baptist Association*, 38–51. New York: E. H. Jones, 1873.

Wilkenfeld, Bruce. "Revolutionary New York." In *New York: The Centennial Years 1676–1976*, 43–74. Edited by Milton M. Klein. Port Washington, N.Y.: Kennikat Press, 1976.

Wood, Gordon. "The Democratization of Mind in the American Revolution." In *The Moral Foundations of the American Republic*, 102–28. Edited by Robert H. Horwitz. Charlottesville: University of Virginia Press, 1977.

198   *Bibliography*

Dissertations

Andrews, Doris. "Popular Religion and the Revolution in the Middle Atlantic Ports: The Rise of the Methodists, 1770–1800." Ph.D. diss., University of Pennsylvania, 1986.

Ashton, Rick J. "The Loyalist Experience: New York, 1763–1789." Ph.D. diss., Northwestern University, 1973.

Balmer, Randall H. "The Dutch Church in an English World: Political Upheaval and Ethnic Conflict in the Middle Colonies." Ph.D. diss., Princeton University, 1985.

Blauvelt, Martha T. "Society, Religion, and Revivalism: The Second Great Awakening in New Jersey, 1780–1830." Ph.D. diss., Princeton University, 1975.

Coalter, Milton J., Jr. "The Life of Gilbert Tennent: A Case Study of Continental Pietism's Influence on the First Great Awakening in the Middle Colonies." Ph.D. diss., Princeton University, 1982.

Cody, Edward J. "Church and State in the Middle Colonies, 1689–1763." Ph.D. diss., Lehigh University, 1970.

Goodfriend, Joyce D. "'Too Great a Mixture of Nations': The Development of New York City Society in the Seventeenth Century." Ph.D. diss., University of California, Los Angeles, 1975.

Howard, Ronald W. "Education and Ethnicity in Colonial New York, 1664–1763: A Study in the Transmission of Culture in Early America." Ph.D. diss., University of Tennessee, 1978.

Jordan, Jean Paul. "The Anglican Establishment in Colonial New York, 1693–1783." Ph.D. diss., Columbia University, 1971.

Lodge, Martin E. "The Great Awakening in the Middle Colonies." Ph.D. diss., University of California, Berkeley, 1964.

Martin, Rogert H. "The Pan-Evangelical Impulse in Britain 1795–1830; With Special Reference to Four London Societies." D. Phil. thesis, Oxford University, 1974.

Mills, Frederick V., Sr. "Anglican Resistance to an American Episcopate 1761–1789." Ph.D. diss., University of Pennsylvania, 1967.

Mol, Johannis Jacob. "Theology and Americanization: The Effects of Pietism and Orthodoxy on Adjustment to a New Culture." Ph.D. diss., Columbia University, 1960.

Nelson, Harvey L. "A Critical Study of Henry Melchior Muhlenberg's Means of Maintaining His Lutheranism." Ph.D. diss., Drew University, 1980.

Roth, Randolph A. "Whence This Strange Fire? Religious and Reform Movements in the Connecticut River Valley of Vermont, 1791–1843." Ph.D. diss., Yale University, 1981.

Sweet, Douglas H. "Church and Community: Town Life and Ministerial Ideals in Revolutionary New Hampshire." Ph.D. diss., Columbia University, 1978.

Tiedemann, Joseph S. "Response to Revolution: Queens County, New York, during the Era of the American Revolution." Ph.D. diss., City University of New York, 1976.

Wingo, Barbara C. "Politics, Society, and Religion: The Presbyterian Clergy of Pennsylvania, New Jersey, and New York, and the Formation of the Nation, 1775–1808." Ph.D. diss., Tulane University, 1976.

INDEX

Abbot, W. C., 90

Accommodationists: defined, 16; arguments of, 17–23; success of, 26–27

Ahlstrom, Sydney, 107

Albany, N.Y., ix, 3, 45, 61, 94

Albany County, N.Y.: settlement in, 3–7 passim; mentioned, 95, 126

Alison, Francis, 85

Amenia Precinct, N.Y., 98, 99

American episcopate: controversy over, 55, 60–64; and imperial policy, 69

American Revolution: reactions to, 75–76; loyalties within, 79–82; impact on church life, 90–101; as divine judgment, 98, 122; and religious cooperation, 101, 114; mentioned, xi, 70

Anglicanism: and traditionalist sympathies, 17; and British loyalty, 69–70. See also Anglicans; Church of England

Anglicans (America): settlement patterns, 2–7 passim; ties to England, 12, 13, 15, 27, 69–70; desire bishop, 24, 27, 60–63; relations with dissenters, 34–35, 49–50, 54–71; theology of, 41, 42, 46; and King's College, 55–59; politics of, 55, 69–70, 79–81, 82; and Protestant pluralism, 60–61; on church charters, 61–62; and religious equality, 66; favor establishment, 68; support voluntarism, 89, 105; during war, 91–92, 93, 96–97; scarcity of clergy among, 106; ecclesiastical restructuring of, 108. See also American episcopate; Anglicanism; Church of England; Episcopalians

Anglicans (British): colonial policies of, 25, 55, 61, 62; evangelical ecumenism of, 131–32

Anglicization, 33–34

Arminian Magazine, 136

Arminianism, 43, 46, 124

Arminians, 134, 136

Asbury, Francis: and religious cooperation, 49, 116, 117–18; travels of, 78, 112; on war's effects, 91, 100; mentioned, 43, 108, 134

Associate Reformed: and religious cooperation, 117, 134, 136, 139; growth of, 128

Associated Westchester Presbytery (Associate Reformed), 122

Auchmuty, Samuel, 61, 77–78

Austerlitz, N.Y., 129

Austin, David, 135

Austin, Samuel, 133

Baird, Robert, 107

Baptists: settlement patterns, 2–7 passim; ties to England, 12; growth of, 21, 45, 78, 109, 110, 113, 119, 139; spiritual fervor among, 38, 128, 129–30; on church-state relations, 65–66, 68; response to Revolution, 79, 81, 82; during war, 91, 92, 95, 99–100; clergy of, 110–11; and religious cooperation, 117, 118, 136; and millennialism, 130–31

Barck, Oscar, 90

Barclay, Henry, 57

Bassett, John, 112

Battenskill, N.Y., 128

Beach, Abraham, 104, 128

Beardsley, John, 92, 96

Bedford, N.Y., 54, 92

Benedict, James, 100

Berkenmeyer, William: as critic, 18, 35; as traditionalist, 20; mentioned, 14

Bern, N.Y., 126

Blacks, 1–2, 38

Boel, Henricus, 42

Bogart, David, 112

Bonomi, Patricia, 30–31, 35

Bostwick, David, 45

Bottskill, N.Y., 95, 100

Bowden, John, 77–78

Bowen, John, 125

Brick Presbyterian Church, N.Y.C.: politics of, 76–77; aid recipient, 116–17

Bridgehampton, N.Y., 126

British army, 79, 91, 94

Broome, John, 76

Brower, Cornelius, 112

Brown, Israel, 60

Bryan, George, 85

Buell, Samuel: revivals of, 45, 120, 127

Burnaby, Andrew, ix